BIBLIOGRAPHY OF AFRICAN WOMEN WRITERS AND JOURNALISTS
(Ancient Egypt – 1984)

Brenda F. Berrian

Mrs. Pamela Kola

Miriam Tlali

ASENATH ODANGA

Grace Ogot

DR. MICERE
GITHAE MUGO

BIBLIOGRAPHY OF AFRICAN WOMEN WRITERS AND JOURNALISTS
(Ancient Egypt – 1984)

Brenda F. Berrian

Three Continents Press
Washington, D.C.

©Brenda F. Berrian 1985

First Edition

Three Continents Press
1346 Connecticut Avenue N.W.
Washington, D.C. 20036

ISBN 0-89410-226-5
ISBN 0-89410-227-3 (pbk)
LC No: 84-52276

All rights reserved. No part of this book may be used or reproduced in any manner whatsoever without written permission of the publisher except for brief quotations in reviews or articles.

ACKNOWLEDGMENTS

I wish to express my appreciation to colleagues and African women writers and journalists who have helped me with this project.

Firstly, I am most grateful to Efua T. Sutherland who provided me with the names of Ghanaian women writers who are known solely within the boundaries of Ghana. In turn, these women responded to my enquiries and sent bibliographical information about their works. Furthermore, in Kenya, Grace Ogot, Pamela Ogot, Marjorie Oludhe-Macgoye, Ellen Ketonga, formerly of Oxford University Press, John Nottingham of Transafrica Publishers, Miriam Kahiga of *The Daily Nation,* and Fibi Munene were quite helpful. Buchi Emecheta, Flora Nwapa, and Mabel Segun of Nigeria must be thanked also.

Secondly, I am indebted to the colleagues who provided bibliographical information: Marie-Elisabeth Bouscarle, Donald Burness, Frederick I. Case, Albert Gerard, Thomas Hammond, Amelia House, Mildred Mortimer, Gideon Mutiso, Bernth Lindfors, Anne Lippert, Nancy Schmidt, Chris Wanjala, Evelyne Accad, and Clarisse Zimra.

Thirdly, for assistance in correcting the spelling of Portuguese names and titles I must extend special thanks to Gerald Moser, Maria Luisa Nunes, and Russell Hamilton.

For locating books and articles the services of the Library of Congress, the Moorland-Springarn Room at Howard University, and the Hillman Library at the University of Pittsburgh were used along with the libraries of the University of Ife, the University of Lagos, the University of Nairobi, the University of Zambia, and the University of California at Los Angeles.

For his patience, tolerance, and guidance I wish to thank Donald Herdeck of Three Continents Press.

For financial support I am very grateful to the Social Science Research Council/American Council of Learned Studies 1979 summer award and the 1980-1981 postdoctoral Southern Fellowships Fund.

TABLE OF CONTENTS

Introduction/ix

I	Autobiography/Biography	1
II	Fiction	
	Children's Literature	4
	Juvenile Literature	14
	Novels/Novelettes	18
	Short Stories	26
III	Drama	
	Published Plays	40
	Performed Plays	46
IV	Poetry	49
V	Folklore	77
VI	Miscellaneous Prose	
	Book Reviews by Authors	83
	Conference Papers/Speeches	86
	Critical Essays/Works	89
	Fragments	96
	Impressionistic Essays	97
	Letters	101
	Vignettes	102
VII	Journalistic Essays	104
VIII	Broadcast Literature	113
IX	Bibliography	118
X	Interviews	119

XI	Criticism of Authors' Works	
	Criticism	126
	Book Reviews of Authors' Works	157
	Commentary	177
	Synopses of Authors' Works	182
	Translation	183
XII	Bibliographical/Biographical Information	186

Appendices

A.	Authors Grouped by Countries	204
B.	Authors Grouped by Genre	216
C.	Journalists Grouped by Genre	228
D.	Forthcoming Works	231
E.	Non-African Women Married to African Men	233
F.	Non-African Journalists Married to Kenyan Men	239
G.	Non-African Women Writers Published by African Publishers	240
H.	Biographical Books on African Women	242
I.	African Women's Magazines	243

Post Addendum/249
Index/259
Biographical Note on Author/281

INTRODUCTION

When references are made to African literature, the names of such well-known writers as Chinua Achebe, Wole Soyinka, and Ngugi wa Thiong'o are mentioned with frequency. These three writers, along with other male African writers, have received international acclaim and attention. Their creative works have appeared in translations, and they have made public appearances at various African or Comparative Literature conferences. However, it is safe to say that an equal amount of international attention had not been granted to their female counterparts until the late 1970s.

In 1980, the late Senegalese writer, Mariama Bâ, became the first African (man or woman) to be awarded the prestigious Japanese literary prize, the Noma Award for her novel, Une si longue lettre. Mercy Owusu - Nimoh of Ghana was runner-up. As a result of these accomplishments, world-wide attention has been drawn to African women writers. This granting of the 1980 Noma Award to Mariama Bâ has also established the credibility of a creative work penned by an African woman. Other African women writers like Buchi Emecheta, Annette M'Baye, and Clémentine Faïk-Nzuji have also won literary prizes. Thus, it is the intent of this bibliography to acquaint the scholar, teacher, librarian, and other Africanists that the old agrument about the paucity of African women writers is not justified.

The majority of the entries in this volume consist of literary works written by African women writers since the twentieth century. The exceptions are Queen Hatshepsut of Egypt of the fifteenth century B.C. and three Swahili poets — Mwana Kupona binti Msham, Nuru binti Abdullah, and Siti binti Saad — of the nineteenth century. Among genres represented are journalistic essays, critical works, folktales, children's literature, novels, short stories, and autobiographies. A total of 386 authors of folklore and creative literary works and 74 journalists are included. The authors come from North, East, West, Central, and Southern Africa. In addition, four women from Madagascar receive mention.

Emphasis is placed upon the novel, poem, play, short story and other types of literature, including the folktale, autobiography, biography, children's fiction, and journalistic essays. Primary works in European languages — English, French, Portuguese — by African women writers reach a total of 913. Original works in African vernacular languages are represented by 52 entries.

Nine appendices are provided to give the reader basic bibliographical tools for studying creative, critical, folkloric, and journalistic works produced by African women writers. The reason for the non-African women sections of the appendix is to correct the misconception that such popular writers as Peggy Appiah and Maria Eugénia Neto are African. Rather they are European women married to African men, but have been accepted within the African context. These women's works, as well as those of a dozen or so more, are read by school children in Ghana and Angola, respectively.

The new category, broadcast literature, is introduced in this volume, for several African women writers have granted recorded interviews and/or produced radio and television plays for the African public through the B.B.C. African Theatre, the Voice of Kenya, Radio Ghana, and local television stations in their countries. Difficulty occurs with the inability to find exact recording dates.

A translation section of this bibliography exists because some of the novels and poetry by African women writers, i.e. Buchi Emecheta have been translated into several foreign languages. This section, therefore, demonstrates that these women's writings are being read, studied, appreciated and discussed in foreign universities on a widespread basis.

The titles of original works in English are capitalized according to general American practice. Works in French and Portuguese have only the first word and proper nouns capitalized; the remaining words are in small letters. Titles in African languages are duplicated from the bibliographical sources in which they were found. Futhermore, after the citation of the original title of a work in an African language, an informal translation in English is offered in parenthesis. In some instances, there is not an English translation because of the inability to gain assistance from native speakers of these various languages.

An impressionistic essay section as opposed to the one on critical essays by African women writers is included. The latter comprise serious analytical discussions of other African writers' works by African women writers, the former, by contrast, consist of vignettes and fragments. These vignettes and fragments are short creative passages composed by the writers in which they explore a single subject in either an amusing or serious manner.

An effort has been made to examine all the entries cited. It has been difficult, however, to know which countries some of the writers are from, because insufficient information was given about them on the jackets of their books and by scholars of African literature. This explains why some of the women are categorized as East African, West African, or simply "unidentified." Further complications arise from the fact that there have been women such as Bessie Head, who were born in one African country but were either granted citizenship or residency in another African nation. This accounts for the listing of two countries beside their names.

The intention here has been to provide a comprehensive coverage of the primary creative works by African women writers along with book reviews and critical articles written about them by critics around the world. Finally, African women have made a mark in the field of African literary criticism; credit is given to them.

Though efforts have been made to compile as accurate and exhaustive a volume as possible, the student, scholar, and professor will be aware that more work is needed, particularly in the general area of journalism and in North and Portuguese African literatures. In some instances, page numbers, dates, and sources of publication were not provided in the initial bibliographies, or primary or secondary texts. Some entries are, therefore, incomplete. Also, some of the women's names, i.e., Romanä Wärq Kasahun or Romanawerk Kasahun of Ethiopia, were spelled two or three different ways in various texts consulted. Other women like Micere Githae - Mugo and Miriam Were were published under their maiden names -the former under Madeleine Githae and the latter Miriam Khamadi. All entries are alphabetized letter by letter. Each writer's country of birth is listed, and the volume has been divided by genre. Obviously, there is a limit to extracting criticism about various African authors. The most useful and available studies on the authors were consulted. As one knows, every good work will provide a stimulus for better scholarship.

Brenda F. Berrian
University of Pittsburgh

I. AUTOBIOGRAPHY/BIOGRAPHY

AMROUCHE, FADHMA AITH MANSOUR (Algeria)

Histoire de ma vie. Paris: Maspero, 1968.

APOKO, ANNA (Uganda)

"At Home in the Village: Growing Up in Acholi," East African Childhood Three Versions: Written by Joseph A. Lijembe, Anna Apoko, J. Mutuku Nzioki. Ed. Lorene Fox. Nairobi: Oxford University Press, 1967, pp. 45-75.

CASELY-HAYFORD, ADELAIDE (Ghana and Sierra Leone)

"Beginning — The Life and Times of Adelaide Casely-Hayford, No. 1," West African Review, 24, 313 (1953), 1058-60.

"The Life and Times of Adelaide Casely-Hayford No. 2," West African Review, 24, 314 (1953, 1169-71.

"The Swallows Homeward Fly No. 3," West African Review, 24, 315 (1953), 1305-11.

"Ships that Greeted Me in Passing No. 9," West African Review, 25, 312 (1954) 533-37.

"American Journey No. 4," West African Review, 25, 316 (1954), 55-58.

"American Journey No. 2," West African Review, 25, 317 (1954), 151-54.

"America Revisited," West African Review, 25, 318 (1954), 239-43, 220.

"Another Visit to England," West African Review, 25, 319 (1954), 353-55.

"Childhood Days," Growing Up. Ed. Deborah Manley. Lagos: African Universities Press, 1967, pp. 18-22.

"Reminiscences," Africa in Prose. Ed. O. R. Dathorne and Willfried Feuser. Middlesex: Penguin Books, 1969, pp. 131-38.

DIALLO, NAFISSATOU (Senegal)

De Tilene au plateau: une enfance dakaroise. Dakar: Les Nouvelles Editions Africaines, 1975. 133 pages.

AUTOBIOGRAPHY/BIOGRAPHY

EMECHETA, BUCHI (Nigeria)

<u>In the Ditch</u>. London: Allison and Busby, 1972. 128 pages [Autobiographical Novel].

<u>Second Class Citizen</u>. London: Allison and Busby; New York: George Braziller, 1975. 175 pages [Autobiographical novel].

"Head Above Water," <u>Kunapipi</u>, 3, 1 (1981), 81-90 (Autobiographical reflections).

JABAVU, NONTANDO NONI (South Africa)

<u>Drawn in Colour: African Contrasts</u>. New York: St. Martins Press, 1962. 208 pages; rpt. London: John Murray, 1963. 261 pages.

<u>The Ochre People: Scenes from South African Life</u>. London: John Murray, 1963 261 pages.

"From the <u>Ochre People</u>," <u>African English Literature</u>. Ed. Anne Tibble. New York: October House, 1965, pp. 156-59.

KEITA, AOUA (Mali)

<u>Femme d'Afrique: la vie d'Aoua Kéita racontée par elle-même</u>. Paris: Présence Africaine, 1975. 397 pages.

KWAMI, MARTHE AFEWELE (Togo)

<u>Autobiographies d'Africaines: onze autobiographies d'indigènes originaires de diverses régions de l'Afrique et representant des métiers et des degrés de culture différents, traduction françaises de L. Homburger</u>. Ed. Diedrich Westermann. Paris: Payot, 1943, pp. 236-37.

MAGIDI, DORA THIZWILANDI, pseudonym (South Africa)

<u>Black Background: The Childhood of a South African Girl</u> [Autobiography of a Girl Known as Dora Thizwilandi Magidi (pseudonym)]. Ed. John Blacking. New York: Abelard-Schuman, 1964.

NWAPA, FLORA (Nigeria)

<u>Golden Wedding Jubilee of Chief and Mrs. C. I. Nwapa, April 20, 1930 - April 20, 1980</u>. Enugu: Flora Nwapa &Co., 1980. 11 pages.

AUTOBIOGRAPHY/BIOGRAPHY

SEGUN, MABEL IMOUKHUEDE JOLAOSA (Nigeria)

"The Unfinished House," Reflections; Nigerian Prose and Verse. Ed. Frances Ademola. Lagos: African Universities Press, 1962, pp. 96-99.

My Father's Daughter. African Reader's Library, 8. Lagos: African Universities Press, 1965. 80 pages.

"The Secret Farm," Growing Up. Ed. Deborah Manley. Lagos: African Universities Press, 1967, pp. 57-67.

SIKAKANE, JOYCE (South Africa)

A Window on Soweto. London: International Defence and Aid Fund, 1977.

SIWUNDHLA, ALICE PRINCESS MSUMBA (Lesotho)

Alice Princess: An Autobiography. Intr. Ralph Edwards. Mountain View, California: Pacific Publishing Association, 1965; rpt. New York: Taplinger, 1967. 166 pages.

SWAARTBOOI, VICTORIA (South Africa)

U-Mandisa [Bringer of Joy]. Lovedale: Lovedale Press, 1933. 57 pages [Xhosa autobiographical novelette].

TORO, PRINCESS ELIZABETH OF (Uganda)

African Princess: The Story of Princess Elizabeth of Toro. London: Hamish Hamilton, 1983. 219 pages.

WACIUMA, CHARITY (Kenya)

Daughter of Mumbi. Nairobi: East African Publishing House, 1969. 96 pages [Autobiographical novelette].

WERE, MIRIAM KHAMADI (Kenya)

A Nurse with a Song. Nairobi: Challenge Publishers and Distributors, 1978. 169 pages [Biography of Margaret O. Wanyonyi].

II FICTION

CHILDREN'S LITERATURE

'ABD ALLAH, SUFI (Egypt)

Baqāyā Rajul (Residues of a Man). Cairo: Al-Tijārī, n.d.

Madrasat Al-Banāt (A Girls' School). Cairo: n. p., 1959.

Alf Mabrūk (A Million Congratulations). Cairo: Al-Kaumiyah, 1965.

Arūsah 'Alā Al-Raff (A Bride on the Shelf). Cairo: Maārif, 1966.

ACQUAH, BARBARA (Ghana)

Ananse and the Wise Men. Accra: n. p., N.d. 24 pages [A Christmas play published in Ghana].

ADDO, DORA YACOBA (Ghana)

Five Lives of Great Ghanaian Pioneers. Accra: Anowao Educational Publications, n.d., illus.

AGADIZI, ANNA (Ghana)

Akwasi Seeks Adventure. Accra: Advance, n.d. 54 pages, illus.

From Poverty to Prosperity. Accra: Advance, 1968. 25 pages, illus.

AJOSE, AUDREY (Nigeria)

Yomi's Adventures. London: Cambridge University Press, 1964. 90 paes.

Yomi in Paris. London: Cambridge University Press, 1968. 81 pages, illus.

AKAPBOT, ANNE (Nigeria)

Aduke Makes Her Choice. London: Nelson, 1966. 20 pages.

Sade and Her Friends. Rapid Reading Series 6. London: Nelson, 1967. 62 pages.

ANIZOBA, ROSE (Nigeria)

The Adventure of Mbugwe the Frog. The Little Bookshelf Series. Ibadan: Oxford University Press, 1965. 94 pages.

ANKRAH, EFUA (Ghana)

Munita Goes Hunting. Lusaka: Neczam, 1972. 24 pages, illus.

CHILDREN'S LITERATURE

APOKO, ANNA (Uganda)

"At Home in the Village: Growing Up in Acholi," East African Childhood: Three Versions. Written by Joseph A. Lijembe, Anna Apoko, J. Mutuku Nzioki. Ed. Lorene Fox. Nairobi: Oxford University Press, 1967.

ASHERI, JEDIDA (Cameroon)

Promise. African Readers Library. Lagos: African Universities Press, 1969. 96 pages, illus.

CASELY-HAYFORD, ADELAIDE (Sierra Leone and Ghana)

"Childhood Days," Growing Up. Ed. Deborah Manley. Lagos: African Universities Press, 1967, pp. 18-22.

"Reminiscences," Africa in Prose. Eds. O. R. Dathorne and Willfied Feuser. Middlesex: Penguin, 1969, pp. 131-38.

CHIFAMBA, JANE (Zimbabwe)

Ngano Dzepasi Chigare (Tales of Old). Oxford: Oxford University Press, in association with the Rhodesia Literature Bureau, 1964. 60 pages.

DAHAL, CHARITY KUGURU (Kenya)

The Orange Thieves, and Other Stories. Nairobi: East African Publishing House, 1966. 72 pages.

The Adventures of Mr. Hyena. Nairobi: East African Publishing House, 1969.

DANKWAH-SMITH, HANNAH (Ghana)

Some Popular Ananse Stories. Accra: Wateville, 1975. 115 page, illus.

DANKYI, JANE OSAFOA (Ghana)

with Kitty Lloyd-Lawrence. Firelight Fables. London: Longman, 1972. 57 pages, illus.

DOGBE, ANNE (Senegal)

Afi à la campagne. Dakar: Les Nouvelles Editions Africaines, 1976. 28 pages.

DRONYI, JOYCE L. (Uganda)

Mother's Pot. Kampala: Uganda Publishing House, 1972. 8 pages, illus.

CHILDREN'S LITERATURE

EMECHETA, BUCHI (Nigeria)

with Alice Emecheta. Titch the Cat. London: Allison and Busby, 1979.

Nowhere to Play. London: Allison and Busby, 1979.

The Wrestling Match. London: Allison and Busby, 1981.

GICORU, NEREAS (Kenya)

with Terry Hirst. Take Me Home. Nairobi: East African Publishing House, 1974. 20 pages, illus.

GITHUKU, MARY (Kenya)

Konyu's Dreams Come True. The African Rope Series. Nairobi: Equatorial, n.d. 96 pages, illus.

GUTU, LAETITIA (Zimbabwe)

Shumba and the He-Goat ... and Other Stories. Gwelo: Mambo Press, with Rhodesia literature Bureau, n.d.

IWUJI, VICTORIA B.C. (Nigeria)

Going to a Midnight Play. Living in Nigeria. Ibadan: African Education Press, 1966. 73 pages, illus.

JOHNSON, RHODA OMOSUNLOLA (Nigeria)

Iyabo of Nigeria. Claremont: Claremont Graduate School, 1973. 79 pages, illus.

KALIMUGOGO, G. (Kenya)

The Pulse of the Woods. Nairobi: East African Literature Bureau, 1973.

The Department. Nairobi: East African Literature Bureau, 1976.

Trials and Tribulations in Sandu's Home. Nairobi: East African Literature Bureau, 1976.

KAVILA, ESTHER (Kenya)

The Three Sons. Nairobi: East African Publishing House, n.d. 48 pages.

KHANGANYA, WILLMESS (Malawi)

The Umbrella. Progress in Reading. London: Longman, 1960. 26 pages, illus.

CHILDREN'S LITERATURE

KIMENYE, BARBARA (Uganda)

The Smugglers. London: Nelson, 1966. 54 pages, illus.

Moses. Nairobi: Oxford University Press, 1969. 73 pages, illus.

Moses and the Camper. Nairobi: Oxford University Press, 1969. 86 pages.

Moses and Mildred. Oxford Library for East Africa. Nairobi: Oxford University Press, 73 pages, illus.

Moses and the Millpede. Nairobi: Oxford University Press, n.d. 14 pages, illus.

Moses in Trouble. Nairobi: Oxford University Press, 1969. 82 pages, illus.

The Winged Adventure. Oxford Library for East Africa. Nairobi: Oxford University Press, 1969. 49 pages, illus.

Moses in a Muddle. Oxford Library for East Africa. Nairobi: Oxford University Press, 1970. 63 pages, illus.

Moses and the Ghost. Nairobi: Oxford University Press, 1971. 84 pages, illus.

Moses and the Penpal. Nairobi: Oxford University Press, 1971. 80 pages.

Moses on the Move. Nairobi: Oxford University Press, 1971. 78 pages.

Paulo's Strange Adventure. Nairobi: Oxford University Press, 1971. 72 pages, illlus.

Sarah and the Boy. Nairobi: Oxford University Press, 1972. 12 pages, illus.

The Runaways. Oxford Library for East Africa. Nairobi: Oxford University Press, 1973. 73 pages, illus.

KYENDO, KALONDU (Kenya)

Cock and Lion. Nairobi: East African Publishing House, 1969. 24 pages.

LAMO, JANET (Uganda)

The Cat Who Went to School. A Crested Crane Book for Children. Kampala: Uganda Publishing House, 1972. 17 pages, illus.

LIKIMANI, MUTHONI (Kenya)

Shangazi na Watoto. (Swahili Children's Stories). Nairobi: East African Publishing House, n.d.

CHILDREN'S LITERATURE

LOUBNA, MAMA, pseudonym Nutaylah Ibrahim Rashid (Egypt)

Hurrah for Life. Cairo: Arab Republic of Egypt, State Information Service, n.d. 94 pages, illus.

MANDAO, MARTHA (Tanzania)

Alone in the City. Dar es Salaam: Africa Christian Press, 1969. Swahili translation: Peke Yangu Mjini. Dar es Salaam: Central Tanganikya Press, 1972. 28 pages.

Musa. Dar es Salaam: Central Tanganikya Press, 1969. n.p., illus.

Anti Opens Her Purse. Dar es Salaam: Africa Christian Press, 1979. Swahili translation: Anti Afungua Mkoba Wake. Dar es Salaam: Central Tanganikya Prss, 1971.

MASSAQUOI, PRINCESS FATIMA (Liberia)

The Leopard's Daughter. Boston: Humphries, 1961. 14 pages, illus. Translated from the Vai.

MATINDI, ANNE (Kenya)

The Lonely Black Pig. Nairobi: East African Publishing House, 1968. 32 pages.

The Sun and the Wind. Nairobi: East African Publishing House, 1969. 24 pages. Swahili translation: Jua na uprepo. Nairobi: East African Publishing House, 1969.

with Cynthia Hunter. The Sun-Men and Other Plays. Nairobi: East African Publishing House, 1971. 80 pages.

MAURA, MARY (Kenya)

Kijanaji's Lucky Escape. Nairobi: Equatorial, 1969. 30 pages, illus.

M'BAYE, ANNETTE d'ERNEVILLE (Senegal)

Les chansons pour Laïty. Dakar: Les Nouvelles Editions Africaines, 1979.

MDOE, JANET N. (Uganda)

Beautiful Namirembe. Progress in Reading. London: Longman, 1969. 25 pages, illus.

CHILDREN'S LITERATURE

MENIRU, THERESA (Nigeria)

The Bad Family and the Catepillar. Evans English Readers. London: Evans Brothers, 1971. 20 pages, illus.

The Carver and the Leopard. Evans English Readers. London: Evans, 1971. 27 pages, illus.

The Melting Girl and Other Stories. Evans English Readers. London: Evans, 1971. 27 pages, illus.

Unoma. London: Evans, 1971.

MFODWO, ESTHER BEKOE (Ghana)

Folk Tales and Stories from Around the World. Children's Library. Accra: Ghana Publishing Corporation, 1971. 30 pages, illus.

MLAGOLA, MARTHA V. (Kenya)

Yasin's Nightmare. Nairobi: East African Publishing House, 1976. 42 pages.

MONEKE, OBIORA (Nigeria)

How Plants Scattered. Read It Yourself Series. Enugu: Flora Nwapa & Co., 1980. 18 pages.

NAGENDA, SALA (Kenya)

Mother of Twins. Nairobi: East African Publishing House, 1971. 32 pages.

NDORO, JOYCE (Kenya)

The Hare's Horns. Nairobi: Est African Publishing House, 1968; rpt. 1972. 32 pages. Kikuyu folk tales.

NTABGOBA, JENINAH (East Africa)

Listening is Fun. Nairobi: East African Publishing House, n.d. 22 pages, illus.

My Goodnight Book. Nairobi: East African Publishing House, n.d. 28 pages, illus.

NWAPA, FLORA (Nigeria)

Emeka-Driver's Guard. London: University of London, 1972. 46 pages.

Mammy Water. Enugu: Flora Nwapa & Co., 1979. 32 pages, illus.

My Animal Colouring Book. Enugu: Flora Nwapa & Co., 1979. 20 pages, illus.

CHILDREN'S LITERATURE

My Tana Colouring Book. Enugu: Flora Nwapa & Co., 1979. 21 pages, illus.

The Adventures of Deke. Enugu: Flora Nwapa & Co., 1980. 15 pages, illus.

The Miracle Kittens. Read It Yourself Series. Enugu: Flora Nwapa & Co., 1980. 19 pages, illus.

My Tana Alphabet Book. Enugu: Flora Nwapa & Co., 1981. 52 pages, illus.

My Animal Number Book. Enugu: Flora Nwapa & Co., 1981 n.p., illus.

NYOKABI, SALLY (Kenya)

The Chameleon Who Couldn't Stop Changing His Mind. Bushbabies. Nairobi: Transafrica Publishers, 1974. 24 pages, illus.

ODAGA, ASENATH BOLE (Kenya)

Jande's Ambition. East Africa Reader's Library 3. Nairobi: East African Publishing House, 1966. 67 pages.

The Hare's Blanket and Other Tales. East Africa Junior Library 3. Nairobi: East African Publishing House, 1967. 28 pages.

The Angry Flames. East Africa Reader's Library 21. Nairobi: East African Publishing House, 1968. 48 pages.

Sweets and Sugar Cane. East Africa Junior Library 10. Nairobi: East African Publishing House, 1971. 24 pages.

Villager's Son. Nairobi: Heinemann Secondary Readers, 1971. 92 pages, illus.

Kip on the Farm. Nairobi: East African Publishing House, 1972. 16 pages.

Kip's Visit to the Coast. Nairobi: East African Publishing House, n.d.

The Diamond Ring. East Africa Junior Library 4. Nairobi: East African Publishing House, 1973. 52 pages.

ODOWELU, VICKI EZINMA (Nigeria)

Beautiful Rose and Her Seventy-Five Husbands. Onitsha: Highbred Maxwell; Student's Own Bookshop, 196?. 73 pages, illus.

CHILDREN'S LITERATURE

OGOT, PAMELA (Kenya)

East African HOW? Stories. Nairobi: East African Publishing House, 1966. 40 pages. Swahili translation: Jinsi chui alipata madoado. Nairobi: East African Publishing House, n.p.

East African WHY? Stories. Nairobi: East African Publishing House, 1966. 40 pages.

East African WHEN? Stories. Nairobi: East African Publishing House, 1968. 32 pages, illus. Swahili translation: Kwa nini fisi hucheka. Nairobi: East African Publishing House, n.d.

The Cunning Tortoise and Other Stories. Nairobi: East African Publishing House, 1980. 16 pages.

OHENE, OOPOKUA (Ghana)

The Frog's Band. Accra: Afram Publications, n.d.

The Invitation. Accra: Afram Publications, 1979.

OKOYE, IFEOMA (Nigeria)

Village Boy. London: Macmillan, 1978 [Won third prize in 1978 Macmillan Children's Literature Contest].

The Adventure of Tulu the Little Monkey. Enugu: Flora Nwapa & Co., 1979.

The Boy Who Liked Only Bread, No Supper for Eze, No School for Eze. Enugu: Fourth Dimensions, 1979 [Collection of three stories].

OMANGA, CLARE (Kenya)

The Girl Who Couldn't Keep a Secret and Other Stories. Nairobi: East African Publishing House, 1969. 34 pages.

OMODING, ANNA (Uganda)

A Fright in the Forest. A Crested Crane Book for Children. Kampala: Uganda Publishing House, 1972. n.p., illus.

CHILDREN' LITERATURE

ONDITI, MARA (East Africa)

Our Alphabet. Nairobi: Foundation Series, 1973. 26 pages, illus.

OWUSU-NIMOH, MERCY (Ghana)

Adventure of Sasa and Esi. Accra: Ghana Publishing Corporation, 1968. 23 pages.

The Walking Calabash and Other Stories. Tema: Ghana Publishing Corporation, 1977. 71 pages, illus.

Rivers of Ghana. Kada: Monin Bookland, 1979.

PHUMLA (South Africa)

Naomi and the Fish. Garden City: Doubleday, 1972. n.p., illus. [A Zulu version of a wicked stepmother story].

SACKEY, JULIANA (Ghana)

The Twins and The Great Water Spirit. Macmillan Controlled Readers from Africa. London: Macmillan, 1972. 54 pages, illus.

SEGUN, MABEL IMOUKHUEDE JOLAOSO (Nigeria)

My Father's Daughter. African Reader's Library 8. Lagos: African Universities Press, 1965. 80 pages.

with Neville Grant. Under the Mango Tree. Books One and Two. London: Longman, 1979.

SOFOLA, ZULU (Nigeria)

King Emene: Tragedy of a Rebellion. Heinemann Secondary Reading Scheme. London: Heinemann, 1974. 46 pagaes, illus.

CHILDREN'S LITERATURE

SUTHERLAND, EFUA THEODORA MORGUE (Ghana)

Playtime in Africa. New York: Atheneum, 1962. 62 pages, illus. Picture essay for children from ages 11-13.

The Roadmakers. London: Newman Neame, 1963.

Vulture! Vulture! and Tahinta. Accra: State Publishing Corporation, 1968. 32 pages, illus. music [Two rhythm plays for children].

UMELO, ROSINA (West Africa)

The Man Who Ate the Money. Oxford: Oxford University Press, 1978. 100 pages.

WACIUMA, CHARITY (Kenya)

The Golden Feather. Nairobi: East African Publishing House, 1966. 48 pages, illus.

Merry-Making. Nairobi: East African Publishing House, 1972, 15 pages.

Mweru, the Ostrich Girl. Nairobi: East African Publishing House, 1973. 23 pages.

Who's Calling? Nairobi: East African Publishing House, 1973. 15 pages.

Mweru, The Ostrich. Nairobi: East African Publishing House, 1974. 23 pages.

WANNE, TEGBO (Ivory Coast)

Enfants d'Afrique. Abidjan: Nouvelles Editions Africaines, 1980.

II FICTION

JUVENILE LITERATURE

AIGBOKHAI, JOSEPHINE (Nigeria)

Olu Martin Goes to See London. Modern English Library. London: University of London, 1972. 63 pages, illus.

BAKALUBA, JANE JAGERS (Uganda)

Honeymoon for Three. African Secondary Readers. Nairobi: East African Publishing House, 1975. 192 pages, illus.

BOBITO, JENIFER (Kenya)

Prescription: LOVE. Afroromance Series, Secondary Level. Nairobi: Afroromance, 1975.

EMECHETA, BUCHI (Nigeria)

The Moonlight Bride. London: Oxford University Press, 1980-. 77 pages, rpt. New York. George Braziller, 1983. 77 pages.

KAGONDU, AGNES (Kenya)

"A Nocturnal Visitor," When I Awoke. Intr. W. G. Bowman. Nairobi: East African Publishing House, 1966, pp. 26-29 (1966 Brooke Bond Essay Competition).

KISANGI, ESTHER (Kenya)

"Story Writing," When I Awoke. Intr. W. G. Bowman. Niarobi: East African Publishing House, 1966, pp. 64-66.

KISE, MARY (Kenya)

Love and Learn. Afroromance Series, Secondary Level. Nairobi: Afroromance, 1975.

JUVENILE LITERATURE

KURIA, R. LUCY (Kenya)

"Out of Disaster," When I Awoke. Intro. W. G. Bowman. Nairobi: East Arican Publishing House, 1966, pp. 48-50.

MAGIDI, DORA THIZWILANDI (South Africa)

Blacking, John. Black Background: The Childhood of a South African Girl. New York: Abelard-Schuman, 1964 [Autobiography of a girl known as Dora Thizwilandi Magidi, pseudonym].

MAKEBA, MIRIAM (South Africa)

The World of African Song. Chicago: Quadrangle, 1971. 119 pages, illus. music scores.

MWANGI, BEATRICE (Kenya)

"Misfortune Never Comes Singly," When I Awoke. Intr. W. G. Bowman. Nairobi: East African Publishing House, 1966, pp. 23-25.

NDONDO, LASSIE (Zimbabwe)

Qaphele Ingane. (Take Care of the Boy) Pietermarizburg: Shuter and Shooter, in association with the Rhodesia Literature Bureau, 1962. 48 pages [Ndebele novel].

NGUYA, LYDIE MUMBI (Kenya)

The 1st Seed. Intr. Taban Lo Liyong. Nairobi: East African Literature Bureau, 1975. 239 pages.

ODAGA, ASENATH BOLE (Kenya)

The Villager's Son. Nairobi: Heinemann Secondary Readers, 1971. 92 pages.

JUVENILE LITERATURE

ODOWELU, VICKI EZINMA (Nigeria)

Beautiful Rose and Her Seventy Five Husbands. Onitsha: Highbred Maxwell; Students' Own Bookshop, 196?. 73 pages, illus.

SOFOLA, ZULU (Nigeria)

King Emene: Tragedy of a Rebellion. Heinemann Secondary Reading Scheme. Nairobi: Heinemann, 1974. 46 pages [Children's play].

WACIUMA, CHARITY (Kenya)

Daughter of Mumbi. Nairobi: East African Publishing House, 1969. 163 pages [Autobiographical novelette].

WANJIRU, PAULINE (Kenya)

"Worm's Turn," When I Awoke. Intr. W. G. Bowman. Nairobi: East African Publishing House, 1966, pp. 20-2.

WARUHIU, DORIS MAY (Kenya)

"Gumba's Reality," When I Awoke. Intr. W. G. Bowman. Nairobi: East African Publishing House, 1966, pp. 36-8.

WERE, MIRIAM KHAMADI (Kenya)

The Boy in Between. Nairobi: Oxford University Library for East Africa, 1970. 101 pages.

The Eighth Wife. Nairobi: East African Publishing House, 1972. 167 pages.

The High School Gent. Nairobi: Oxford University Press, 1973. 173 pages.

Your Heart Is My Altar. Modern African Library 37. Nairobi: East African Publishing House, 1980. 159 pages.

JUVENILE LITERATURE

YAOU, REGINA (Ivory Coast)

<u>Lezou Marie ou les écueils de la vie</u>, Abidjan: Nouvelles Editions Africaines, 1982.

II. FICTION

NOVELS/NOVELETTES

ADIAFFI, ANNE-MARIE

Une vie hypothèquée. Dakar: Nouvelles Editions Africaines, 1984. 128 pages.

AFONSO, MARIA PERPETUA CANDEIAS DA SILVA (Angola)

Navionga, filha de branco. Lisboa: Agência-Geral do Ultramar, 1966. 155 pages.

AIDOO, CHRISTINA AMA ATA (Ghana)

Our Sister Killjoy or Reflections from a Black-Eyed Squint. London: Longman, 1978: rpt. New York: NOK Publishers, 1979.

ANDRIA, AIMEE (Madagascar)

Brouillard. Paris: Louis Soulanges, 1967. 109 pages.

L'esquif. Paris: Louis Soulanges, 1968. 127 pages.

BA, MARIAMA (Senegal)

Une si longue lettre. Dakar: Le Nouvelles Editions Africaines, 1979, 131 pages.

Un chant écarlate. Dakar: Les Nouvelles Editions Africaines, 1981, 251 pages.

BABISIDYA M. (Tanzania)

Shida. Dar-es-salaam: Tanzania Publishing House, n.d.

BENSKINA, PRINCESS ORELIA (Ghana)

i have loved you already. New York: Exposition Press, 1975.

BITTARI, ZOUBEIDA (Algeria)

O mes soeurs musulmanes, pleurez! Paris: Gallimard, 1964.

BOAHEMAA, BEATRICE YAA (Ghana)

My Runaway Husband. Accra: Facts and Fiction Agency, 1972.

NOVELS/NOVELETTES

CHAIBI, AICHA (Tunisia)

Rached. Tunis: Maison Tunisienne de l'Edition, 1975. 350 pages.

CHEDID, ANDREE (Egypt)

Terre regardée. Paris: Gallimard, 1957. 48 pages.

Le Sixième jour. Paris: Flammarion, 1960.

Le Survivant. Paris, Julliard, 1963. 217 pages.

L'Autre. Paris: Flammarion, 1969. 213 pages.

La Cité fertile. Paris: Flammarion, 1972. 171 pages.

Nefertiti et le rêve d'Akhnaton. Paris: Flammarion, 1974. 230 pages.

Le sommeil délivré. Paris: Flammarion, 1976. 226 pages.

DEBECHE, DJAMILA (Algeria)

Leila, jeune fille algérienne. Alger: Charras, 1947.

Aziza. Alger: Imbert, 1955.

DJEBAR, ASSIA (Algeria)

La soif. Paris: Julliard, 1957. 165 pages.

Les Impatients. Paris: Julliard, 1958. 239 pages.

Women of Islam. London: Deutsch, 1961.

Les Enfants du nouveau monde. Paris: Julliard, 1962. 219 pages.

Les Alouettes naïves. Paris: Julliard, 1967.

La Nouba des femmes du mont Chenoua. Paris: Des Femmes, 1979.

DOOH-BUNYA, LYDIE (Cameroon)

La Brise du jour. Yaoundé: Editions CLE, 1977.

NOVELS/NOVELETTES

EMECHETA, BUCHI (Nigeria)

The Bride Price. London: Allison and Busby; New York: George Braziller, 1976.
168 pages.

The Slave Girl. London: Allison and Busby; New York: George Braziller, 1977.
179 pages.

The Joys of Motherhood. London: Allison and Busby; New York: George Braziller, 1979. 224 pages.

Destination Biafra. London: Allison and Busby, 1982. 272 pages.

Double Yoke. London: Ogwugwu Afor Co., Ltd., 1982; rpt. New York: George Braziller, 1983. 162 pages.

FAKUNLE-ONADEKO, OLUFUNMILAYO (Nigeria)

The Sacrificial Child. n.p., n.d.

FONSECA, LILIA DA (Angola)

Panguila. Lisboa: Parceria António Maria Pereira, 1944. 307 pages.

FUTSHANE, ZORA, Z. T. (South Africa)

U-Jujuju (Magic). Lovedale: Lovedale Press, 1938. 76 pages; rpt. 1943.
48 pages; rpt. 1962. [Xhosa Novel].

Ujuju no Mhla ngenqaba (Jujuju; and Mhla in Trouble). Lovedale: Lovedale Press, 1960. 67 pages, illus. [Xhosa Novel].

GEBRU, SENEDDN (Ethiopia)

Yelibbe Meshaf (The Book of My Heart). Addis Ababa: n. p., 1942.

HEAD, BESSIE (South Africa and Botswana)

When Rain Clouds Gather. London: Gollancz, 1969. 188 pages; New York: Simon and Schuster, 1969. 188 pages.

Maru. African Writers Series 101. London: Heinemann, 1977; New York: Humanities Press, 1977.

NOVELS/NOVELETTES

A Question of Power. African Writers Series 149. London: Heinemann; New York: Humanities Press; New York: Pantheon Press, 1977.

HIGIRO, J. (Kenya)

Voice of Silence. Nairobi: East African Literature Bureau, 1975. 70 pages.

KAKAZA, LILLITH OR LOTA G. (South Arica)

Intyatyambo yomzi (The flower in the home). Gcuwa: n.p., 1913. 31 pages [Xhosa Novelette].

KALIMUGOGO, G. (Kenya)

Trials and Tribulations in Sandu's Home. Nairobi: East African Literature Bureau, 1976. 146 pages.

KAYA, SIMONE (Ivory Coast)

Les Danseuses d'Impé-Eya: jeunes filles à Abidjan. Abidjan: Indades, 1976. 120 pages.

KUOH-MOUKOURY, THERESE (Cameroon)

Les couples dominos. Paris: Julliard, 1973. 250 pages.

LEMSINE, AICHA (Algeria)

La chrysalide: chroniques algériennes. Paris: Editions des Femmes, 1976.

Ciel de Porphyre. Paris: Jean Claude Simoen, 1978.

LIKIMANI, MUTHONI (Kenya)

They Shall Be Chastised. Nairobi: East African Literature Bureau, 1974; rpt. 1977. 231 pages.

What Does a Man Want? Nairobi: East African Literature Bureau, 1974; rpt. 1977. 209 pages.

NOVELS/NOVELETTES

MAHUHUSI, M. A. (South Africa)

Xikotikoti wa Matshotsho. n.p., (1970) [Tsonga Novel].

MAKURA, TENDAI (Zimbabwe)

Vatete Vacmabuepi (Where Will the Aunt Come From?). Gwelo: Mambo Press, 1977.

MANDEBVU, STELLA (Zimbabwe)

Ndochema Naani (It's All My Fault). Essex: Longman, 1974. 118 pages.

MITCHELL, ELIZABETH M. (Liberia)

The Last Rites and Ceremonies. Monrovia: MS, 1972.

MKHOMBO, JOY FLORENCE CHRESTOPHENE (South Africa)

Ntsakisi wa Tahani — n'wanjiyani (Good Fellow of Tahani, A Boaster). Pretoria: Van Schaik, 1962. 95 pages [Tsonga Novel].

MUGOT, HAZEL DE SILVA (Seychelles)

Black Night of Quiloa. Nairobi: East African Publishing House, 1971. 90 pages.

NGCOBO, LAURETTA (South Africa)

Cross of Gold. London: Longman, 1981. 289 pages.

NJAU, REBEKA (Kenya)

Ripples in the Pool. African Writers Series 203. London: Heinemann, 1978. 152 pages.

NWAPA, FLORA (Nigeria)

Efuru. African Writers Series 26. London: Heinemann, 1966. 288 pages.

NOVELS/NOVELETTES

Idu. African Writers Series 56. London: Heinemann, 1970. 218 pages.

Never Again. Enugu: Nwamife Publishers, 1975. 80 pages.

One Is Enough. Enugu: Tana Press, 1983. 154 pages.

OGOT, GRACE AKINYI (Kenya)

The Promised Land. Nairobi: East African Publishing House, 1966. 193 pages.
    Swahili translation: Nehi Bila Ngurumo. Nairobi: Longman, 1979. 43 pages.

OKOYE, IFEOMA (Nigeria)

Behind The Clouds. London: Longman; Washington, D.C.: Three Continents Press, 1982. 119 pages.

Men Without Ears. Essex: Longman - Drumbeat Series, 1983. 160 pages.

OLIVESI, DJAMILA (North Africa)

Les enfants de polisario. Paris: Edition des femmes, 1979.

OWINO, ROSEMARIE (Kenya)

Sugar Daddy's Lover. Nairobi: Spear, 1975. 75 pages.

RAKOTOSON, MICHELE (Malgache)

Dadabé. Paris: Edition Karthala, 1984. 100 pages.

RAMALA, MAGGIE (Lesotho)

Lukas Motšheletšhele. n.p., 1963. [Based on a Jekyll and Hyde story in Sotho].

RATSIFANDRIHAMANANA, CLARISSE (Madagascar)

Ny zanako (Ma fille). Tananarivo: Printim-Pirenena, 1969. 2 vols.

NOVELS/NOVELETTES

SEBBAR, LEILA (Algeria)

On tue les petites filles. Paris: Editions Stock, n.d.

Fatima ou les Algériennes au square. Paris: Editions Stock, n.d.

Le Chinois vert d'Afrique. Paris: Editions Stock, 1984.

SOW FALL, AMINATA (Senegal)

La grève des battù. Dakar: Les Nouvelles Editions Africaines, 1979; rpt.
    The Beggars' Strike. Translated Dorothy Blair. London: Longman; Washington, D. C.: Three Continents Press, 1981.

Le revenant. Dakar: Les Nouvelles Editions Africaines, 1980.

L'Appel des arènes. Dakar: Les Nouvelles Editions Africaines, 1982. 144 pages.

TAOS-AMROUCHE, MARGUERITE (Algeria)

Jacinthe noire. Paris: Charlot, 1947. Reedit. Paris: 1972.

La Rue des tambourins. Paris: La Table Ronde, 1960.

L'Amant imaginaire. Paris: Morel, 1975. 435 pages.

TLALI, MIRIAM (South Africa)

Muriel at Metropolitan. Johannesburg: Ravan Press, 1975; rpt. Washington, D.C.: Three Continents Press, 1979. 190 pages.

Amandla. Johanneburg: Ravan Press, 1980.

NOVELS/NOVELETTES

TSOGO, DELPHINE ZANGA (Cameroon)

Vies des femmes. Yaoundé: CLE, 1983. 121 pages.

ULASI, ADAORA LILY (Nigeria)

Many Things You No Understand. London: Michael Joseph, 1971. 190 pages.
   [A detective novel].

Many Things Begin to Change. New York: Collier/Macmillan, 1975. 156 pages.
   [A detective novel].

The Man from Sagamu. New York: Collier/Macmillan, 1978. 124 pages.
   [A detective novel].

WILLIAMS, KATE NGOWO (Cameroon)

The Love Seat. Yaoundé: n.p., 1978. [a government press - paid for by her father].

II. FICTION

SHORT STORIES

'ABD ALLAH, SUFI (Egypt)

Madrasat Al-Banāt [A Girls's School]. Cairo: n.p., 1959.

Alf Mabruk [A Million Congratulations]. Cairo: Al-Kaumiyah, 1965.

Arūsha 'Alā Al-Raff [A Bride on the Shelf]. Cairo: Maärif, 1966.

Bagāyä Rajul [Residues of a Man]. Cairo: Al-Tijārī, n.d.

ACHOLA (East Africa)

"A Letter to Rufus," Darlite, 4, 2 (1970), 25-31.

ADEMOLA, FRANCES (Ghana and Nigeria)

Reflections: Nigerian Prose and Verse. Pref. Ezekiel Mphahlele. Lagos: African Universities Press, 1962. 123 pages; rpt. Forward Nnamdi Azikiwe. Lagos: African Universities Press, 1965. 119 pages.

AFONSO, MARIE PERPETUA CANDEIAS DA SILVA (Angola)

A Mulher de duras cores. Falsos trilhos. Lisboa: Ganda, 1959. 62 pages.

O homen enfeitçado. Coleçāo Imbondeiro 20. Sá da Bandeira: Publicaçōes Imbondeiro, 1961. 31 pages, illus.

AIDOO, CHRISTINA AMA ATA (Ghana)

"No Sweetness Here," Black Orpheus, No. 12 (1963), 27-36; rpt. Rhythms; Selected Short Stories and Poems. Ed. Charlotte Brooks. New York: Washington Square Press, 1974, pp. 209-27; rpt. Ghanaian Writing Today. Vol. I. Ed. B. S. Kwakwa. Accra: Ghana Publishing Corporation, 1974, pp. 98-118.

"In the Cutting of a Drink," Pan African Short Stories. Ed. Neville Denny. London: Nelson, 1965, pages 43-54.

"A Gift from Somewhere," Journal of New African Literature, 2 (1966), 36-44; rpt. New African Literature and the Arts, Vol. I. Ed. Joseph Okpaku. New York: Thomas Y. Crowell, 1966, pp. 177-88.

SHORT STORIES

"Certain Winds from the South," Black Orpheus, No. 20 (1966), 8-13; rpt. Political Spider. Ed. Ulli Beier. New York: Africana Publishing Corporation, 1969, pp. 101-9.

"The Late Bud," Okyeame, 2, 2 (1966), 33-40.

"Story-Telling in an African Village," The New African, October 1966, p. 166.

"The Message," Okyeame, 3, 1 (1966), 33-40; rpt. African Writing Today, Ed. Ezekiel Mphahlele. Middlesex: Penguin, 1967, pp. 87-95; rpt. Ghanaian Writing: Ghana as Seen by Her Own Writers as Well as by German Authors. Ed. A. W. Kayper-Mensah and Horst Wolff. Tubingen: Erdmann, 1972, pp.101-109; rpt. Fragment From a Lost Diary and other Stories: Women of Asia, Africa, and Latin America. Ed. Naomi Katz and Nancy Milton. Boston: Beacon Press, 1973, pp. 118-26.

"Cut Me a Drink," Modern African Stories. Ed. Ellis Komey and Ezekiel Mohahlele. London: Faber and Faber, 1968. pp. 13-19.

"Everything Counts," Zuka, 3 (1969), 9-13; rpt. Giant Talk: An Anthology of Third World Writing. Ed. Quincy Troupe. New York: Random House, 1975, pp. 35-39; rpt. Straight Ahead International, 1, 1 (1980), 13, 16.

"Other Versions," The Literary Review, 11, 4 (1969), 459-68; rpt. The New African, 7, 2 (1969), 44-45; rpt. African Writing Today. Ed. John Povey and Charles Angoff. New York: Manyland Books, 1969, pp 199-206; rpt. Contemporary African Literature. Ed. Edris Makward and Leslie Lacy. New York: Random House, 1972, pp. 109-16.

"Two Sisters," Modern African Stories. Ed. Charles Larson. New York: Collier/Macmillan, 1970, pp. 108-17.

No Sweetness Here. New York: Doubleday, 1971. 166 pages.

"Satisfaction?" University of Cape Coast English Department Workpapers, 2 (1972), 2-12.

AKELLO, GRACE (Uganda)

"A Manly Nightmare," Viva, March 1978, pp. 28-9.

AMARILIS, ORLANDA (Cape Verde)

Cais-do-Sodre te Salamansa. Ciombra: Centelha, 1974. 124 pages.

SHORT STORIES

"Canal Gelado," Colóquio/Letras, No. 39 (1977)

"Luísa Filha de NIca," África, 1, 1 (1978), 19-24.

ANTHONY, MONICA (South Africa)

"Night Train to Johannesburg," Zonk, 9 , 12 (1957).

ATTARAH, CHRISTINA (Sierra Leone)

"Tangled Web," Black Orpheus, No. 13 (1963), 27-31.

BANNUNA, KHANATA (Morocco)

Liy-askut Al-Samt [Down with Silence]. Beirut: Al-Tijari, 1968.

Al-Nār Wal-Ikhtiyār [Fire and Choice]. Beirut: Al-Tijari, 1969.

CASELY-HAYFORD, ADELAIDE (Sierra Leone/Ghana)

"Kobina," West African Review, 22, 283 (1951), 385, 387.

"Mista Courifer," An African Treasury. Ed. Langston Hughes. New York: Crown, 1960, pp 134-43; rpt. West African Narrative. Ed. Paul Edwards. Edinburg: Nelson and Sons, 1963, pp. 164-80; rpt. Modern African Stories. Ed. Ellis Komey and Ezekiel Mphahlele. London: Faber and Faber, 1964, pp. 50-9, rpt. The African Assertion. Ed. Austin J. Shelton. New York: The Odyssey Press, 1968, pp. 153-63; rpt. Africa Speaks: A Prose Anthology. Ed. John P. Berry. London: Evans Brothers, 1970, pp. 8-9.

"Childhood Days," Growing Up. Ed. Deborah Manley. Lagos: African Universities Press, 1967, pp. 18-22.

"Reminiscences," Africa in Prose. Ed. O. R. Dathorne and Willfried Feuser. Middlesex: Penquin, 1969, pp. 131-38.

CASELY-HAYFORD, GLADYS (Sierra Leone/Ghana)

"Shadow of Darkness," African Voices. Ed. Anna Rutherford. New York: Grosset and Dunlap, 1970, pp. 134-39.

SHORT STORIES

CHEDID, ANDREE (Egypt)

Les Corps et le temps, suivi de L'étroite peau. Paris: Flammarion, 1978.

DJEBAR, ASSIA (Algeria)

"Il n'y a pas d'exil," La Nouvelle Critique, No. 112 (1960), 97-108.

"8 mai 1945;" "L'Affrontement du danger;" "Bilan d'un amour;" Anthologie des écrivains maghrébins d'expression française. Ed. Albert Memmi. Paris: Présence Africaine, 1965, pp. 103-5; 107-12 [from Les Enfants du nouveau monde.]

"Chapter from Les impatients," North African Writing. Ed. Len Ortzen. London: Heinemann, 1970.

"Images douces pour fillettes arabes," Des Femmes Hebdo, décembre 1979. p. 21.

Femmes d'Alger dans leur appartement. Paris: Editions des femmes, 1980.

DOVE-DANQUAH, MABEL (Ghana)

"Anticipation," African New Writing: Short Stories by African Authors. Ed. T. Cullen Young. London: Lutterworth, 1947, pp. 37-42,; rpt. An African Treasury. Ed. Langston Hughes. New York: Crown, 1960; pp. 163-67; rpt. The African Assertion. Ed. Austin J. Shelton. New York: The Odyssey Press, 1968, pp. 100-4; rpt. Ghanaian Writing Today. Vol I. Ed. B. S. Kwakwa. Accra: Ghana Publishing Corporation, 1974, pp. 120-24.

"Payment," African New Writing: Short Stories by African Authors. Ed. T. Cullen Young. London: Lutterworth, 1947, pp. 37-42; prt. An African Treasury. Ed. Langston Hughes. New York: Crown, 1960, pp. 163-67; rpt. The African Assertion. Ed. Austin J. Shelton. New York: The Odyssey Press, 1968, pp. 100-4; rpt. Ghanaian Writing Today. Vol I. Ed. B. S. Kwakwa. Accra: Ghana Publishing Corporation, 1974, pp. 120-24.

"The Torn Veil," African New Writing: Short Stories by African Authors. Ed. T. Cullen Young. London: Lutterworth, 1947, pp. 43-50; rpt. A Selection of African Prose. Ed. W. H. Whiteley. Oxford: The Clarendon Press, 1964, pp. 43-48.

with Phebean Itayemi-Ogundipe. The Torn Veil and Other Stories. London: Evans Brothers, 1975. 44 pages.

DUBE, VIOLET (South Africa)

Wozanazo izindaba zika Phoshozwayo [Tell us the stories of Phoshozwayo]. London: Oxford University Press, 1935.

SHORT STORIES

FAIK-NZUJI, CLEMENTINE MADIYA (Zaire)

"Ditetembwa," Jazz and Palm Wine. Ed. Willfried Feuser. London: Longman, 1981, pp. 26-30.

FONSECA, LILIA DA (Angola)

Filha de Branco. Sa da Bandeira: Edicoes Imbondeiro, 1960. 26 pages.

GITHAE, MADELEINE, also known as MICERE GITHAE-MUGO (Kenya)

"The Innocent," Penpoint, No. 16 (1964), 19-21.

HEAD, BESSIE (South Africa/Botswana)

"Collector of Treasures," MS June 1977, pp. 56-61, 90-2, 95-6.

"For Serowe, A Village in Africa," The New African, 4, 10 (1965), 230.

"Snowball;" "Looking for a Rain-God," New African, 3, 5 (1966), 65, 100-01.

"The Old Woman," Classic 2,3 (1967), 20-1.

"Sorrow Food," Transition, 6, 30 (1967), 47-8.

"Village People, Botswana," Classic, 2,3 (1967), 19-25.

"The Woman from America," Classic, 3, 1 (1968), 14-6.

"Chief Sekoto Holds Court," Voices of Africa. Ed. Barbara Nolen. New York: Fontana/Collins, 1972, pp. 36-40.

"Heaven Is Not Closed," Black World, 25, 2 (1975), 54-60; rpt. Forced Landing. Staffrider Series #3. Ed. Mothobi Multoatse. Johannesburg: Ravan Press, 1980, pp. 73-9.

"The Prisoner Wore Glasses," Opaque Shadows and Other Stories from Africa. Ed. Charles Larson. Washington, D.C.: Inscape, 1975, pp. 42-8; rpt. More Modern African Stories. Ed. Charles R. Larson. New York: Fontana/Collins, 1975.

"Witchcraft," MS, November 1975, pp. 72-7, 121

The Collector of Treasures and Other Botswana Village Tales. London: Heinemann, 1977. 109 pages.

SHORT STORIES

HOUSE, AMELIA (South Africa)

"Awakening," Staffrider, 2, 1 (1979), 8-10.

"Hunted," African Writing Today. Ed. Peter Nazareth. Hamilton: Outrigger Publications, 1981, pp. 209-17.

ITAYEMI-OGUNDIPE, PHEBEAN (Nigeria)

"Nothing So Sweet," African New Writing. Ed. T. Cullen Young. London: Lutterworth, 1947.

with Mabel Dove-Danquah. The Torn Veil and Other Stories. London: Evans Brothers, 1975. 44 pages.

JABBEH, PATRICIA D. M. (Liberia)

"The Nocturnal Being," New Voices from West Africa; The First Major Anthology of Contemporary Liberian Short Stories. Ed. S. Henry Cordor. Monrovia: The Liberian Literary and Educational Publications, 1979, pp. 74-82.

KALEBU, BETTY (Uganda)

"The Blacksmith and the Chief," Ghala, July 1970, p. 45.

KALIMUGOGO, G. (Kenya)

Dare to Die. Nairobi: East African Literature Bureau, 1978.

KIMENYE, BARBARA (Uganda)

Kalasandra. London: Oxford University Press, 1965. 103 pages.

Kalasandra Revisited. London, Nairobi: Oxford University Press, 1966. 110 pages.

"Pius Wins the Pools," Africa Speaks: A Prose Anthology. Ed. John P. Berry. London: Evans Brothers, 1970, pp. 1-3 [from "The Winner" in Kalasanda].

KIYINGI, ELIZABETH (East Africa)

"A Hunting Expedition," Penpoint, No. 20 (1966), 20-2.

SHORT STORIES

KOKUNDA, VIOLET (Uganda)

"Kefa Kazana," Penpoint, No. 16 (1964), 3-5; rpt. Origin East Africa: A Makerere Anthology. Ed. David Cook. London: Heinemann, 1965, pp. 1-3.

"Kenda," Ghala, 9, 7 (1973), 10-6.

KWAKU, ROSEMARY (Ghana)

"The Sad Part of His Life," The Mirror, March 1971, p. 11

"While His Body Laid in State," Weekly Spectator, July 1971.

LARA, ALDA (Angola)

Tempo de chuva. Lobito: Capricórnio, 1973. 36 pages.

LOBO, MARIA MANUELA DE SOUSA (Mozambique)

"Amejoe," Africa, 1, 1 (1978), 43-4.

MALAKA, MAUD (South Africa)

"One Bride — Three Grooms," Zonk, 2 (1959).

MASCARENHAS, MARIA MARGARIDA (Cape Verde)

"Nha Vicencia;" "Paciência;" Raizes, No. 2 (1977), 65-72.

MBONI, SARAH (Kenya)

"Stranger at the Wedding," Viva, 2, 1 (1976), 27-34.

MENSAH, GRACE OSEI (Ghana)

Eight Delightful Short Stories. Accra: Waterville, n.d.

SHORT STORIES

MHELEMA, MARJORIE (East Africa)

"A Child is Born," Zuka, No. 3 (1969), 39-41.

MITCHELL, ELIZABETH M. (Liberia)

"Swehe is Triumphant," New Voices from West Africa: The First Major Anthology of Contemporary Liberian Short Stories. Ed. S. Henry Cordor. Monrovia: The Liberian Literary and Educational Publications, 1979, pp. 9-24.

MOKWENA, JOAN (South Africa)

"My Husband Was a Flirt," Drum, May 1953.

MULI, ANNE KEERU (Kenya)

"Mwelu and I," Africa Woman, No. 19 (1979), 54-5.

"The Waiting Game," Viva, 6,9 (1980), 49-52.

NABWIRE, CONSTANCE (Uganda)

"Teda," East Africa Journal, 6, 1 (1969), 19-22.

NAKITWE, ANGELA NASHAKOMA (East Africa)

"Circumcision," Dhana, 5, 1 (1975), 3-6.

NDEGWA, CATHERINE D. (Kenya)

"The Revelation," Busara, 2,3 (1970), 3-6.

"The Last Christmas Present," Busara, 4, 2 (1971).

SHORT STORIES

NDELE, SERENA (Kenya)

"The Woman Who Dared," Viva, 6,8 (1980), 24-7.

NDELE, SUSAN (Kenya)

"The Beautiful Guerilla Fighter (Part I)," Viva, February-March 1979, pp. 36-42.

"The Beautiful Guerilla Fighter (Part II)," Viva, April 1979.

NJAU, REBEKA (Kenya)

"Muma," Présence Africaine, 22, 50 (1964), 215-20.

"Along with a Fig Tree," Zuka, 1 (1969), 27-31 [A chapter from a novel which developed into Ripples in a Pool and was awarded the East African Writing Committee Prize].

The Hypocrite. Nairobi: Uzima Press, 1977. 63 pages.

"Karuri and the Hawking Business," East African Literature: An Anthology. Ed. Arne Zetterstein. London: Longmans, 1983, pp. 86-9.

NORONHA, LYDIE (East Africa)

"Same Ends," Penpoint, No. 21 (1966), 34-4.

NSANZUBUHORO, VICTOIRE (Rwanda)

Nta byera (Nothing Can Be Spotless). Kigale: Editions Rwandaises, 1972.

NWAGBOSO, ROSALINE (Nigeria)

"My Real Mother," West Africa, 28 June 1982, pp. 1701-5.

"Somebody Else's Wife," West Africa, 11 July 1983, pp. 1611-13.

NWAPA, FLORA (Nigeria)

"My Spoons Are Finished," Présence Africaine, No. 63 (1967), 227-35.

"Idu," African Arts/ Arts d'Afrique, 1, 4 (1968), 50-52 [Extract from the novel, Idu].

SHORT STORIES

This is Lagos and Other Stories. Enugu: Nwankwo-Ifejika, 1971. 117 pages.

"The Campaigner," The Insider: Stories of War and Peace from Nigeria. Ed. Chinua Achebe. Enugu: Nwankwo-Ifejika Publishers, 1971, pp. 73-78; rpt. African Rhythms: Selected Stories and Poems. Ed. Charlotte Brooks. New York: Washington Square Press, 1974, pp. 136-55.

"Ada," Black Orpheus, 3, 4 (1970), 20-20 [Chapter from a forthcoming novel].

Wives at War and Other Stories. Enugu: Flora Nwapa & Co., 1980. 96 pages.

OGADA, PENNIAH A. (Kenya)

"A Case for Inheritance," Opaque Shadows and Other Stories from Contemporary Africa. Ed. Charles Larson. Washington, D. C.: Inscape, 1975, pp. 133-40.

OGOT, GRACE AKINYI (Kenya)

"The Year of the Sacrifice," Black Orpheus, No. 11 (1962), 41-50.

"Ward Nine," Transition, 3,13 (1964), 41-4.

"The Rain Came," Modern African Stories. Ed. Ezekiel Mphahlele. London: Faber and Faber, 1964, pp. 180-89; rpt. Pan African Short Stories. Ed. Neville Denny. London: Nelson, 1965, pp. 12-27; rpt. Lotus: Afro-Asian Writings, No. 1 (1971), 73-9; rpt. African Rhythms: Selected Stories and Poems. Ed. Charlotte Brooks. New York: Washington Square Press, 1974, pp. 198-209.

"Elizabeth," East Africa Journal, 3,6 (1966), 11-8.

"The Bamboo Hut," East Africa Journal, 3; 10 (1967), 40-4.

"The Hero," Nexus, 1, 2 (1967), 5-8.

"The Old White Witch," East Africa Journal, 4, 6 (1967), 15-22.

"Tekayo," African Writing Today. Ed. Ezekiel Mphahlele. Middlesex: Penguin, Books, 1967, pp. 109-20.

"Pay Day," East Africa Journal, 5,7 (1968), 26-8; rpt. East African Literature: An Anthology, Ed. Arne Zetterstein. London: Longman, 1983, pp. 78-81.

SHORT STORIES

Land Without Thunder. Nairobi: East African Publishing House, 1968. 204 pages.

"Island of Tears," East Africa Journal, 6,8 (1969), 20-5.

"The Promised Land," Palaver: Modern African Writings. Ed. Wilfred Cartey. New York: Nelson, 1970, pp. 83-92.

"The Other Woman," Ghala, 7,7 (1970), 6-13.

"The Family Doctor," Ghala, July 1971, pp. 6-14.

"The Middle Door," Ghala, 9, 1 (1973), 59-60.

"Ayiembo's Ghost," Viva, 1, 1 (1974), 51-5.

The Other Woman. Nairobi: Transafrica Publishers, 1977.

"The Wayward Father," Femina (Bombay), 8-12 September 1979, pp. 45,47.

"The Fisherman," Folketi Bilk-Kulturfront (Stockholm), 21 November 1979, pp. 15-21.

The Island of Tears. Nairobi: Uzima Press, 1980.

OLIMBA, MAUDE (Kenya)

"The Whore," Joe, 15 January 1976, pp. 19-22.

PONTI-LAKO, AGNES (Sudan)

"The Son-In-Law," Sudan Now, June 1978, pp. 57-9.

QUTB, AMINA (Egypt)

Al-tyāf Al-Arb'ah (The Four Ghosts). Cairo: n.p., n.d.

Min Tayyār Al-Hayāt (From the Course of Life). Cairo: n.p., n.d.

ROBERTS, MAIMA (Liberia)

"The Book Woman of Zua Town," New Voices from West Africa: The First Major Anthology of Contemporary Liberian Short Stories. Ed. S. Henry Cordor. Monrovia: The Liberian Literary and Educational Publications, 1979, pp. 156-65.

ROSEMARY, pseudonym (Kenya)

"The Witness," Viva, September 1978, pp. 49-57.

SHORT STORIES

SEGUN, MABLE IMOUKHUEDE JOLAOSA (Nigeria)

"The Unfinished House," Reflections: Nigerian Prose and Verse. Ed. Frances Ademola. Lagos: African Universities Press, 1962, pp. 96-9.

"The Secret Farm," Growing Up. Ed. Deborah Manley. Lagos: African Universities Press, 1967, pp. 57-67.

"The New Confidante,"Nigerian Magazine, No. 97 (1969), 151-54.

SELLO, DORIS (South Africa)

"I Broke Their Hearts," Drum, August 1953.

SETIDISHO, EDITH (South Africa)

Induku ayinamzi (A stick has no name). Cape Town: Oxford University Press, 1961. 107 pages, illus. [Xhosa].

SIBANE, NONA (South Africa)

"Narrow Is The Way," Our Africa, 1, 12, and 2, 3 (1959).

"No Way in the Wilderness," Our Africa, 4,5-6 (1962).

"Let It Be Forgotten," Our Africa, 4, 10 (1962).

SIGANGA, JENIFER (Kenya)

"Second Meeting," Viva, 2,7 (1976), 16-18.

SILVA, MARIA DE JESUS NUNES DA (Angola)

"Se nao fosse a Victoria," Mensagem, Nos. 2-4 (1952), 29-30.

SUMBANE, NATALA (Mozambique)

Litcher im Dunkeln Erzahlungen aus Mocambique. Intr. J. Badertscher. Zürich: Wandererverlag, 1950. 90 pages, illus.

SHORT STORIES

SUTHERLAND, EFUA THEODORA MORGUE (Ghana)

"Samataase Village," Okyeame, 1 (1961), 53-8.

"New Life at Kyerefaso," An African Treasury. Ed. Langston Hughes. New York: Crown, 1960, pp. 111-17; rpt. Modern African Prose. Ed. Richard Rive. London: Heinemann, 1964, pp. 79-86; rpt. English African Literature. Ed. Anne Tibble. New York: October House, 1965, pp. 245-50; rpt. Pan African Short Stories. Ed. Neville Denny. London: Nelson, 1965, pp. 1-11; rpt. An African Assertion. Ed. Austin J. Shelton. New York: The Odyssey Press, 1968, pp. 100-4; rpt. Lotus: Afro-Asian Writings. 5 (1970), 67-71; rpt. Nommo: An Anthology of Modern Black African and Black American Literature. Ed. William H. Robinson. New York: Macmillan, 1972, pp. 238-87; rpt. Ghanaian Writing Today, 1. Ed. B. S. Kwakwa. Accra: Ghana Publishing Corporation, 1974, pp. 80-6.

TAOS-AMROUCHE, MARGUERITE (Tunisia/Algeria)

"Pourquoi fallait-il que je fusse toujours...en marge?" Anthologie des écrivains maghrébins d'expression française. Ed. Albert Memmi. Paris: Présence Africaine, 1965, pp. 279-81 [from Rue des tambourins].

THOMAS, GLADYS (South Africa)

"The Promise." Staffrider, 4,1 (1981), 5-8.

TIALI, MIRIAM (South Africa)

"Soweto Hijack," Staffrider, 1, 1 (1978), 12-20; rpt. Rikka, 6,1 (1979), 24-41.

"The Point of No Return," Staffrider, 1, 2 (1978),; rpt. Forced Landing. Ed. Mothobi Mutloatse. Johannesburg: Ravan Press, 1980, pp. 137-49; London: Heinemann, 1981.

'Amandla," Staffrider, 3,2 (1980), 37-38, 41 [Excerpt from the novel, Amandla].

"The Hunting Melancholy of Kilpvoor Dam," Staffrider, 4,1 (1981), 13-6.

TULAY, ELIZABETH LOVO JALLAH (Liberia)

"The Disguised Wife," New Voices from West Africa: The First Major Anthology of Contemporary Liberian Short Stories. Monrovia: The Liberian Literary and Educational Publications, 1979, pp. 74-82.

SHORT STORIES

UREY-NGARA, ABIGAIL (Unidentified)

"Deceived in Love," Africa Woman, No. 15 (1978), 60-1, 63.

WANJIRU, L. MUMBI (Kenya)

"One Woman's Solution," Viva, 2, 8 (1976), 44-5.

WERE, JANE (Kenya)

"A Broken Promise," Viva, March 1978, pp. 26-7.

WERE, MIRIAM KHAMADI (Kenya)

"For Old Time's Sake," Joe, October 1974, pp. 16-21.

YEBOAH-AFARI, ADJOA (Ghana)

The Sound of Pestles. Accra: n.p., n.d.

ZIRIMU, ELVANIA NAMUKWAYA (Uganda)

"The Hen and the Groundnuts," Origin East Africa: A Makerere Anthology. Ed. David Cook. London: Heinemann, 1965, pp. 137-39.

"Land of the Hills," Dhana, November 1971, pp. 52-5.

"Nvanungi," Dhana, 2,2 (1972), 1-7.

"Lutambi," Dhana, 4,2 (1974), 9-11.

"The Robber and the Robbed," Dhana, 5, 2 (1975), 18-21.

III. DRAMA

PUBLISHED PLAYS

ACQUAH, BARBARA (Ghana)

Ananse and the Wise Men. Accra: n.p., n.d. 24 pages [A children's Christmas play].

ADDO, PATIENCE (Ghana)

"Company Pot: A Concert Party Performance," Nine African Plays for Radio. Ed. Gwenyth Henderson and Cosmos Pieterse. London: Heinemann, 1973, pp. 163-85.

AIDOO, CHRISTINA AMA ATA (Ghana)

The Dilemma of a Ghost. London: Longmans and Green, 1965. 50 pages; rpt. New York: Collier/MacMillan, 1971.

"Prezelozyla Malgorzata Semil 'Christina Ama Ata Aidoo Duch Na Rozdrozu'," Dialog, No. 6 (1968), 65-90 [Translation of The Dilemma of a Ghost into Polish].

Anowa. London: Longmans and Green, 1970. 66 pages; rpt. Washington, D.C.: Three Continents Press, 1979.

"Anua," Okyeame, 4, 1 (1970), 41-50.

"The Dilemma of a Ghost (extract)," Ghanaian Writing Today, 1. Ed. B.S. Kwakwa. Accra: Ghana Publishing Corporation, 1974, pp. 88-97.

CHEDID, ANDREE (Egypt)

Le Montreur. Paris: Editions du Seuil, 1969. 95 pages.

CHOGO-WAPAKABULO, ANGELINA (Tanzania)

Wala Mbivu. Nairobi: East African Publishing House, 1974.

Kawambwa na Kamchape. Nairobi: East African Publishing House, n.d.

Kortini Mtu Huya. Nairobi: East African Publishing House, n.d.

Kijiji Chetu. Dar-es-Salaam: Tanzania Publishing House, n.d.

PUBLISHED PLAYS

CLEMS, DARLENE (Ghana)

"The Prisoner, The Judge, and The Jailer," Nine African Plays for Radio. Ed. Gwenyth Henderson and Cosmo Pieterse. London: Heinemann, 1973, pp. 71-86.

"Scholarship Woman," African Theatre. African Writers Series #127. Ed. Gwenyth Henderson. London: Heinemann, 1973, pp. 67-86.

DIKE, FATIMA (South AFrica)

"Sacrifice of Kreli," Theatre One. Johannesurg: A.D. Donker, 1977.

The First South African. Johannesburg: Ravan Press, 1979.

DJEBAR, ASSIA (Algeria)

Rouge l'aube. Alger: SNED, 1969.

KAMA-BONGO, JOSEPHINE (Gabon)

Obali (Pièce en 5 actes). Libreville: n.p., 1975. 64 pages [Presented for the first time on March 25, 1974 at the First Gabonese Cultural Festival in Libreville].

KASAHUN, ROMANA WARQ (Ethiopia)

The Light of Science. Addis Ababa: n.p., 1955 (A play dedicated to the memory of Princess Tshay Haile Selassie).

KHAKETLA, CAROLINE NTSELISENG 'MASECHELE R. (Lesotho)

Mosali eo u'neileng eena (The Woman You Gave Me). Morija; Morija Sesuto Book Depot, 1956. 90 pages (In Sotho).

Pelo ea Monna (The Heart of a Man). Maseru: the author, 1976 [Sotho drama set in Sophiatown and Lesotho].

KWAKU, ROSEMARY (Ghana)

"Two Troubles, One God," Railport, 1, 10 (1973), 17.

PUBLISHED PLAYS

LIBONDO, JEANNE NGO (USA/Cameroon)

"Oh, How Dearly I Detest Three," Nine African Plays for Radio. African Writers Series #134. Ed. Gwenyth Henderson and Cosmo Pieterse. London. Heinemann, 1973.

LIHAMBA, AMANDINA (Tanzania)

Hawada la Fedha. Dar-es-Salaam: Tanzania Publishing House, n.d.

with Penina Muhando and M. Bahsidya Harakoti za Ukombuzi. Dar-es-Salaam: Tanzania Publishing House, n.d.

LIKING, WEREWERE (Cameroon)

Orphée-Dafric, roman. Orphée d'Afrique, théâtre rituel. Paris: L'Harmattan, 1981, pp. 9-122. "Collection Encres Noires, 14."

MATENJWA, CHRISTINE (Kenya)

"Little Muya and Big Muya," The Cooking Pan and Other Plays. Ed. Margaret Macpherson. London: Heinemann, 1979.

MATINDI, ANNE (Kenya)

with Cynthia Hunter. The Sun-Men and Other Plays. Nairobi: East African Publishing House, 1971. 80 pages.

MUGO, MICERE GITHAE (Kenya)

"The Long Illness of Ex-Chief Kiti," The Fiddlehead, 90 (1971), 3-37.

The Long Illness of Ex-Chief Kiti. Nairobi: East African Literature Bureau, 1976. 61 pages [Expanded version].

with Ngugi wa Thiong'o. The Trial of Dedan Kimathi. London: Heinemann, 1976. 85 pages.

MUHANDO, PENINA (Tanzania)

Hatia (Guilt). Nairobi: East African Publishing House, 1972. 41 pages.

Tambueni Haki Zetu (Recognize our rights). Dar-es-Salaam: Tanzania Publishing House, 1975. 34 pages.

PUBLISHED PLAYS

with Ndyanao Balisidya. Fasihi na Sanaa Za Maonyesho. Dar-es-Salaam: Tanzania Publishing House, 1976. 86 pages.

Heshima Yangu. Nairobi: East African Publishing House, n.d. 19 pages.

Pambo. Dar-es-Salaam: Foundation, 1976. 64 pages.

NJAU, REBEKA (Kenya)

"The Scar," Transition, 3,8 (1963), 23-28; rpt. Eleven Short African Plays. Ed. Cosmo Pieterse. London: Heinemann, 1971.

The Scar: A Tragedy In One Act. Moshi, Tanzania: Kibo Art Gallery, 1965. 32 pages.

NJOYA, RABIATOU (Cameroon)

La dernière aimée. "Collection Théâtre" Yaoundé: CLE, 1980. pp. 6-61.

OGOT, GRACE AKINYI (Kenya)

Mphahele, Ezekiel. "Oganda's Journey," Staffrider. 2,3 (1979), 38-47 (A dramatization of a short story by Grace Ogot).

RAKOTOSON, MICHELE (Malgache)

L'Histoire de Koto, 1979.

Sambany, 1980 (3e prix du concours théâtral inter-africain de Radio France Internationale).

RAMALA, MAGGIE (Lesotho)

Rangwane ke go paletse (Uncle, I have beaten you). [A three-act Sotho play published in 1971].

PUBLISHED PLAYS

SOFOLA, ZULU (Nigeria)

The Deer Hunter and the Hunter's Pearl. London: Evans Brothers, 1969.

"Wedlock of the Gods: A Play," Nigeria Magazine, 106 (1970), 206-18.

The Disturbed Peace of Christmas. Ibadan: Dayster Press, 1971.

Wedlock of the Gods. Evans African Plays. London: Evans Brother, 1972. 56 pages.

The Sweet Trap. Ibadan: Oxford University Press, 1977. 76 pages.

SUTHERLAND, EFUA THEODORA MORGUE (Ghana)

"Anansegoro," Présence Africaine, No. 50 (19645), 221-36 [One-act play].

"Foriwa," Okyeame, 3,1 (1964), 40-47.

"You Swore an Oath Anansegoro," Présence Africaine, 22, 50 (1964), 231-47.

"Edufa," Okyeame, 3, 1 (1966), 47-49; rpt. Plays from Black Africa. Ed.
    Frederic Litto. New York: Hill and Wang, 1968, pp. 209-72; rpt.
    Ghananian Writing Today, 1. Ed. B. S. Kwakwa. Accra: Ghana Publishing
    Corporation, 1974, pp. 68-79.

Foriwa: A Play in Three Acts. Accra-Tema: State Publishing Corporation,
    1967. 67 pages. A community play.

Odasani. Accra: Anowuo Educational Publications, 1967.

Vulture! Vulture! and Tahinta. Accra: State Publishing Corporation, 1968.
    32 pages, illus. music [Two children's rhythm plays].

"The Marriage of Anansewa [excerpt], "Okyeame, 4,2 (1969), 63-9.

Edufa. London: Longmans and Green, 1969. 62 pages; rpt. Washington, D.C.:
    Three Continents Press, 1979 [A tragedy].

The Original Bob. Makers of Ghanaian Theatre Series. Accra; Anowuo Educational
    Publications, 1969 [The story of Bob Johnson].

The Marriage of Anansewa. London: Longman, 1977. 66 pages [A fantasy].

PUBLISHED PLAYS

UDENSI, UWA (Nigeria)

"Monkey on the Tree," African Plays for Playing. 2 Ed. Michael Etherton. London: Heinemann, 1976, pp. 7-32.

ZIRIMU, ELVANIA NAMUKWAYA (Uganda)

"Keeping Up with the Mukasas," Origin East Africa: A Makerere Anthology. Ed. David Cook. London: Heinemann, 1965, pp. 140-51.

"Family Spear," African Theatre. Ed. Gwenyth Henderson. London: Heinemann, 1974, pp. 109-29 [Prize winning radio play].

When the Hunchback Made Rain and Snoring Strangers. Nairobi: East African Publishing House, 1975. 87 pages.

"Keeping Up with the Mukasas (excerpt), " In Black and White: Writings from East Africa with Broadcast Discussions and Commentary. Ed. David Cook. Nairobi: East African Literature Bureau, 1976, pp. 37-8.

PERFORMED PLAYS

ADDO, JOYCE (Ghana)

"History of the Roman Catholic Church in Ghana," Peformed at the Kwame Nkrumah Cultural Centre in Accra, Ghana in 1981.

ADDO, PATIENCE (Ghana)

"Anansewa," Cultural Events in Africa, No. 72 (1971), 2 [A play performed at the Vandyck Theatre, University of Bristol, U.K.].

CLEMS, DARLENE (Ghana)

"The Prisoner, The Judge, and The Jailer," Cultural Events in Africa, No. 74 (1971), 4 [Broadcast by B.B.C. African Theatre, 8-10 August 1971].

"The Big Boss Cometh," Cultural Events in Africa, No. 78 (1971), 4 [Broadcast on 12 December 1971 by B. B.C. African Theatre].

DIKE, FATIMA (South Africa)

"The Glass House," Performed in New York at the Theatre at St. Peter's Church in 1980.

EMECHETA, BUCHI (Nigeria)

"A Kind of Marriage," Performed for B.B.C. TV and Radio.

"The Juju Landlord," Performed for B.B.C. Radio

"Tanya, a Black Woman," Performed for B.B.C. Radio

ENEM, EDITH (Nigeria)

"Ransom," Performed by the National Theatre of the University of Ife, Ile-Ife, Nigeria in June 1982.

ESAN, YETUNDE (Nigeria)

"Don't Say It in Writing," P.R.: Nigeria, June 1960 [A play in Pidgin English].

PERFORMED PLAYS

GATHII, HANNAH (Kenya)

"The Debt," Performed at the 1965 Uganda Festival in Kampala

JOHN-ROWE, JULIANA (Sierra Leone)

"E de E no du [There is but not enough]," A Krio play on Family Planning performed in Freetown, Sierra Leone in 1970.

"I Dey I Noh Du," Krio play performed in Freetown in 1972.

"I Dohn Rich Tem," A Krio play which premiered in Freetown in January 1975 at the State House.

"Na Mami Bohn Am," [A Krio play].

KHAKETLA, CAROLINE N.M.R. (Lesotho)

"Mahlopha-a-senya (Both good and bad at the same moment) Won the 1954 play competition of the Johannesburg publisher, Afrikaanse Pers-Boek-handel.

KWAKU, ROSEMARY (Ghana)

"Ghana Moves Right," Performed by the Puppetry Section of the Ghana Information Services Department in 1974.

"Oh, How Dearly I Love Thee," Cultural Events in Africa, No. 73 (1971), 5; No. 74 (1971), 4 [Broadcast by B.B.C. African Theatre on 25-27 June 1971].

LOKKO, SOPHIA (Ghana)

"Lai Momo," Cultural Events in Africa, No. 81 (1971), 3 [An adaptation of Lorca's Blood Wedding].

NAKACWA, THERESA (Uganda)

"Empologoma," Play performed in 1965 at the Uganda National Theatre in Kampala

NJAU, REBEKA (Kenya)

"In Round Chain," One-act play first performed in 1964

PERFORMED PLAYS

PEARCE, ESTHER TAYLOR (Sierra Leone)

"Bad Man bettah pas empty ose," [A bad husband is better than an empty house]

"Jargoon say e wan marrade," [Jargoon wants to get married].

"Who dat nor woke nor go eat," [Whoever does no work shall not eat].

SUTHERLAND, EFUA THEODORA MORGUE (Ghana)

"Nyamekye"

"The Pineapple Child," Performed children's play.

ZIRIMU, ELVANIA NAMUKWAYA (Uganda)

"Taabu of Asungwe," Dhana, 3,1 (1973), 24 [Play performed in August 1973 at the National Theatre in Kampala].

IV. POETRY

ABDULLAH, NURU BINTI (East Africa)

"Peke Peke (By Herself)," An Anthology of Swahili Love
  Poetry. Ed. and Tr. Jan Knappert. Los Angeles: University of California
  Press, 1972, pp. 16-7 (Swahili Poetry).

ABREU, MANUELA DE (Angola)

"Six Poems," No Reino de Caliban. Vol II. Ed. Manuel Ferreria. Lisboa:
  Seara Nova, 1976, pp. 372-75.

ACHEBE, CHRISTIE CHINWE (Nigeria)

"Black Dragons," Okike No. 11 (1976), 154.

ACHOLONU, CATHERINE (Nigeria)

"Lost Virtue;" "Song of Beauty;" Okike, No. 17 (1980), 82-3.

"Going Home," Présence Africaine, No. 120 (1981), 63-5.

ADDO, JOYCE (Ghana)

"Poem," Voices of Ghana: Literary Contributions to the Ghana Broadcasting
  System, 1955-1957. Ed. Henry Swanzy. Accra: Ministry of Information and
  Broadcasting, 1958.

"Memories of an Old Friend," Présence Africaine, No. 80 (1971), 93-94.

"Kleman Revisited," Ghanaian Writing: Ghana as Seen by Her Own Writers
  as Well as by German Authors. Ed. A. W. Kayper-Mensah and Horst Wolff.
  Tubingen: Erdmann, 1972, pp. 145-48.

ADEMOLA, FRANCES (Ghana/Nigeria)

Reflections: Nigerian Prose and Verse. Pref. Ezekiel Mphahlele. Lagos:
  African Universities Press, 1962. 123 pages; rpt. Foreword Nnamdi
  Azikiwe. Lagos: African Universities Press, 1965. 119 pages.

AIDOO, CHRISTINA AMA ATA (Ghana)

"The Last of the Proud Ones," Okyeame, 2,1 (1964), 9-10.

POETRY

"The Reward;" "The Awakening;" The New African 4 (1965), 10.

"Poem;" "Prelude;" "Sebonwoma'" Présence Africaine, No. 57 (1966), 300-02.

"Of Love and Commitment," Zuka, No. 4 (1969), 9-11.

"For Kinna," Zuka, No. 5 (1970), 15-16.

"Challenging Yours;" "Greetings from London;" Zuka, No. 6 (1972), 66-7.

"Cornfields in Accra," The Word Is Here: Poetry from Modern Africa. Ed. Keoraptse Kgositsile. New York: Anchor/Doubleday, 1973, pp. 113-16; rpt. Aftermath: An Anthology of Poems in English from Africa, Asia and the Caribbean. Ed. Robert Weaver and Joseph Bruchac. Greenfield: Greenfield Review Press, 1977, pp. 9-12.

"Poem," You Better Believe It: Black Verse in English from Africa, the West Indies, and the United States. Ed. Paul Breman. New York: Penquin, 1973, pp. 472-73.

"Sebonwoma," Poems from Africa. Ed. Samuel Allen. New York: Thomas Y. Crowell, 1973, p. 17.

"Our Sister Killjoy on Why We Die Like Flies," Asemka, 1, 2 (1974), 105-6.

"Poems," Nimrod, 21, 2; 22, 1 (1977).

Dancing Out Doubts. Vols. 1-2. New York: NOK Publishers, 1981.

AKAFIA, WOTSA (Togo)

"J'ai marché...," Présence Africaine, No. 86 (1973), 89-90.

AKELLO, GRACE (Uganda)

My Barren Song. Arusha: Eastern Africa Publications Company, 1979. 140 pages.

"New Steps...Old Steps," African Writing Today. Ed. Peter Nazareth. Hamilton: Outrigger Publications, 1981, pp. 20-23 [Special edition of Pacific Moana Quarterly, 6, 3-4 (1981)].

"Only a Child," West Africa, 30 November 1982, p. 2865.

POETRY

ALLOTEY, ALICE (Ghana)

"To Sleep," Okyeame, 4, 2 (1969), 22.

ALMEIDA, DEOLINDA RODRIQUES DE (Angola)

"Poems," O Canto Armado: Antologia Tematica de Poesia Africana. Ed. Mario de Andrade. Lisboa: Sa da Costa Editora, 1979.

"Christmas Feast," Poems from Angola. Ed. Michael Wolfers. London: Heinemann, 1979, pp. 67-8.

"Mamu," Lavra & Oficina, No. 6 (1979).

AMEGASHIE, SUSAN (Ghana)

"Abortion," Africa Woman, No. 36 (1981), 17.

AMRANI, DANIELE (Algeria)

"Poems," Espoir et parole: poèmes algériens. Ed. Denise Barrat. Paris: Seghers, 1964, pp. 38, 51, 134, 147, 158, 200.

APIO, LYDIE M. (East Africa)

"Beyond the Grave," Dhana, 3,2 (1973), 45.

"The Last Echoes," Dhana, 4, 1 (1974), 75-6.

ASIBONG, ELIZABETH E. (Nigeria)

"Hogan Kid Bassey-Eren owo akan eren owo" (A Man Who Conquers a Man) (1975) [An Efik epic poem].

ATTIK, MRIRIDA N'AIT (Morocco)

Songs of Mririda, Courtesan of the High Atlas. Trs. Daniel Helpern and Paula Paley. Greensboro: Unicorn, 1974. 54 pages.

"Poem," The Penguin Book of Women Poets. Ed. Carol Cosman, Joan Keefe and Katheleen Weaver. New York: Penguin, 1978.

POETRY

AVERY, GRETA (Sierra Leone)

"Expatriates," Aureol 70 Poems. Intr. Julian Croft. Freetown: Fourah Bay College, 1970 p. 8.

BA, OUMAR (Senegal)

"Mon Afrique;" "Courage;" "Sécheresse;" Présence Africaine, No. 57 (1966), 128-29.

"Drought," The Penguin Book of Women Poets. Ed. Carol Cosman, Joan Keefe and Kathleen Weaver. New York: Penguin, 1978, p. 310.

BABUKIKA, JUSTINE (East Africa)

"The Lament," Dhana, 5, 1 (1975), 22.

BATEYO, JULIET M. (East Africa)

"Silent Bottle;" "Patience;" Dhana, 2, 2 (1972), 37-8.

"The Bounds;" "My Cherished Garden;" Dhana, 4, 1 (1974), 51, 94.

BISHAI, NADIA (Egypt)

"Two (Untitled) Poems," African Writing Today. Ed. Peter Nazareth. Hamilton: Outrigger Publications, 1981, p. 28.

BOITUMELO (South Africa)

"When I Die," Staffrider, 1, 3 (1978), 49.

"My Smile," Staffrider, 1, 4 (1978), 44.

"Tribute to Mapetha," Staffrider, 2, 1 (1979), 49.

"Didimala;" "Black Mother;" Staffrider, 2, 4 (1979), 36, 49.

"Here I Stand with No Child in Sight," Staffrider, 2,4, (1979), 60.

BONNY, ANNE - MARIE (Cameroon)

"Hymne à la veuve du Biafra;" "Il était assis;" Abbia, No. 25 (1971), 160-61.

POETRY

CHEDID, ANDREE (Egypt)

Terre et poésie. Paris: Gallimard, 1956.

Fêtes et lubies: petits poèmes pour les sans-âges. Paris: Flammarion, 1973. 80 pages.

"Poem," Mudus Artium, 7,2 (1974).

Cérémonial de la violence. Paris: Flammarion, 1976. 51 pages.

Fraternité de la parole. Paris: Flammarion, 1976. 108 pages.

Les Corps et le temps [poetry]. L'Etroite peau: récits. Paris: Flammarion, 1978. 268 pages.

"Poems," Women of the Fertile Crescent: Modern Poetry by Arab Women. Ed. Kamal Boullata. Washington, D. C.: Three Continents Press, 1981, pp.1-12.

"The Future and the Ancestor," Women of the Fertile Crescent: Modern Poetry by Arab Women. Ed. Mirene Ghossein and Samuel Hazo. Washington, D. C.: Three Continents Press, 1981; rpt. Women Poets of the World. Ed. Joana Bankier and Deirdre Lashgari. New York: Macmillan, 1983, p. 99.

CHIMA, SIMMA (East Africa)

"Maimed," "My Heroine;" Faces at Crossroads: A 'Currents' Anthology. Ed. Chris Wanjala. Nairobi: East African Literature Bureau, 1971, pp. 99-101.

CHIRWA, NELLIE (Malawi)

"Poems," Mau: 30 Poems from Malawi. Blantyre: Hetherwick Press, 1971. 36 pages.

CHRISTIE, PHILLIPA (Zimbabwe)

"Mhandu (Shona Poem)." Madetembedzo Akare Namatsua (Traditional and Modern Poems). Ed. Musa Shamuyarira, Solomon M. Mutswairo, and Wilson E. Chivoura. London: Longman, in association with the Rhodesia Literature Bureau, 1959; rpt. 1962.

POETRY

CHUKWUMA, HELEN (Nigeria)

"The Appeal," The Muse, (1964).

"Biafra for Biafra," New African Literature and the Arts. Ed. Joseph Okpaku. New York: Third Press, 1974.

COGE, MAIMUNA BARMANI (Nigeria)

"Wakar Kungiyar Hausa (Song for the Hausa Conference) Bayero University in Kano, Nigeria 1980. Edited by Beverly Mack in Contemporary African Literature. Washington, DC: Three Continents Press, 1983.

DATTA, SOROJ (Uganda)

"The Block;" "The Dead Bird;" East Africa Journal, 3, 10 (1967), 11, 36.

"The Dead Bird," Poems from East Africa. Ed. David Cook and David Rubadiri. London: Heinemann, 1971, p. 35; rpt. Aftermath: An Anthology of Poems in English from Africa, Asia, and the Caribbean. Ed. Robert Weaver and Joseph Bruchac. Greenfield: Greenfield Review Press, 1977, p. 114.

DIAKHATE, NDEYE COUMBA (Senegal)

Filles du Soleil. Dakar: Les Nouvelles Editions Africaines, 1979.

DIAMONEKE, CECILE-IVELYSE (Unidentified)

Voix des cascades. Paris: Présence Africaine, n. p.

DJABALI, LEILA (Algeria)

"Poems," Espoir et parole; poèmes algériens. Ed. Denise Barrat. Paris: Seghers, 1964, pp. 99-100.

"For My Torturer, Lieutenant D -," Women Poets of the World. Ed. Joana Bankier and Deirdre Lashgari. New York: Macmillan, 1983, p. 283.

DJEBAR, ASSIA (Algeria)

"Tous les matins," Espoir et parole: poèmes algériens. Ed. Denise Barrat. Paris: Seghers, 1964, pp. 156-57.

Poèmes pour l'Algérie heureuse. Alger: SNED, 1969.

POETRY

DOUTS, CHRISTINE (South Africa)

"Eight Poems," Black Voices Shout. Ed. James Matthews. Athlone Cape: Black Publishing House, 1974; Austin: Troubadour Press, 1975.

EGBE, PAULINE (Cameroon)

"My Mother," Abbia, Nos. 14-15 (1966), 230-31.

EL-MISKERY, SHEIKHA (Uganda)

"The Crack;" "Just a Word;" Poems from East Africa. Ed. David Cook and David Rubadiri. London: Heinemann, 1971, 36-7.

EMECHETA, BUCHI (Nigeria)

"Nostalgia," Africa Woman, No. 19 (1979), 30.

ERONINI, FAUSTINA NWACHI (Nigeria)

"African Maid;" "My Love;" "Lumumba;" Présence Africaine, No. 36 (1961), 87-8.

ESAN, YETUNDE (Nigeria)

"Ololu-An Egunyun," You Better Believe It: Black Verse in English from Africa, the West Indies, and the United States. Ed. Paul Breman. Harmondsworth: Penguin, 1973, pp. 440-41.

ESPIRITO SANTO, ALDA DE (Sao Tome e Principe)

"Poems," Caderno de poesia negra de expressao portuguesa. Ed. Mario de Andrade. Lisboa: Livraria Escolar Editora, 1953.

"Poems," Antologia da poesia negra de espressào portuguesa. Ed. Mario de Andrade. Paris: Jean-Pierre Oswald, 1958, pp. 23, 34-5, 92-3.

"Dort in Agua Grande;" "Jenseits des Strandes;" "Wo sind die gejagten menschen?;" Poesia Negra. Ed. Mario de Andrade. Nymphenburger Verlagshandlung, 1962, pp. 43-4, 46.

POETRY

"Where Are the Men Seized in This Wind of Madness?," <u>Modern Poetry from Africa</u>. Ed. Alan F. C. Ryder. Harmondsworth: Penguin Poets, 1963; rpt. <u>Modern Poetry from Africa</u>. Eds. Ulli Beier and Gerald Moore. Baltimore: Penguin, 1965, pp. 191-93. rpt. <u>Women Poets of the World</u>. Ed. Joana Bankier and Deirdre Lashgari. New York: Macmillan, 1983, pp. 284-86.

"Poems," <u>Poetas de São Tomé e Príncipe: Antologia</u>. Lisboa: Casa dos Estudiantes do Imperio, 1963.

"Poems," <u>Présence Africaine</u>, No. 57 (1966), 490-98.

"Ou sont-ils les hommes chassés par ce vent de folie?;" "Au Loin de la plage;" <u>La Poésie africaine d'expression portugaise</u>. Ed. Mario de Andrade. Paris: Jean-Pierre Oswald, 1969, pp. 139-43.

"Far from the Beach," <u>The Other Voice: Twentieth Century Women's Poetry in Translation</u>. Ed. Joana Bankier and als. New York: W. W. Norton, 1976, pp.148-49.

<u>O Jorgal das Ilhas</u>. São Tomé: n. p., 1976. 4 pages.

<u>E Nosso o Solo Sagrado de Terra</u>. Lisboa: Ulmeiro, 1978. 184 pages.

"The Same Side of the Canoe," <u>The Penguin Book of Women Poets</u>. Ed. Carol Cosman, Joan Keefe and Kathleen Weaver. New York: Penguin, 1978, pp. 303-5.

FAIK-NZUJI, CLEMENTINE MADIYA (Zaire)

<u>Murmures. Poèmes</u>. Kinshasa: Editions Lettres Congolaises, Office National de la Recherche et du Développement, 1968. 15 pags.

<u>Le temps de amants</u>. Kinshasa: Editions Mandore, 1969. 48 pages.

<u>Kasala: poèmes</u>. Kinshasa: Editions Mandore, 1969. 58 pages.

"Impressions — poèmes," <u>Anthologie des écrivains congolais</u>. Kinshasa: S.N.E.C., Ministère de la Culture, 1969, pp. 99-104.

<u>Gestes interrompus</u>. Lubumbashi: Editions Mandore, 1976.

"Chute (extrait de <u>Gestes interrompus</u>);" "Rupture;" "Mushamasha (extrait de <u>Kasala</u>);" <u>Présence Africaine</u>, No. 104 (1977), 95-6.

POETRY

Impressions. Paris: n. p., 1978 [Won the Prix L.S. Senghor in 1978].

Lianes. Kinshasa: Editions du Mont Noir, n.d.

FALL, KINE KIRAMA (Senegal)

Chants de la rivière fraîche. Dakar: Les Nouvelles Editions Africaines, 1979.

FLORA (Mozambique)

"Eu te saudo Josina (1972)," Poesia de Combate. Maputo: FRELIMO, 1977, p. 128.

GASHE, MARINA, pseudonym for Rebeka Njau (Kenya)

"The Village," Poems from Black Africa. Ed. Langston Hughes. Bloomington: Indiana University Press, 1963, p. 47.

GEBRU, SENEDDU (Ethiopia)

Yelibbe Meshaf (The Book of My Heart). Addis Ababa: n. p., 1942 [Consists of a verse essay and two plays].

GITHAE, MADELEINE, maiden name for Micere Githae-Mugo (Kenya)

"Is Judgement Come?," Penpoint, No. 20 (1966), 16-7.

GREKI, ANNA (Algeria)

Algérie, capitale Alger. Tunis: SNED, 1963. 146 pages [en français et en arabe].

"Poems," Espoir et parole: poèmes algériens. Ed. Denise Barrat. Paris: Seghers, 1964, pp. 123-24; 136-37; 152-55; 162-64; 198-99; 205-7.

Temps fort. Paris: Présence Africaine, 1966.

"The Nights, the Day," Lotus: Afro-Asian Writings, No. 8 (1971), 134-35.

GRIFFIN, MARY ABENA (Ghana)

"The Index Number," The Gar, No. 32 (1978), 25.

POETRY

GUENDOUZ, NADIA (Algeria)

"Poems," Espoir et parole: poèmes algériens. Ed. Denise Barrat. Paris: Seghers, 1964, pp. 62-63; 173-74.

Amal. Alger: SNED, 1968.

GWARAM, HAUWA (Nigeria)

"Wakar Jama'iyas Matan Arewa ("Song for the Association of the Women of the North"), Edited by Beverly Mack in Contemporary African Literature. Washington, DC: Three Continents Press, 1983.

HOUSE, AMELIA, pseudonym Blossom Pegram (South Africa)

"You Are Born in your Coffin;" "Mark of My Birth" The Literary Review: South Africa, 15, 1 (1971).

"Deliverance;" "For South Africa;" AthensA (1977).

"Poems," The Gar, No. 31 (1977).

"Sunrise;" "Hard Labour;" "Exile;" "Deliverance;" Staffrider, 1,2 (1978).

"Five Poems," The Gar, No. 31 (1977), 28.

"Sunrise," The Gar, No. 31 (1977), 16.

"For South Africa," The Gar, No. 32 (1978), 31.

'Four Poems," Staffrider, 1, 2 (1978).

"Awakening," Staffrider, 2, 1 (1979).

"Eight Poems," Minority Voices, 2, 1 (1979)

"Five Poems," The Gar, No. 34 (1980), 30.

"Mr. White Discoverer," Staffrider, 3, 4 (1980-81), 2.

"Birth of the Blues," Inside the Turret, March 1980.

IBINGIRA, GRACE (Kenya)

Bitter Harvest. Modern African Library 36. Nairobi: East African Publishing House, 1981.

POETRY

JORDAN, NANDI (South Africa)

"Nineteen Poems," Quixote, 7, 2, (1968).

KAHAKU, PAULINE W. (Kenya)

"African Man," Viva, 6, 7 (1980), 15-6.

KANIE, ANOMA (Ivory Coast)

"All That You Have Given Me, Africa," The Penguin Book of Women Poets. Ed. Carol Cosman, Joan Keefe and Kathleen Weaver. New York: Penguin, 1978, pp. 305-6.

KAPHWIYO, JOSEPHINE (Malawi)

"Poems," Mau: 39 Poems from Malawi. Blantyre: Hetherwick Press, 1971. 36 pages

KARANJA, PAULA (Kenya)

"Unnatural", Viva, August, 1978, p. 89.

KARIBO, MINJI (Nigeria)

"Supersition," Nigerian Student Verse. Ed. Martin Banham. Ibadan: Ibadan University Press, 1960; rpt. A Book of African Verse. Ed. John Reed and Clive Wake. London: Heinemann, 1964, pp. 34-5; rpt. African Poetry for Schools. Ed. W. L. Radford. Nairobi: East African Publishing House, 1970, p. 30; rpt. Women Poets of the World. Ed. Joana Bankier and Deirdre Lashgari. New York: Macmillan, 1983, pp. 288-89.

KASESE, MEDARD (Zambia)

"A Spectacle," "An Angler's Treaty;" New Writing from Zambia, No. 2 (1969), 18-9.

"Mother Bird;" "The Desolate Woman;" New Writing from Zambia, 7, 1 (1971), 30-1.

"Prisoner of Inactivity;" "Black Mother;" New Writing from Zambia, 7, 2 (1971), 22-4.

POETRY

KATSINA, BINTA (Nigeria)

"Wakar Matan Nijeriya (Song for the Women of Nigeria)" Performed on 14 March 1980 at the annual Bayero University Hausa Conference in Kano, Nigeria. Edited by Beverly Mack. Contemporary African Literature. Washington, DC: Three Continents Press, 1983.

kaXHOBA, NTOMBIYAKHE kaBIYELA (South Africa)

"Poem," Staffrider, 2, 4 (1979), 61.

"When Did I Last Have a Good Laugh?," Staffrider, 2, 2 (1979).

KGOSITSILE, BALEKA (South Africa)

"Poem," Sechaba, October 1974.

KHAKETLA, CAROLINE N.M.R (Lesotho)

Mantsopa. Capetown: Oxford University Press, 1963. 88 pages.

"The White and the Black," The Penguin Book of South African Verse. Ed. Jack Cope and Uys King. Middlesex: Penguin, 1968, p. 261: rpt. The Other Voice: Twentieth-Century Women's Poetry in Translation. Ed. Joana Bankier and als. New York: W. W. Norton, 1976, p. 151.

KHAMADI, MIRIAM, also Miriam K. Were (Kenya)

"They Ran Out of Mud;" "On Wings;" "Zygote;" Transition, 5, 25 (1966), 22, 42.

"Zygote;" "They Ran Out of Mud;" "My Daughter is Not Yet Back;" Zuka, No. 4 (1969), 34-5.

KICHWA, MORENA HALIM (South Africa)

Bushman's Brew. Toronto: Goothair Press, 1974. 18 pages.

KIMENYI, LUCI W. (Kenya)

"A Secretary's Prayer," Viva, 6, 3 (1980), 13.

POETRY

KING, DELPHINE (Sierra Leone)

Dreams of Twilight. Apapa: Nigerian National Pres, 1962. 71 pages.

"The Child," Aftermath: An Anthology of Poems in English from Africa, Asia, and the Caribbean. Ed. Robert Weaver and Joseph Bruchac. Greenfield: Greenfield Review Press, 1977, p. 73.

KUMAH, SYLVIE (Ghan)

"Home Comfort," Africa Woman, No. 11(1977), 52.

"Hair (Dedicated to Alice)," Africa Woman, No. 12 (1977), 52.

Facing I. Germany: Literarisches Colloquium, 1980.

KURANKYI-TAYLOR, DOROTHY (Ghana)

Reflected Thoughts. Ilfracombe: Arthur H. Stockwell, 1959. 39 pages.

KWAKU, ROSEMARY (Ghana)

"Awudeme," Radio & TV Times, 13, 38 (1972).

"Rago Adagie," Radio & TV Times, 13, 42 (1972).

"The Forgotten Ones," The Daily Graphic, No. 6721 (1972), 5.

"Blood Tears," The New Ghana, 2, 4 (1973), 16.

"Path of Peace," Radio & TV Times, 14, 1 (1973).

"Second Invitation," Radio & TV Times, 14, 3 (1973).

"The Afrikan Dream," Radio & TV Times, 14, 12 (1973).

"A Birthday Token," Ideal Woman, January 1973.

"A Cry from the Countryside;" "Blessed Civilization;" "Stolen Love;" Ideal Woman, 4, 10 (1975), 10.

"Four Poems," The Ghana Review, 3, 1 (1978), 25.

"Poverty," Okike, No. 16 (1979), 70.

POETRY

LALUAH, ACQUAH, pseudonym for Gladys May Casely-Hayford (Ghana/Sierra Leone)

"Creation;" "Art Pure and True," The Philadelphia Tribune, 14 October 1937.

Take Um So. Freetown: New Era Press, 1948. 7 pages [Krio poetry].

"The Serving Girl," An African Treasury. Ed. Langston Hughes. London: Gollancz 1961, p. 187.

"Nativity;" "Shadow of Darkness;" Poems from Black Africa. Ed. Langston Hughes. Bloomington: Indiana University Press, 1963, pp. 75-7.

"The Serving Girl;" "African School-Girls Song;" "African School-Boys Song;" "Rainy Season Love Song;" Our Poets Speak. Ed. Donald St. John-Parsons. London: University of London Press, 1966, pp. 25, 28-31.

LARA, ALDA (Angola)

Poemas. Sá da Bandeira: Edições Imbondeiro, 1966. 198 pages.

Poesia. Launda: Caderinos Lavra & Oficina, No. 18, 1979. 53 pages.

LIMA, MARIA EUGENIA (Angola)

Entre a pantera e o espelho. Porto: Tipografia Nunes, 1964. 53 pages.

LWANGA, SUSAN (East Africa)

"Daybreak," Poems of Black Africa. Ed. Wole Soyinka. New York: Hill and Wang, 1975, p. 260.

MABUZA, LINDIWE (South Africa)

'Insomnia;" "Listening to Mbaquanga;" "The Day You Left for L.A.;" "Tribute to Mazizi Kunene;" "Summer 1970;" Confrontation, 1, 3 (1974).

"Insomnia:" "Listening to Mbaquanga;" Giant Talk: An Anthology of Third World Writing. Ed. Quincy Troupe and Rainer Schulte. New York: Random House, 1975, pp. 488-91.

"Poem," Freedom Ways, 15, 4 (1975).

POETRY

"Two Poems," Mandus Artium, 7, 2 (1976)

"Ten Poems," Speak Easy Speak Free. Ed. S. K. Mberi and Cosmo Pieterse. New York: International Press, 1975.

"Two Poems," Vurtnyaland, 4 (1979).

"Six Poems," Poets to the People: South African Freedom Songs. Ed. Barry Feinberg. London: George Allen and Unwin Ltd., 1974; London: Heinemann, 1980, pp. 89-100.

"Summer 1970," Speak Easy Speak Free. Ed. Cosmos Pieterse and Antar Sudan Katara Mberi. New York: International Publishers, 1977; rpt., Women Poets of the World. Ed. Joana Bankier and Deirdre Lashgari. New York: Macmillan, 1983, pp. 290-91;

MACHEL, JOSINA (Mozambique)

"E Neste Momento," As Armas Estao Acesas nas Nossas Mâos: Antologia Breve da Poesia Revolucionária de Mocambique. Pref. Papiniano Carlos. Porto: Ediçōes "Apesar de Tudo." 1976.

"This Is the Time," If You Want to Know Me: Reflections of Life in South Africa. Ed. Peggy L. Halsey, Gail J. Morlan and Melba Smith. New York: Friendship Press, 1976, p. 42.

"O Nosso Dia Histórico," Poesia de Combate. Maputo: FRELIMO, 1977, p. 51.

MACKAY, ILVA (South Africa)

"Seven Poems," Black Voices Shout. Ed. James Matthews. Athlone Cape: Black Publishing House, 1974; Austin: Troubadour Press, 1975.

"Free Yourself;" "No More;" The Gar, No. 31 (1977), 22.

"Poem," Sechaba, June 1979.

MAI, JEANNE NGO (Cameroon)

Poèmes sauvages et lamentations. Monte Carlo: Palais Miami, 1967. 111 pages [Collection Le Cahier des poètes de notre temps].

POETRY

MALAFA, EFOSI (Cameroon)

"A Man Will Turn You Down;" " What is Imporant;" "Love a Woman;" Africa Woman, No. 9 (1977), 52.

MALL, JASMINE (South Africa)

"On Mayfair Station," Staffrider, 2, 3, (1979).

MANDELA, ZINDZI (South Africa)

with Peter Magubane. black as i am. Los Angeles: The Guild of Tutors Press, 1978. 119 pages.

"My Country," If You Want to Know Me: Reflections of Life in South Africa. Ed. Peggy L. Halsey, Gail J. Morlan and Melba Smith. New York: Friendship Press, 1976, p. 13.

MAOKA, SHIMANE (South Africa)

"An African Woman," Staffrider, 2, 1 (1979), 36.

MARGARIDO, MARIA MANUELA CONCEICAO CARVALHO DA (Sao Tome e Principe)

Alto como o silêncio. Lisboa: Publicacoes Europa - America, 1957. 36 pages.

"Poems," Antologia da poesia de Sao Tomé e Príncipe. Ed. Alfredo Margarido. Lisboa: no. p., 1963.

"Memoria de ilha do Príncipe," Poetas e contistas africanos de espressao portuguesa. Sao Paulo: Editora Bresiliense, 1963.

"Socope;" "Vos que ocupais a nossa terra;" Présence Africaine, No. 57 (1966), 499-500.

"You Who Occupy Our Land," Woman Poets of the World. Ed. Joana Bankier and Deirdre Lashgari. New York: Macmillan, 1983, p. 284.

POETRY

MARWA, RAVI (Kenya)

"The Pattern;" "Strange;" "Choice:" Faces at Crossroads: A 'Currents' Anthology. Ed. Chris Wanjala. Nairobi: East African Literature Bureau, 1971, pp. 119-21.

MASEKELA, BARBARA (South Africa)

"Earth Has no Fury;" "Wishes and Facts;" "Flowers from You;" "Changes;" "U'Tamsi;" Confrontation, 1, 3 (1974).

MASEMBE, HARRIET (East Africa)

"Embalasasa," Dhana, 1, 1 (1971), 46.

MASHISHI, KEDISALETSE (South Africa)

"I Am the Equator," Staffrider, 2, 4 (1979).

MATENJWA, CHRISTINE (Kenya)

"The Worm," Dhana, 4, 2 (1974), 54.

"Rosemary Anne Rita Any More;" "Walking;" Dhana, 5, 2 (1975), 11-14, 24.

MATIP, MARIE-CLAIRE (Cameroon)

Ngonda. Bibliothèque du jeune africain. Douala-Yaoundé: Librairie au Messager, 1958. 48 pages, illus.

MATLOU, REBECCA (South Africa)

"Five Poems," Poets to the People: South African Freedom Poems. Ed. Barry Feinberg. London: George Allen and Unwin, Ltd., 1974; London: Heinemann, 1980, pp. 123-28.

M'BAYE, ANNETTE D'ERNEVILLE (Senegal)

Poèmes africains. Paris: Centre d'art national français, 1965. 20 pages.

Kadda. Dakar: Imprimerie A. Diop, 1966. 28 pages.

POETRY

"Poems," Présence Africaine, No. 57 (1966), 136-37.

"Poem," Poems from Africa. Ed. Samuel Allen. New York: Thomas Y. Crowell, 1973, p. 179.

"Silhouette," The Penguin Book of Women Poets. Ed. Carol Cosman, Joan Keefe and Kathleen Weaver. New York: Penguin, 1978, p. 302.

MBOWA, ROSE (Uganda)

"That Game," Penpoint, No. 20 (1966), 24.

"The Moon;" "Kind Face;" "The Easter Bull;" "The Real She;" Penpoint, No. 21 (1966), 13, 15, 19-20, 45.

"Light," East Africa Journal, 3, 10 (1967), 44.

"Ruin;" "That Game;" Poems from East Africa. Ed. David Cook and David Rubadiri. London: Heinemann, 1971, pp. 100-1.

"Those Birds," Dhana, 2, 1 (1972), 20.

"Ruin," In Black and White: Writings from East Africa with Broadcast Discussions and Commentary. Ed. David Cook. Nairobi: East African Literature Bureau, 1976, pp. 20-1; rpt. Aftermath: An Anthology of Poems in English from Africa, Asia, and the Caribbean. Ed. Robert Weaver and Joseph Bruchac. Greenfield: Greenfield Review Press, 1977, p. 119.

MHANDO, BLANDINA (Tanzania)

"The Passage: A Ritual that Never Took Place," Darlite, 6 (1970), 12-25.

MHLONGO, MAUREEN (South Africa)

"Singumhlobiso;" "Umvuzo Wakungalaleli;" Staffrider, 1, 4 (1978), 28 [Poetry in Zulu].

MOHAMEDALI, HAMIDA (Kenya)

"The Retreat;" "The Wayward Soul;" Drum Beat. Ed. Lennard Okala. Nairobi: East African Publishing House, 1967, pp. 88-9.

POETRY

MOKHOMO, MAKHOKOLOTSO A. (South Africa)

"When He Speaks to Me of Love [extract from "Moratuwa — Lerato la me" (My Beloved, My Love)]," The Penguin Book of South African Verse. Ed. Jack Cope and Uys Krige. Midelesex: Penguin, 1968, p. 273.

MOKOROSI, EMELY SEMELENG (Botswana?)

Bolebali (Forgetfulness). Morija: Morija Sesuto Book Depot, 1951. 47 pages [Sotho].

MORAIS, DESI (Mozambique)

"Eu, Tu, Nos Somos o Povo (1975);" "Retalhos (1975);" "Mulher Mocambicana;" Armas Estao Acesas nas Nossas Maos: Antologia Breve da Poesia Revolucionaria de Mocambique. Pref. Pepinano Carlos. Porto: Ediçoes Apesar de Tudo, 1976.

MORAZZO, YOLANDA (Cape Verde)

Cântico de Ferro. Lisboa: Oficinas Gráficas N.A., 1976. 77 pages.

MORITI, PALESA (South Africa)

"Farewell My Friend," Staffrider, 1, 4, (1978), 48.

MOROLO, WINNIE (South Africa)

"Thula Sana Lwam," Staffrider, 1, 4 (1978), 48.

"Courage, African Woman," Staffrider, 2, 4 (1979), 60.

MPHAHLELE, TERESA K. (South Africa)

"The Drag On of East Africa," Okike, No. 8 (1975), 66-8.

"Kikuyu Sunset;" "Kikuyu Love Affair;" Okike, No. 10 (1976), 73-5.

"Just Remembering," Okike, No. 11 (1976), 110.

POETRY

MPONGO, MARIE-EUGENIE (Zaire)

"Masikini (poème dramatique en quatre tableaux)," Anthologie des écrivains congolais. Kinshasa: S. N. E. C., Ministère de la Culture, 1969, pp. 41-5.

MTUNGWA, GLORIA (South Africa)

"Militant Beauty," Sechaba, 12 (1978).

MUCAVALE, JOANA MATEUS (Mozambique)

"Farol," Poesia de Combate. Maputo: FRELIMO, 1977, pp. 124-25.

MUGO, MICERE GITHAE (Kenya)

"Wife of a Husband," Okike, No. 4 (1973), 78.

"Poems," Fiddlehead, 96 (1974), 40-6.

"I Took My Son by the Hand," An Introduction to East African Poetry. Ed. Jonathan Kariara and Ellen Kitonga. Nairobi: Oxford University Press, 1976, pp. 115-18.

Daughter of My People Sing. Nairobi: East African Literature Bureau, 1976. 60 pages.

MUKWAYA, JEAN B. (East Africa)

"One More Favour," Dhana, 2, 2 (1972), 37.

MUTEMBA, MAUDE (Zambia)

"Cause No-one to Suffer," The Jewel of Africa, 1, 4-5 (1968), 6.

"The Mask," The Jewel of Africa, 3, 1-2 (1970), 2-6.

MUTSILA, IRENE (South Africa)

"Your Cross," Staffrider, 2, 4 (1979).

POETRY

MVEMVE, LINDIWE (South Africa)

"Poems," Staffrider, 3, 3 (1980), 47.

MWAKALA, MARIA (Mozambique)

"Mulher Mocambicana (1971), Poesia de Combate. Maputo: FRELIMO, 1977, p. 127.

NACHALE, JOANA (Mozambique)

"Poesia (1971)," Poesia de Combate. Maputo: FRELIMO, 1977, p. 126.

NAKITWE, ANGELA NASHAKHOMA (East Africa)

"Approaches to Love," Dhana, 4, 1 (1974), 22-3.

NCHWE, MANOKO (South Africa)

"My Tears," Staffrider, 2, 4 (1979), 60.

NDAAYA, CITEKU (Zaire)

"from Ndaaya Kasala," The Penguin Book of Women Poets. Ed. Carol Cosman, Joan Keefe and Kathleen Weaver. New York: Penguin, 1978, pp. 306-8.

NENE, AMELIA (Unidentified)

Fleurs de vie. Paris: Présence Africaine, n.p.

NGATHO, STELLA (Kenya)

"Footpath;" "The Kraal;" "A Young Tree;" Poems from East Africa. Ed. David Cook and David Rubadiri. London: Heinemann, 1971, pp. 109-11.

"The Kraal," Aftermath; An Anthology of Poems in English from Africa, Asia and the Caribbean. Eds. Robert Weaver and Joseph Bruchac. Greenfield: Greenfield Review Press, 1977, p. 27.

"Footpath," Women Poets of the World. Ed. Joana Bankier and Deirdre Lashgari. New York: MacMillan, 1983, pp. 289-90.

POETRY

NIRINA, ESTHER (Madagascar)

"Prière;" "Granil;" Présence Africaine, Nos. 101-102 (1977), 164-65.

NJAU, REBEKA (Kenya)

"Prayer of a Rural Woman," The Target, 15-20 October 1978, p. 5.

"The Cry of a Young Girl," The Target, 26 November - 9 December 1978, p. 3.

"Prayer of an Affluent Woman," The Target, 24 December - 16 January 1979, p. 8.

"Gebet eines Kindes," Nordelbische Mission, 20, 3 (1979), 11.

NORONHA, LYDIE (East Africa)

"The Crowning Glory," Penpoint, No. 21 (1966), 33.

OBI, DOROTHY (Nigeria)

"Winds of Africa," Black Orpheus, 1, 10 (19), 10; rpt. Women Poets of the World. Ed. Joana Bankier and Deirdre Lashgari. New York: Macmillan, 1983, p. 288.

OGUNDIPE-LESLIE, OMOLARA (Nigeria)

"Birthday Song;" "Those Rags...My Rags of Time;" Okike, No. 13 (1979), 9-10.

O'LANSEN, MALIKA (Algeria)

"Poems," Espoir et parole: poemes algériens. Ed. Denise Barrat. Paris: Seghers, 1964, pp. 64-5, 81.

OLISA, MARGARET (East Africa)

"Poems," Black Orpheus, No. 14 (1964), 46-7.

PEREIRA-EMANUEL, FRANCESCA YETUNDE (Nigeria)

"The Paradox;" "Mother Dark;" "The Burden;" "Two Strange Worlds;" Poems from Black Africa. Ed. Langston Hughes. Bloomington: Indiana University Press, 1963, pp. 90-5.

POETRY

PHIRI, IRENE (Zambia)

"A Wish after Death," New Writing from Zambia, 7, 4 (1971), 27.

PHUNGULA, NOMUSA, CYNTHIA (South Africa)

"Xola," Staffrider, 1, 4 (1978), 27 [Poem in Zulu].

QUEEN HATSHEPSUT (Egypt)

"From the Obelisk Inscriptions," 45 lines, Ancient Egyptian Literature, Vol II. Ed and Tr. Miriam Lichtheim. Berkeley: University of California Press, 1971; rpt. Women Poets of the World. Joana Bankier and Deirdre Lashgari. New York: Macmillan, 1983, pp. 277-78.

RIBEIRO, MARIANA MARQUES, pseudonym Ytchyana (Guinea - Bissau)

"Poems," Antologia dos Jovens Poetas: Momentos Primeiros da Construcao. Bissau: Conselho Nacional de Cultura, 1978.

ROBY, MARIA EMILIA (Mozambique)

"Hino a Mocambique," As Armas Estao Acesas nas Nossas Maos: Antologia Breve de Poesia Revolucionaria de Mocambique. Pref. Papinano Carlos. Porto: Edições Apesar de Tudo, 1976.

RUSH, BRENDA UTAMU (Unidentified)

"A Good Man is the Next Thing to God," Africa Woman, No. 11 (1977), 52.

RWAKYAYA, PROSCOVIA (Uganda)

"The Beard," African Writing Today. Ed. John Povey and Charles Angoff. New York: Manyland Books, 1969, p. 214.

"The Beard;" "The Inmates;" Poems from East Africa. Ed. David Cook and David Rubadiri. London: Heinemann, 1971, pp. 147-48.

"April 1966;" "More Poems;" In Black and White: Writings from East Africa with Broadcast Discussions and Commentary. Ed. David Cook. Nairobi: East African Literature Bureau, 1976, pp. 48-50.

POETRY

SA' ADU, A. B. (Nigeria)

"The Slogan," FESTAC Anthology of Nigerian New Writing. Ed. Cyprian Ekwensi. Lagos: Cultural Division of the Federal Ministry of Information, 1977, p. 10.

SEGUN, MABEL IMOUKHUEDE JOLAOSA (Nigeria)

"Conflict," Odu, No. 3 (1962), 35.

"The Pigeon Hole;" "Conflict;" "Corruption;" "A Second Olympus;" Reflections: Nigerian Prose and Verse. Ed. Frances Ademola. Lagos: African Universities Press, 1966, pp. 56-9.

"Conflict;" "Pigeon Hole;" Poems from Africa. Ed. Samuel Allen. New York: Thomas Y. Crowell, 1973, pp. 80, 82.

"The Pigeon Hole," Aftermath: An Anthology of Poems in English From Africa, Asia and the Caribbean. Ed. Robert Weaver and Joseph Bruchac. Greenfield: Greenfield Review Press, 1977, p. 60.

SHUAIB, YINKA (Nigeria)

"Giant Afrikanus," FESTAC Anthology of Nigerian New Writing. Ed. Cyprian Ekwensi. Lagos: Cultural Division of the Federal Ministry of Information. 1977, pp. 16-9.

SIGWILI, NOKUGCINA (South Africa)

"Persecution;" "The Building Fell;" Staffrider, 4, 1 (1980), 44.

SOUSA, NOEMIA CAROLINA ABRANCHES SOARES DE (Mozambique)

"Negra," Mensagem (1952).

"Ruf;" "Magaica;" "Lab mein volk ziehn;" Poesia Negra. Ed. Mario de Andrade. West Germany: Nymphenburger Verlagshandlung, 1962, pp. 104, 106, 108.

"Deixa passar meu povo." Antologia de poesia negra espressao portuguesa. Ed. Mario de Andrade. Paris: Jean Pierre Oswald, 1958, pp. 92-3.

POETRY

"Appeal," Modern Poetry from Africa. Ed. Gerald Moore and Ulli Beier.
 Baltimore: Penguin, 1965, pp. 239-40; rpt. African English Literature.
 Ed. Anne Tibble. New York: October House, 1965, pp. 288-89; rpt. 3000 Years
 of Black Poetry. Ed. Alan Lomax and Raoul Abdul. New York: Dodd, Mead and
 Company, 1970, pp. 188-89.

"Poema da infância distante;" "Se me quiseres conhecer;" "Sangue negro;"
 "Não matas;" Présence Africaine, No. 57 (1966), 465-71.

"Appel;" "Laisse passer mon peuple;" "Notre voix;" La poésie africaine
 d'expression portuguaise: anthologie. Ed. Mario C. P. de Andrade. Paris:
 Jean-Pierre Oswald, 1969, pp. 137-43.

"If You Want to Know Me," Poems of Black Africa. Ed. Wole Soyinka. New
 York: Hill and Wang, 1975, pp. 84-5; rpt. Attachments to the Sun. Ed. Douglas
 Blackburn, Alfred Horsfall and Chris Wanjala. London: Edward Arnold, 1978,
 p. 69.

"The Poem of Joao," Poems of Black Africa. Ed. Wole Soyinka. New York:
 Hill and Wang, 1975, pp. 197-99.

"Poem of Distant Childhood," The Penguin Book of Women Poets. Ed. Carol
 Cosman, Joan Keefe and Kathleen Weaver. New York: Penguin, 1978, pp.
 298-301.

SUTHERLAND, EFUA THEODORA MORGUE (Ghana)

"Mumunde My Mumunde;" "An Ashanti Story;" "Little Flowers;" "It Happened;" An
 Anthology of West African Verse. Ed. Olumbe Bassir. Ibadan: Ibadan
 University Press, 1957, pp. 7; 13-6; 22-3; 42-7.

"The Redeemed;" "Once Upon a Time;" "The Dedication;" "Song of the Fishing
 Ghosts;" Messages: Poems from Ghana. Ed. Kofi Awoonor and G. Adoli-Mortty.
 London: Heinemann, 1971, pp. 158-69.

"Song of the Fishing Ghosts;" "Our Songs Are About It;" Ghanaian Writing as
 Seen by Her Own Writers as Well as by German Authors. Ed. A. A. Kayper-
 Mensah and Horst Wolff. Tubingen: Erdmann, 1972, pp. 127-28.

"A Professional Beggar's Lullaby;" Aftermath: An Anthology of Poems in
 English from Africa, Asia, and the Caribbean. Ed. Robert Weaver and Joseph
 Bruchac. Greenfield: Greenfield Review Press, 1977, p. 23.

TADJO, VERONIQUE (Ivory Coast)

Latérite. Coll. Monde Noir Poche No. 24. Paris: Hatier/Agence, 1983. 94 pp
 [Won le Prix littéraire 1983 de l'ACCT].

POETRY

TAOS-AMROUCHE, MARGUERITE (Algeria/Tunisia)

Le grain magique: contes, poèmes et proverbes de Kabylie. Paris: Maspero, 1965.

TEAGE, HILARY (Liberia)

"Hymn," Banks-Henries, A. Doris. "Survey of Liberian Literature," Liberian Writing: Liberia as Seen by Her Own Writers as well as by German Authors. Foreword William V. S. Tubman. Tubingen: Horst Erdmann, 1970, pp. 14-6.

TELIKO, RAHMATOULLAHI (Guinea)

"Majjaado (Whoever Ignores God is Lost)," La femme, la vache, la foi: écrivains et poètes. Ed. Alfa Ibrahim Sow. Paris: Julliard. 1966, pp. 88-101 [Translated from the Peul by Christiane Seydou Amadu].

"Who Does Not Know That God is Lost?," Trs. and Ed. Christiane Seydou. Gérard, Albert. African Language Literatures: An Introduction to the Literary History of Sub-Saharan Africa. Washington, D.C.: Three Continents Press; London: Longman, 1980, p. 56.

TEMBE, ROSARIA (Mozambique)

"Josina Machel, Cidada do Mundo (1971)," Poesia de Combate. Maputo: FRELIMO, 1977, p. 122.

THOMAS, GLADYS (South Africa)

"Leave Me Alone," If You Want to Know Me: Reflections of Life in South Africa. Ed. Peggy L. Halsey, Gail J. Morlan, and Melba Smith. New York: Friendship Press, 1976, p. 22.

TLALI, SOPHIA (Lesotho)

"Poem," Staffrider, 2, 1 (1979), 49.

TOL'ANDE, ELISABETH FRANCOISE MWEYA (Zaire)

Remous de feuilles. Paris: Editions du Mont Noir, n.d.

"Poème," Dombi, No. 2 (1970), 4.

"Partir du jour," Afrique Chrétienne, No. 31 (1970), 24-5; No. 4 (1971), 17.

POETRY

VEIGA, AMELIA (Angola)

Destinos. Sa da Bandeira: Publicacoes Imbondeiro, 1962. 63 pages.

Poemas. Sa da Bendeira: Publicacoes Imbondeiro, 1963. 102 pages.

Libertacao. Sa do Bandeira: Tipografia Imprex, 1974. 178 pages.

WANGECI, AGATHA (Kenya)

"For Zanzibar;" "The Congolese;" Drum Beat. Ed. Lennard Okola. Nairobi: East African Publishing House, 1967, pp. 148-49.

WARE, REBECCA J. N. (Liberia)

"Home." Poems of Liberia 1836-1961. Ed. A. Doris Banks-Henries. London: Macmillan, 1963, p. 31.

WHEATLEY, PHILLIS (Senegal/USA)

Poems of the Various Subjects, Religious and Moral, by Phillis Wheatley, Negro Servant to Mr. Wheatley of Boston. London: A. Bell, 1773.

Memoir and Poems of Phillis Wheatley, A Native African and Slave. Ed. Margaretta Matilda Odell. Boston: I. Knapp, 1838. 155 pages; Miami: Mnemosyne Publishing Company, 1969. 155 pages.

The Poems of Phillis Wheatley. Ed. Julian Mason. Chapel Hill: University of North Carolina Press, 1966. 113 pages.

Phillis Wheatley. Poems and Letters. Ed. Charles F. Heartman. Miami: Mnemosyne Publishing Company, 1969. 111 pages.

"Poems," Black Insights. Ed. Nick Aaron Ford. Waltham: Xerox College Publishing 1971, pp. 1-4.

"Poems." Black Writers of America. A Comprehensive Anthology. Ed. Richard Barksdale and Kenneth Kinnamon. New York: Macmillan, 1972, pp. 38-44.

WILLIAMS, DAPHNE B. E. (Sierra Leone)

"Envoys of King Mosque," Aureol 70 Poems. Intr. Julian Croft. Freetown: Fourah Bay College, 1970, p. 11.

POETRY

WILSON, BEVERLY R. (Liberia)

"Liberia;" "Happy Land;" Poems of Liberia 1836-1961. Ed. A. Doris Banks-Henries. London: Macmillan, 1963, pp. 4-5.

XAVIER, EMELINDA PEREIA (Angola)

"Poems," Antologia des Novos Poetas Angolanos. Luanda: n. p., 1950.

"Poems," Poetas Angolanos. Ed. C. Eduardo. Luanda: n.p., 1959.

"Poems," No Reino de Caliban. Vol II. Ed. Manuel Ferreira. Lisboa: Seara Nova, 1976.

ZAGBEDE, JOSEPHINE (Ghana)

"Legbagbo," Okyeame, 4, 2 (1969), 23.

ZELLEKE, SERK-ADDIS (Ethiopia)

"Diamonds," New African, July 1981, p. 59.

ZERARI, ZEHOR (Algeria)

"Poems," Espoir et parole: poèmes algériens. Ed. Denise Barrat. Paris: Seghers, 1964, pp. 131-33, 195-97.

ZINONDO, TOKOZILE (Mozambique)

"Juntou as Criancas de Diversas Partes (1972)," Poesia de Combate. Maputo: FRELIMO, 1977, p. 123.

ZIRIMU, ELVANIA NAMUKWAYA (Uganda)

"Lament of the Orphans," Dhana, 1, 2 (1971), 20-2.

"Fighting in the Village;" "Unto Thy Hands;" Dhana, 2, 2 (1972), 47-8.

"Paradise Refugee," Dhana, 3, 1 (1973), 21-4.

"Unto Thy Hands," An Introduction to East African Poetry. Ed. Jonathan Kariara and Ellen Kitonga. Nairobi: Oxford University Press, 1976, pp. 46-8 [with notes].

V. FOLKLORE

AL-HASAN, SUSAN (Ghana)

Two Tales. Accra: n.p., 1965 [Children's folklore].

AMOOTI, BEATRICE TINKAMANYIRE (East Africa)

"The Leper," Dhana, 3, 2 (1973), 34-6.

AMROUCHE, MARIE-LOUISE also Marguerite Taos-Amrouche (Algeria/Tunisia)

"Folklore Kabyle," Revue d'Alger, No. 3 (1944), 81-6 [Two Kabyle narratives].

"Le chêne et l'orge," Forge, 3 (1947), 21-3 [One Kabyle narrative].

"Conte Kabyle: Loundja: fille de Tseriel," Algeria, No. 6 (1949), 47-50 [One Kabyle narrative].

ANTIRI, JANET ADWOA (Ghana)

"Akan Combs," African Arts, 8, 1 (1974), 32-5.

ANYANGWE, GLADYS NGWI (Cameroon)

"Master Trickster," The Mould,, No. 3 (1979), 63-6.

APPIAH, PEGGY (Britain/Ghana)

Ananse the Spider: Tales from an Ashanti Village. New York: Pantheon Books, 1966. 152 pages, illus.

Tales of an Ashanti Father. London: Deutsch, 1967. 157 pages.

The Children of Ananse. Evans Children Library. London: Evans, 1968. 176 pages, illus.

Why There Are So Many Roads. African Junior Series. Lagos: Pilgrim, 1972. 62 pages, illus.

Why The Hyena Does Not Care for Fish and Other Tales from the Ashanti Gold Weights. London: Deutsch, 1977. 77 pages, illus.

FOLKLORE

ATTIK, MRIRIDA N'AIT (Morocco)

Songs of Mririda, Courtesan of the High Atlas. Trs. Daniel Halpern and
 Paula Paley. Greensboro: Unicorn, 1974. 54 pages.

BAETA, LILY (Ghana)

Da to gli nam (Tell me a story, Mother). London, Accra: Longman Vernacular
 Literature Bureau, 1951 [An Ewe folktale].

BANKS-HENRIES, A. DORIS (USA/LIBERIA)

Liberian Folklore. New York: Macmillan, 1966. 152 pages.

CHIFAMBA, JANE (Zimbabwe)

Ngano Dzepasi (Tales of Old). Oxford University Press, in association with
 the Rhodesia Literature Bureau, 1964. 60 pages.

DAHAL, CHARITY KUGURU (Kenya)

The Orange Thieves and Other Stories. Nairobi: East African Publishing House,
 1966.

The Adventures of Mr Hyena. Nairobi: East African Publishing House, 1969.

DANKWAH-SMITH, HANNAH (Ghana)

Some Popular Ananse Stories. Accra: Waterville, 1975. 115 pages, illus.

DANKYI, JANE OSAFOA (Ghana)

with Kitty Lloyd-Lawrence. Firelight Fables. London: Longman, 1972. 57 pages,
 illus.

DUBE, VIOLET (South Africa)

Woza nazo (Come along with Them). Cape Town: Oxford University Press,
 1935 [Collection of Zulu traditional tales].

FOLKLORE

FAIK-NZUGI, CLEMENTINE M. (Zaire)

Kasala: Chant héroïque luba. Pref. Leo Stappers. Lubumbashi: Presses Universitaires, 1974. 250 pages.

Kasala: Chant poétique luba. Lubumbashi: Presses Universitaires Zaïre, 1974.

Lenga et autres contes d'inspiration traditionnelle. Lubumbashi: Editions St. Paul-Afrique, 1976. 78 pages.

KAGODA, NUMULUUTA (East Africa)

"Mother Never Ate the Bananas," Dhana, 1, 2 (1971), 12-5 [A Kisoga folk story].

KAKAZA, LILLITH (South Africa)

Utandiwe wakawa gcaleka (Tandiwe, a Damsel of Gaikaland). Cape Town: Methodist Book Room, 1914.

MENIRU, THERESA (Nigeria)

The Bad Family and the Caterpillar. Evans English Readers. London: Evans Brothers, 1971. 20 pages, illus.

The Carver and the Leopard. Evans English Readers. London: Evans Brothers, 1971. 27 pages, illus.

The Melting Girl and Other Stories. Evans English Readers. London: Evans Brothers, 1971. 27 pages, illus.

MESSENGA, pseudonym (Kenya)

"Struggle for Existence," Darlite, 4, 2 (1970), 2-5.

MFODWO, ESTHER BEKOE (Ghana)

Folktales and Stories from Around the World. Children's Library. Accra: Ghana Publishing Corporation, 1971. 30 pages, illus.

FOLKLORE

MVUNGI, MARTHA (Tanzania)

Three Solid Stones. African Writers Series #159. London: Heinemann, 1975.

MWANGI, ROSE GECAU (Kenya)

Kikuyu Folktales. Nairobi: East African Literature Bureau, 1970; 1976. 131 pages.

NDORO, JOYCE (Kenya)

The Hare's Horns. Nairobi: East African Publishing House, 1968; 1972. 34 pages [A Kikuyu folktale].

NJOROGE, LIZZIE NYAMBURA (Kenya)

Kiria gitumaga hiti itheke. Nairobi: East African Publishing House, n.d. [Kikuyu folktales].

Mburi yetagwo nijiru. Nairobi: East African Publishing House, n.d. 40 pages [Kikuyu folktales].

Wakonya. Nairobi: East African Publishing House, n.d. 40 pages [Kikuyu folktale].

NZERIBE, EJINE (Nigeria)

"The King and His Ten Wives," Africa Woman, No. 16 (1978), 62.

NZUJI, CAROLINE BALEKA BAMBA (Zaire)

"Igname mystérieuse ," [Une histoire mionirique, mi-lyrique], Anthologie des écrivains congolais. Kinshasa: S.N.E.C., Ministère de la Culture, 1969, pp. 27-37.

ODAGA, ASENATH BOLE (Kenya)

The Hare's Blanket and Other Tales. East Africa Junior Library No. 3. Nairobi: East African Publishing House, 1967. 28 pages.

FOLKLORE

OGOT, PAMELA (Kenya)

East African HOW Stories. Nairobi: East African Publishing House, 1966. 44 pages; rpt. Swahili translation: Jinsi chui alipata madoado. Nairobi: East African Publishing House, n.d.

East African WHY? Stories. Nairobi: East African Publishing House, 1966. 44 pages; rpt. Swahili translation: Mauti yalianza lini? Nairobi: East African Publishing House, n.d.

East African WHEN Stories. Nairobi: East African Publishing House, 1968. 35 pages; rpt. Swahili translation: Kwa nini fisi hucheka. Nairobi: East African Publishing House, n.d.

OMANGA, CLARE (Kenya)

The Girl Who Couldn't Keep a Secret and Other Stories. Nairobi: East African Publishing House, 1969. 28 pages.

SEYDOU AMADU, CHRISTIANE (West Africa)

Silâmaka et Poullôri: récit épique peul raconté par Tinguidji. Classiques Africaines, 13. Paris: Armand Colin, 1972.

SUMBANE, NATALA (Mozambique)

Swa rivala a swi heli (There are so many happenings in the life of today) n.p., n.d. (1967) [Tsonga folktales].

TAOS-AMROUCHE, MARGUERITE (Tunisia)

Le grain magique: contes poèmes et proverbes berbères de Kabylie. Paris: Maspero, 1965 [23 Kabyle narratives].

TOOKARAM, MERYL (Unidentified)

"How the Dog Came to Live with Man," African Woman, No. 11 (1977), 53 [Fable].

"How the Old Man's Dreams Come True," Africa Woman, No. 12 (1977), 53 [Fable].

"Why the Cat and Mouse Hate Each Other," Africa Woman, No. 16 (1978), 63.

FOLKLORE

"The Last Journey to Mondola Falls," <u>Africa Woman</u>, No. 23 (1979), 58-59.

ULASI, ADAORA LILY (Nigeria)

<u>The Night That Harry Died</u>. Lagos: n.p., 1974 (Tale).

WACIUMA, CHARITY (Kenya)

<u>The Golden Feather</u>. Nairobi: East African Publishing House, 1966. 48 pages.

<u>Mweru, The Ostrich Girl</u>. Nairobi: East African Publishing House, 1973. 23 pages.

ZIRIMU, ELVANIA NAMUKWAYA (Uganda)

"Kintu and Nambi," <u>East Africa Journal</u>, 5, 7 (1968), 32-6 [A Ganda Folktale].

VI. MISCELLANEOUS PROSE

BOOK REVIEWS BY AUTHORS

AIDOO, CHRISTINA AMA ATA (Ghana)

"Gerald Moore's Seven African Writers," Transition, 4, 10 (1963), 45-6.

"Mokwugo Okoye's African Responses," Transition, 5 , 24 (1966), 55-6.

"Oginga Odinga's Not Yet Uhuru," Présence Africaine, No. 64 (1967), 179-81.

"Wole Soyinka's Idanre and Other Poems," West Africa, 13 January 1968, pp. 40-1.

"Davis Sebukima's A Son of Kabira," Zuka, No. 5 (19709), 69-70.

CHUKWUMA, HELEN (Nigeria)

"John E. Eberegbulam's A Dictionary of Igbo Names, Culture and Proverbs," Research in African Literatures, 12, 1 (1981), 121-25.

EGEJURU, PHANUEL A. (Nigeria)

"Ernest Emenyonu's The Rise of the Ibgo Novel," Research in African Literatures, 13, 1 (1982), 78-82.

EMECHETA, BUCHI (Nigeria)

"Peter Fryer's Staying Power: This History of Black People in Britain," New Society, 24 May 1984, p. 323.

GICORU, NEREAS (Kenya)

"Ngugi wa Thiong'o's Petals of Blood," JOE, August 1977, pp. 25-6.

"Maya Angelou's I Know Why the Caged Bird Sings; Mari Evans' I Am a Black Woman; Angela Davis' Angela Davis: An Autobiography," JOE, September 1977, pp. 28-9.

"Ndabaningi Sithole's Frelimo Militant," JOE, November 1977, p. 29.

BOOK REVIEWS BY AUTHORS

GITHAE-MUGO, MICERE (Kenya)

"Muthoni Likimani's What Does a Man Want?" Viva, August 1975, p. 45.

"Peninah Muhando's Hatia, " African Literataure Today, 8. Ed. Eldred Jones. New York: Africana Publishing Corporation, 1976, pp. 139-40.

HOUSE, AMELIA (South Africa)

"R. L. Petini's Hill of Fools," Staffrider, 2, 2 (1979).

HUNYA, JANET (Kenya)

"Nkem Nwankwo's My Mercedes is Bigger Than Yours," JOE, 29 April 1976, p. 27.

ITAYEMI-OGUNDIPE, PHEBEAN (Nigeria)

"For What Audience," Ibadan, 6 June 1959, pp. 29-30 (Review of Wole Soyinka's The Swamp-Dwellers).

JABAVU, NONI (South Africa)

"T. M. Aliko's One Man One Wife," West Africa, 2 May 1959.

KAHIGA, MIRIAM (Kenya)

"Jacqueline Pierce's Leopard in a Cage," JOE, March 1977, pp. 25-6.

"Wole Soyinka's Ogun Abibiman," JOE, April 1977, p. 25.

"Ousmane Sembene's Xala and Meja Mwangi's Going Down River," JOE, May 1977, pp. 26-7.

"DeGraft Salute with Own Play," The Daily Nation, 21 February 1979, p. 18 (About the production of Joe De Graft's play Through a Film Darkly at the Kenya Cultural Centre).

"Murder and Its Many Meanings." The Daily Nation, 7 July 1978, p. 11 (about Robert Serumaga's Majangwa).

BOOK REVIEWS BY AUTHORS

MOHAMEDALI, HAMIDA (Kenya)

"Wole Soyinka's The Interpreters," Nexus, 1, 3 (1968), 37-9.

NJAU, REBEKA (Kenya)

"Wole Soyinka's Poems of Black Africa," JOE, 15 January 1976, pp. 25-6.

OGUNDIPE-LESLIE, OMOLARA (Nigerian)

"Charles Larson's The Emergence of African Fiction," Okike, No. 4 (1973), 81-9; rpt. Ba Shiru, 5, 1 (1973).

OKONKWO, JULIET L. (Nigeria)

"Michael J. C. Echeruo's Mortality," The Muse, 4 (1972), 36-8.

"Cyprian Ekwensi's Survive the Peace," Okike, No. 13 (1979), 57-65.

"Festus Iyayi's Violence and Sable Sellassie's Firebrands," Okike, No. 17 (1980), 124-29.

SEGUN, MABEL IMOUKHUEDE JOLAOSA (Nigeria)

"Amos Tutuola's Life in the Bush of the Ghosts," Odu, No. 1 (1955), 42-3.

ZIRIMU, ELVANIA NAMUKWAYA (Uganda)

"James Ngugi's A Grain of Wheat," Mawazo, 1, 2 (1967), 92-4.

"Okot p'Bitek's Two Songs: Song of A Prisoner and Song of Malaya," Mawazo, 3, 1 (1971), 73-5.

"Ola Rotimi's The Gods Are Not to Blame and Robert Serumaga's The Elephants," Mawazo, 3, 3 (1972), 48-9.

CONFERENCE PAPERS/SPEECHES

ADDO, JOYCE (Ghana)

"Television Drama in Ghana," African Literature Conference, University of Ibadan Ibadan, Nigeria, 1978.

AIDOO, CHRISTINA AMA ATA (Ghana)

Issue, 6 1 (1976), 51-52 (Untitled speech on drama and its oral traditions at the first African Literature Association Conference at Northwestern University, Evanston, Illinois).

"Images of Women," Woman and Work in Africa Symposium No. 6, University of Illinois at Urbana, Urbana, Illinois, 29 April 1979.

CHUKWUMA, HELEN (Nigeria)

"The Prose of Neglect," Third Ibadan Annual African Literature Conference, University of Ibadan, Ibadan, Nigeria, 10-14 July 1978.

EMECHETA, BUCHI (Nigeria)

"Building on Tradition: Can the Past Provide Direction for the Future?" Women and Work Symposium No. 6, University of Illinois at Urbana, Urbana, Illinois, 29 April 1979.

"Tradition vs Modernism in Nation Building," Graduate School of Public and International Affairs, University of Pittsburgh, Pittsburgh, Pennsylvania, 3 May 1979.

"The Problem that an African Novelist Faces in the Publishing World," Department of Black Studies, University of Pittsburgh, Pittsburgh, Pennsylvania, 4 May 1979.

"Discussion of The Rape of Sharvi," Workshop on Commonwealth Women Novelists, Commonwealth Institute, London, Saturday 7 January 1984.

"Speech for the Feminist Book Week," Pimlico Library, London, 13 June 1984.

CONFERENCE PAPERS/SPEECHES

GITHAE-MUGO, MICERE (Kenya)

"Sources of a Common Black Aesthetic in Literature on the Continent and in the Diaspora," The Second African Diasporan Studies Institute Conference, Kenyatta International Conference Centre, Nairobi, Kenya, 24-26 August 1981.

ODAGA, ASENATH BOLE (Kenya)

"Giriama Oral Literature," Seminar on the Coast Province of Kenya, Insititute of African Studies, University of Nairobi, Nairobi, Kenya, February 1977, 13 pages.

"Literature, African Writers and Africa's Dependence: Causes and Remedies," Mila, No. 125 (1979), 12 pages (Speech delivered on 3 October 1979 at the Institute of African Studies, University of Nairobi.)

"Traditions: Past Growth and Future Development in East Africa," Kisumu, Kenya, 18-22 April 1979, 34 pages.

OGUNDIPE-LESLIE, OMOLARA (Nigeria)

"The Poetry of Christopher Okigbo," Colloquium on the African Presence, Northwestern University, Evanston, Illinois, April 1972.

"Notes on Issues in African Aesthetics," Conference of the Association of African Literary Critics, University of Ife, Ile-Ife, Nigeria, 1975.

"The Uses of Modern African Poetry," Nigeria English Studies Association Conference, Zaria, Nigeria, 1975.

"And Still the Narcissist: Soyinka and Senghor," Ibadan Annual Lierature Conference, Ibadan, Nigeria, July 1979.

"A Marxist Reading of The Interpreters by Wole Soyinka," Conference on Literature, Language and Ideology, University of Benin, Cotonou, Dahomey, March 1980.

"In Search of Depth, Immediacy and Context: The Teaching of Literature in English in African Universities," joint author Dr. Felix Mnthali. Fifth Ibadan Annual African Literature Conference, University of Ibadan, Ibadan, Nigeria, 29 July - 1 August 1979.

"Is Violence by Festus Iyayi the First Nigerian Proletarian Novel?" Fifth Ibadan Annual African Literature Conference, University of Ibadan, Ibadan, Nigeria, 29 July - 1 August 1979.

CONFERENCE PAPERS/SPEECHES

OKONKWO, JULIET I. (Nigeria)

"The Essential Unity of Soyinka's The Interpreters and Season of Anomy," Third Ibadan Annual African Literature Conference, University of Ibadan, Ibadan, Nigeria, 10-14 July 1978.

SOFOLA, ZULU (Nigeria)

"The Concept of Tragedy in African Experience," FESTAC Literature Colloquium, Lagos, Nigeria, 15 January - 12 February 1977, 23 pages.

CRITICAL ESSAYS/WORKS

ABADA, ESSOMBA ROSE (Cameroon)

Le femme vue par Sembène Ousmane dans ses cinq premiers romans. Yaoundé: Université de Yaoundé, Faculté des lettres et sciences humaines. Département de littérature africaine comparée, 1974. 126 pages.

ACHEBE, CHRISTIE C. (Nigeria)

"Social Limitations of the Academic Woman to the Pursuit of Education," Nigerian Journal of Education, 2, 1 (1979), 112.

"Continuities, Changes and Challenges: Women's Roles in Nigerian Society," Présence Africaine, No. 120 (1981), 3-16.

ADEMOLA, FRANCES (Ghana)

"J. P. Clark and His Audience," African Forum, 1, 2 (1965), 84-6.

AIDOO, CHRISTINA AMA ATA (Ghana)

"The African Poet, His Critics and His Future," Legonite, (1964), 57-9.

"No Saviours," New African, 52 (1969), 37-9; rpt. African Writers on African Writing. Ed. G. D. Killam. New York : Africana Publishing Corporation, 1973, pp. 14-8.

"Introduction," The Beautiful Ones Are Not Yet Born, Ayi K. Armah. New York: Collier-Macmillan, 1969, pp. i-iv.

"Commitment," University of Cape Coast English Department Workpapers, 1 (1971), 10-4.

AVERY, GRETA M. K. (Sierra Leone)

"African Oral Traditions," Africana Research Bulletin, 1, 1 (1970)

BOITUMELO (South Africa)

"Women Writers Speak," Staffrider, 2, 4 (1979), 60-1; rpt. Black Women Writers from South Africa: A Preliminary Checklist. Ed. Amelia House. Evanston: Northwestern University Program on Women, 1980, pp. 19-21.

CRITICAL ESSAYS/WORKS

CASELY-HAYFORD, GLADYS MAY (Ghana/Sierra Leone)

"The Progress of African Drama and Literature," West African Review, 22, 285 (1951), 661, 663.

EGEJURU, PHANUEL A. (Nigeria)

Black Writers, White Audience: A Critical Approach to African Literature. Hicksville: Exposition Press, 1978. 255 pages.

"Who Is the Audience of Modern African Literature?" Obsidian, 5, 1-2 (1979), 51-8.

with David Dorsey and Stephen Arnold. Design and Intent in African Literature. Selected papers from the 1979 African Literature Association in Bloomington. Washington, DC: Three Continents Press, 1981.

ENEM, EDITH (Nigeria)

"Kwagh-hir Theatre," Nigeria Magazine, No. 120 (1976); rpt. Drama and Theatre in Nigeria: A Critical Source Book. Ed. Yemi Ogunbiyi. Lagos: Nigeria Magazine, 1981, pp. 249-51.

ESPIRITO SANTO, ALDA DO (São Tomé e Príncipe)

"Presença cultural," África, 1, 2 (1978), 189 - 95.

ESSILFIE, NAA AFARLEY (Ghana)

'The Africanisation of the English Language Syllabus," Asemka, No. 3 (1973), 91-100.

FAIK-NZUJI, CLEMENTINE MADIYA (Zaire)

with Illunga Kabongo. "Au premier festival culturel panafricain d'Alger. Impressions du symposium," Congo-Afrique, 4 (1969), 383-99.

"Proverbes. Essai d'une étude analytique et perspectives pédagogiques," Etudes Congolaises, 12, 2 (1969).

"Discordances Sémantiques dans le language proverbial," Cahiers de littérature et de linguistique appliquée, No. 2 (1970).

"Procédés de violement dans l'énigme luba," Poétique, 19 (1974), 333-39.

CRITICAL ESSAYS/WORKS

"Le Kasala et ses traits essentiels dans la littérature traditionelle orale luba," Cahiers d'Etudes Africaines, 15 (1975), 457-80.

"Art traditionnel au Zaïre: I. Le Proverbe," Zaïre-Afrique, 16, 103 (1976), 155-70.

"Art traditionnel au Zaïre: I. La Devinette à inférence au énigme," Zaïre-Afrique, 16, 104 (1976), 235-42.

"Art traditionnel au Zaïre: III. La Devinette à parallélismes," Zaïre-Afrique, 16, 105 (1976), 299-303.

"Art traditionnel au Zaïre: IV. La Situation piégée," Zaïre-Afrique, 16, 107 (1976), 427-38.

"Art traditionnel au Zaïre: V. Noms amplifiés," Zaïre-Afrique, 16, 108 (1976), 475-87.

"Art traditionnel au Zaïre (suite et fin): VI. Les Textes magiques," Zaïre-Afrique, 16, 109 (1976), 557-64.

Devinettes tonales tusumwinu. Paris: Société d Etude Linguistique et Anthropologie de France, 1976. 93 pages.

La Mère dévorante: Essai sur la morphologie des contes africaines. Paris: Editions Gallimard, 1976. 321 pages.

with Tzevetan Todorov. "La Voix du cyondo le soir à travers la savane: Le Langage tambourine chez les lubas," Recherche, Pédagogie et Culture, Nos. 29-30 (1977), 19-30.

"L'Amplification dans la littérature orale: L'Exemple des anthroponymes," African Perspectives, 1 (1977), 85-97.

GACHUKIA, EDDAH (Kenya)

"The Role of Women in Ngugi's Novels," Busara, 3,4, (1971), 30-3.

"Chinua Achebe and Tradition," Chris L. Wanjala, ed. Standpoints on African Literature: A Critical Anthology. Nairobi: East African Literature Bureau, 1973, pp. 172-87.

Notes on Ngugi wa Thiong'o "The River Between." Nairobi: Heinemann Educational Books, 1976. 32 pages.

CRITICAL ESSAYS/WORKS

with S. Kichama Akivaga. The Teaching of African Literature in Schools. Vol. I. Nairobi: Kenya Literature Bureau, 1978.

GITHAE-MUGO, MICERE (Kenya)

"Taban Lo Liyong: Eating Chiefs," New African Literature and the Arts, Vol. III. Ed. Joseph Okpaku. New York: The Third Press, 1973, pp. 235-41.

"Patterns of Communications in Edward Braithwaite's Masks." The Teaching of African Literature in Schools. Vol. I. Eds. Eddah Gachukia and S. Kichama Akivaga. Nairobi: Kenya Literature ureau, 1978, pp. 240-45.

"Children's Literature in Kenya," East African Literature: An Anthology. Ed. Arne Zettersten. London: Longman, 1983, pp. 206-11.

KITAMBI, BERNADETTE (Tanzania)

Hadithi Zetu. Dar-es-Salaam: Tanzania Publishing House, n.d. (oral literature).

MLAMA, PENNINA (Tanzania)

"Modern African Theatre with Special Emphasis on East Africa," Umma, 5 (1975), 1-11.

MUDIMBE-BOYI, MBULAMWANZA ELISABAETH (Zaire)

"Béatrice du Congo de Bernard Dadié, signe du temps ou pièce à clé?" L'Afrique littérature et artistique, No. 35 (1975), 19

L'Oeuvre romanesque de Jacques-Stephen Alexis écrivain haïtien. Lumbumbashi: Editions du Mont-Noir, 1975, 128 pages.

NZUJI, CAROLINE BALEKA BAMBA (Zaire)

"De l'oralité à l'écriture," Notre Librairie, 44 (1977), 37-53.

ODAGA, ASENATH BOLE (Kenya)

"Children's Literature in Kenya: Literature as an Image Forming Force," Mila, 5, 1 (1976), 3-12.

CRITICAL ESSAYS/WORKS

The Teaching of Oral Literature in Schools. Nairobi: East African Publishing House, 1981.

OGOT, GRACE AKINYI (Kenya)

"Family Planning for African Women," East Africa Journal, 4, 4 (1967), 19-23.

"The African Writer," East Africa Journal, 5, 9 (1968), 35-7.

Co-author of A Glossary in English-Kiswahili, Kikuyu and Dholuo. London: Cassell, 1972.

OGUNDIPE-LESLIE, OMOLARA (Nigeria)

"'The Palm-Wine Drinkard' A Reassessment of Amos Tutuola," Présence Africaine, 71 (1969), 99-108; rpt. Journal of Commonwealth Literature, 9 (1970), 48-56; rpt. Critical Perspectives on Amos Tutuola. Ed. Bernth Lindfors. Washington, DC: Three Continents Press, 1975, pp. 145-54.

"Chinua Achebe: His Vision and His Craft," Black Orpheus, 2, 7 (1971-72), 34-41.

"Nigeria, Alienation and the Novels of Achebe," Présence Africaine, 84 (1972), 99-108; rpt. Black World, 22, 8 (1973), 34-43.

"African Aesthetics and Literature," Ufahamu, 4, 1 (1973), 4-7.

"Christopher Okigbo: Creative Rhetoric," The Conch Review of Books, 1 (1973), 67-74.

"Malignant Schizophrenia in After-Africa," Ba Shiru, 4, 2 (1973), 81-6; rpt. as "The Trial of Christopher Okigbo and the Novel of Ideas," Nigeria Magazine, 13 (1974), 54-8.

"The Poetry of Christopher Okigbo: Its Evolution and Significance," Studies in Black Literature, 4, 3 (1973), 1-8; rpt. West Africa, 2 April 1973, pp. 427-29; rpt. Ufahamu, 4, 1 (1973), 47-54.

"Christopher Okigbo: The Development of a Poet," New Horn, 1, 2, (1974), 17-32.

"Nigerian Writers and Political Commitment," Ufahamu, 5, 2, (1974), 20-50.

"Ten Years of Tutuola Studies," Text and Context in Africa: Methodological Explorations in the Field of African Literature. Leiden: Afrika-Studie-Centrum, 1976, pp. 67-76.

CRITICAL ESSAYS/WORKS

"The Poetics of Fiction by Yoruba Writers: the Case of Ogboju Ode Ninu Igbo Irunwale," CLA Journal, 22 (1979), 240-53.

OKONKWO, JULIET IL. (Nigeria)

"Adam and Eve: Igbo Marriage in the Nigerian Novel," Conch, 3, 11 (1971), 137-51.

"The Talented Woman in African Literature," Africa Quarterly, 15, 4 (1975), 36-47.

"African Literature and Its Language of Expression," Africa Quarterly, 15, 4 (1976), 56-66.

"The Missing Link in African Literature," African Literature Today, Vol 10. Ed. Eldred Jones. New York: Africana Publishing House; London: Heinemann, 1979, pp. 86-105.

"The Essential Unity of Soyinka's The Interpreters and Season of Anomy," African Literature Today, Vol 11. Ed. Eldred Jones. London: Heinemann, 1980, pp. 110-21.

PALA, O. (Tanzania)

"Go Back to the Soil," Lotus: Afro-Asian Writings, No. 1 (1971), 22-7.

SACKEY, JULIANA, A. (Ghana)

"Bilingualism in Ghana: A Socio-Linguistic Perspective," Asemka, 3 (1973), 101-08.

SEGUN, MABEL IMOUKHUEDE JOLAOSA (Nigeria)

"On Being a West African Writer," Ibadan, 12 (1961).

SEYDOU AMADU, CHRISTIANE (West Africa)

"Comment définir le genre épique? Un example: l'épopée africaine," Journal of the Anthropological Society of Oxford, 13, 1 (1982), 84-98.

"A Few Reflexions on Narrative Structures of Epic Texts: A Case Example of Bambara and Fulani Epics," Research in African Literatures, 14, 3 (1983), 312-31.

CRITICAL ESSAYS/WORKS

SOFOLA, ZULU (Nigeria)

"Jane Eyre" Notes. Lagos: Onibonoje, 1968. 120 pages.

"The Playwright and Theatrical Creation," Nigeria Magazine, 128-129 (1979), 68-74.

"The Theater in the Search for African Authenticity," African Theology En Route. Ed. Kofi Appiah-Kubi and Sergio Torres. Maryknoll, New York: Orbis, 1979, pp. 126-36.

SUTHERLAND, EFUA THEODORA MORGUE (Ghana)

"Venture into Theatre," Okyeame, 1, 1 (1961), 47-8.

Anansegoro: Story-Telling Drama in Ghana. African Studies Library Series. Accra: Afram, 1975.

TAOS-AMROUCHE, MARGUERITE (Tunisia)

"From Algerian Kabyle Folklore: The Seven Ogres," Lotus: Afro-Asian Writings No. 1 (1971), 112-18.

THIAM, AWA (West Africa)

La Parole aux négresses. Paris: Denoel-Gonthier, 1978. 119 pages.

FRAGMENTS

LUSINDE, RUTH (East Africa)

"That Day;" "Through a Hospital Ward," Penpoint, 15 (1963), 14-5.

NAMUBIRU, MARGARET (East Africa)

"View from My Window," Dhana, 6, 2 (1976), 123.

TLALI, MIRIAM (South Africa)

"Soweto Speaking (column)," Staffrider, 1, 1 (1978), 2-6.

"Soweto Speaking No. 5 Rev. Tsolo," Staffrider, 1, 3 (1978), 2.

"Soweto Speaking No. 6 Mrs. B. Makau," Staffrider, 1, 3 (1978), 3.

"Soweto Speaking No. 9 Sergeant Moloi," Staffrider, 2, 3 (1979), 2-3.

"Soweto Speaking New Horizons," Staffrider, 1, 4 (1978), 2-5.

"The First Train to Faraday," Staffrider, 3, 4 (1980-81), 3-4.

IMPRESSIONISTIC ESSAYS

ALIFAIJO, MARGARET (East Africa)

"A Neglected Village," In Black and White: Writings from East Africa with Broadcast Discussions and Commentary. Ed. David Cook. Nairobi: East African Literature Bureau, 1976, p. 124.

SISTER ANSELM (Uganda)

"What Frequently Happens in Karamoja," In Black and White: Writings from East Africa with Broadcast Discussions and Commentary. Ed. David Cook. Nairobi: East African Literature Bureau, 1976, pp. 56-8.

DAMANI, CHARU (East Africa)

"A Neglected Village," In Black and White: Writings from East Africa with Broadcast Discussions and Commentary. Ed. David Cook. Nairobi: East African Literature Bureau, 1976, p. 125.

EMECHETA, BUCHI (Nigeria)

A. Articles from West Africa.

"Another Fear of Flying," 25 June 1979, pp. 1119-20.

"A Question of Dollars," 30 July 1979, pp. 1367-68.

"A Time Bomb," 30 October 1978, pp. 2139-40.

"An African View in Church of England," 24 April 1978, pp. 805-6.

"Christmas is For All," 25 December 1978, pp. 2590-91.

"Darry and a Bouquet of Flowers," 9 July 1979, pp. 1215-16.

"Give Us This Day Our Daily Bread," 4 December 1978, pp. 2410-11.

"The Human Race Decides to March through London," 19 June 1978, pp. 1177-80.

"Language Difficulties," 16 July 1979, pp. 1267-68.

"Out of the Ditch and into Print," 3 April 1978, pp. 669-72.

"Language Difficulties," 16 July 1979, pp. 1267-68.

IMPRESSIONISTIC ESSAYS

"US Longing for Roasted Yams," 27 August 1979, pp. 1560-62.

"US Police Convince Me I Am Lost," 24 September 1979, pp. 1761-62.

"What the Carol Singers are Missing," 24-31 December 1979, pp. 2385-86

"A Week of Ghana," 13 October 1980, pp. 2015-16.

"Calabar Contrasts and Complaints," 12 January 1981, pp. 71-72.

"Lagos Provides a Warm Welcome," 19 January 1981, pp. 110-11, 113.

"Simpler Than Sociology," 10 August 1981, pp. 1813-14.

"Nigeria: Experiencing a Cultural Lag," 2 November 1981, pp. 2582-83.

B. EXCERPTS FROM IN THE DITCH

"Baptism by Socialization —In the Ditch-1," New Statesman, 8 January 1971, pp. 43-4.

"Down to the Dole House — In the Ditch - 2," New Statesman, 15 January 1971, pp. 77-8.

"The Ministry's Visiting Day — In the Ditch — 3," New Statesman, 22 January 1971, p. 110.

C. OTHER ESSAYS

"Should Husbands Control a Wife's Salary?", African Weekly Review (Nigeria), 1, 3 (1967), 8.

"Buchi's Social Column — Marriage Does It Pay?", African Weekly Review, 20 October 1967, p. 12.

"Mixed Marriage," African Weekly Review, 1, 17 (1968), 13.

"Through West African Eyes," CMS Magazine, October-December 1978, pp. 18-9.

"A Writer's Day," New Fiction, No. 20 (1979), p. 3.

"African Woman," Root, 2, 6 (August 1981), pp. 22-5, 30.

"Women of Pittsburgh," Root, February 1982, pp. 14-5, 25.

"Black and a Woman," New Society, July 1984.

IMPRESSIONISTIC ESSAYS

IFUDU, THEODORA (Nigeria)

"Did I Fall in Love with Jerry...," West Africa, 15 October 1979, pp. 1888-89.

JETHA, NAZARA (East Africa)

"A Neglected Village," In Black and White: Writings from East Africa with Broadcast Discussions and Commentary. Ed. David Cook. Nairobi: East African Literature Bureau, 1976, pp. 126-27.

KAGONDU, AGNES (Kenya)

"A Nocturnal Visitor," When I Awoke. Intr. W. G. Bowman. Nairobi: East Africa Publishing House, 1966, pp. 26-9 (1966 Brooke Bond Essay Competition).

KAHIGA, HANNAH (Kenya)

"A Model Day During the Emergency," In Black and White: Writings from East Africa with Broadcast Discussions and Commentary. Ed. David Cook. Nairobi: East African Literature Bureau, 1976, pp. 58-61.

"Wandegeya," In Black and White: Writings from East Africa with Broadcast Discussions and Commentary. Ed. David Cook. Nairobi: East African Literature Bureau, 1976, pp. 54-6.

KISANGI, ESTHER (Kenya)

"Story Writing," When I Awoke. Intr. W. G. Bowman. Nairobi: East African Publishing House, 1966, pp. 64-6.

KURIA, R. LUCY (Kenya)

"Out of Disaster," When I Awoke. Intr. W. G. Bowman. Nairobi: East African Publishing House, 1966, pp. 48-50.

LEHAI, JOY (East Africa)

"A Neglected Village," In Black and White: Writings from East Africa with Broadcast Discussions and Commentary. Ed. David Cook. Nairobi: East African Literature Bureau, 1976, pp. 128-29.

IMPRESSIONISTIC ESSAYS

MWANGI, BEATRICE (Kenya)

"Misfortune Never Comes Singly," When I Awoke. Intr. W. G. Bowman. Nairobi: East African Publishing House, 1966, pp. 23-5.

WANJIRU, PAULINE (Kenya)

"Worm's Turn," When I Awoke. Intr. W. G. Bowman. Nairobi: East African Publishing House, 1966, pp. 20-2.

WARUHIU, DORIS MAY (Kenya)

"Gumba's Reality," When I Awoke. Intr. W. G. Bowman. Nairobi: East African Publishing House, 1966, pp. 36-8.

YEBOAH-AFARI, AJOA V. (Ghana)

The Best of Yaa Yaa. Accra: n. p., n. d. [Collection from column in "The Mirror"].

LETTERS

AIDOO, CHRISTINA AMA ATA (Ghana)

"Thank You Mr. Howe," Transition, 6, 29 (1967), 5-6.

HEAD, BESSIE (South Africa/Botswana)

"For a Friend, 'D.B'," Transition, 3, 11 (1963), 40.

"Letter to Transition 16," Transition, 4, 17 (1964), 6.

VIGNETTES

CHITE, HELEN, pseudonym for Enid S. Sibajene (Zambia)

"Expecting Too Much in Marriage," Times of Zambia, 2 February 1979.

"The Day My Husband Fell Ill...," Times of Zambia, 9 February 1979.

"How I Almost Got Divorced," Times of Zambia, 19 February 1979.

"Life Changes When Mother Visits Our Home," Times of Zambia, 23 February 1979.

"Saturday Fishing Trip Went Wrong," Times of Zambia, 2 March 1979.

"At 11, My Son Thought He Was a Man," Times of Zambia, 9 March 1979.

"My Uncle's Death Sobered Eddie," Times of Zambia, 23 March 1979.

"He is Still the Jealous Old Eddie," Times of Zambia. 6 April 1979.

"May Brenda Rest in Peace," Times of Zambia, 13 April 1979.

"My Curiosity Embarrasssed Me," Times of Zambia, 27 April 1979.

"The Day Eddie and I Play Counsellors," Times of Zambia, 4 May 1979.

"The Friend We Didn't Need," Times of Zambia, 18 May 1979.

"Why Mr. Mwanza Wanted a Baby Girl," Times of Zambia, 23 May 1979.

"Our Guest Was Really Not All That Impressed," Times of Zambia, 22 June 1979.

"Niece Would Not Take Our Advice," Times of Zambia, 29 June 1979.

GICORU HIRST, NEREAS (Kenya)

"My Friend...Joe?" Joe, September 1977, pp. 4-5.

LUSINDE, RUTH (East Africa)

"Skill of Harmony," Penpoint, No. 16 (1964), 9.

VIGNETTES

MATENJWA, CHRISTINE (Kenya)

"The Life of Maggie Taabu-A Song of Love," Joe, May 1976, p. 13.

"The Life of Maggie Taabu-Start Your Day With A Smile," Joe, June 1976, p. 13.

"The Life of Maggie Taabu-When in Doubt-Ask Your Father," Joe, August 1976, p. 15.

VII. JOURNALISTIC ESSAYS

ADEMU-JOHN, CECILIA (Sierra Leone)

"Women's Network," Africa Woman, No. 16 (1978), 10.

"What Can Society Do for the Physically Handicapped?," Africa Woman, No. 19 (1979), 18.

AMEGASHIE, SUSAN (Ghana)

"CAM Is Just the Beginning," Africa Woman, No. 30 (1980), 9.

ANYIKO, GRACE (Kenya)

"Marriage: Should It Be Just a Contact?," The Daily Nation, 19 August 1981, p. 11.

CHARLES, MOU (Kenya)

"Mzee: A Chronology," Viva, September 1978, pp. 21-5.

"On the Sets of 'Ashanti';" "The Right Foods;" Viva, October 1978, pp. 23-4; 49.

"Christmas Is on the Wane," Viva, November 1978, p. 42A.

CHISHIBA, DOROTHY (Zambia)

"Women and Crime," Africa Woman, No. 36 (1981), 54.

COLE, BERNADETTE (Sierra Leone)

"Women of the World Unite," West Africa, 28 July 1980, pp. 1376-77.

"Africa's Hot Seat," West Africa, 28 July 1982, pp. 1686-88.

DIALLO, ASSIATOU (Guinea)

"Le Fashion Rally de la Reine Polou," Amina, No. 69 (1978), 10-17.

JOURNALISTIC ESSAYS

"Comment évoluent les rapports des couples africains (rapport de Souleymane Cisse, le cinéaste malien);" "Un beau succès professionel: Fatou Sylla;" "La Beauté par les plantes;" Amina, No. 74 (1978), 9-11; 29; 33.

GABBA, ANNA (Unidentified)

"Ambassador Tatu Fatuma Nuru," Africa Woman, N0. 20 (1979), 17.

GETHI, ANGELINA (Kenya)

"Helping Plan Families," Viva, November 1978, pp. 45-6.

GITONGA, BIRGITA (Kenya)

"An Overtime Family," Viva, October 1978, p. 88.

HOUSE, AMELIA (South Africa)

"A Special Page for Women?," Staffrider, 5, 3 (1980), 45.

IBRU, EMIE (Unidentified)

"New Trends in Black Hair-Care," Africa Woman, No. 19 (1979), 39-41.

IKPEAZU, NGOZI (Nigeria)

"Widows Society's Victims," Africa Woman, No. 36 (1981), 20-1.

KAHIGA, MIRIAM (Kenya)

"The Women of Mathare," Viva, 11, 1 (1976), 52-4.

"The Dating Game," Joe, March 1977, p. 11.

"No Man Is an Uncle," Joe, April 1977, pp. 13-4.

"The Urban Nomads," Joe, May 1977, p. 20.

"Good News," Joe, August 1977, p. 14.

"Talking about Theatre — Decorating the Bar," Joe, August 1977, p. 26.

JOURNALISTIC ESSAYS

"Miss-Taken Identity?," Joe, September 1977, p. 18.

"University Players Go To Berlin," The Daily Nation, 4 July 1979, p. 20.

"YWCA Gets a Feminine Touch," The Daily Nation, 18 August 1981, p. 8.

"US Blacks Hit by Disunity," The Daily Nation, 19 August 1981, p. 13.

KATUMBA, REBECCA (Uganda)

"Rural Education in Uganda," Africa Woman, No. 26 (1980), 62-3.

"The Plight of the Women of Karamoja," Africa Woman, No. 32 (1981), 10-1.

KIARIE, MIRIAM (Kenya)

"At Home Abroad - Talks to Janet Mwangle," Viva, 6, 1 (1980), 34-5.

"Saving Marriages," Viva, 6, 4 (1980), 11-4, 84.

"Business Women;" "Children's Ulcers, The Other Side of Marriage;" Viva, 6, 5 (1980), 9-13; 39-41.

"The Illegitimate' Child," Viva, 6, 7 (1980) 12.

"Depression," Viva, 6, 8 (1980), 9-13.

"The Alcoholics Battle," Viva, 6, 9 (1980), 10-3.

"Activist Profile: Khalida Dar," Viva, 6, 10 (1980), 53-4.

"Being Parents," Viva, 7, 3 (1980), 9-11.

"Kenya's Bar Culture," Viva, 7, 6 (1981), 8-10, 12-3.

KUOH-MOUKOURY, THERESE (Cameroon)

"La journée internationale des femmes à Bamako," Afrique contemporaine, No. 78 (1977), 6-10.

JOURNALISTIC ESSAYS

KUTTA, SARAH KALA-LOBE (Senegal)

"Le rôle éducatif du jeu dans le développement intellectuel de l'enfant," Amina, No. 69 (1978), 28-31.

KWAKU, ROSEMARY (Ghana)

"$300,000 for Valco Fund," Voltascope, 2, 12 (1971), 2.

"Movement to Unite African Youth," The Daily Graphic, No. 6778 (1972), 10.

"SRC Honour at Stake," Torch, 2, 3 (1972), 62.

"Fashions for the New Year," Ideal Woman, 2, 5 (1973), 20-22.

"The Akonnedi Shrine," Ideal Woman, 2, 7 (1973), 9, 17.

"UN Survives," Ghanaian Times, No. 4947 (1973), 6.

"New Hope for Kidney Patients," Ghanaian Times, No. 4964 (1973), 6.

"Women Beyond the Home," The Daily Graphic, No. 7246 (1974), 5.

"To Marry or Not to Marry," Ideal Woman, 5, 7 (1974), 16-20.

"Modern Marriages - Much 'I Do' About Nothing," Chit-Chat, No. 0056 (1974), 5, 8, 9.

"Modern Marriage — What Future?," Ghanaian Times, No. 5143 (1974), 4.

"FESTAC 1977," Ghana Review, 2, 4 (1977), 22, 23.

MAJALE, IRENE (Kenya)

"The Massive Dancing Festival Flop?," Joe, April 1977, p. 28.

MASEKELA, BARBARA (South Africa)

"Women under Apartheid," New African, May 1981, pp. 19-20.

M'BAYE, ANNETTE D'ERNEVILLE (Senegal)

"Promotion de la femme sénégalaise," Développement et Civilisation, décembre 1962, pp. 67-71.

JOURNALISTIC ESSAYS

"Une victoire des Sénégalaises," Jeune Afrique, No. 367 (1968), 34-5.

"Mère et enfant au Sénégal," Actuel développement, No. 6 (1975), 33-6.

MBUGUA, ISABEL (Kenya)

"You Can Be 'Skinned Alive' If You Don't Watch Out," The Daily Nation, 19 August 1981, pp. 12-3, 15.

"Night Lives," Viva ,6, 1 (1980), 4-7.

"Women's Groups Are Not Genuinely Helping," Viva, 6, 3 (1980), 18-20.

"What Women Like," Viva, 6, 4, (1980), 71-2.

MOREL, MARION (South Africa)

"Girls about Town," An African Treasury. Ed. Langston Hughes. New York: Pyramid, 1961, pp. 78-9.

MUNENE, FIBI (Kenya)

"Anything Men Can Do We Can Do," Target, 23 February 1975, p. 9.

"Women in Africa - A Kenyan Perspective," Africa Report, January-February 1977.

"What's Wrong with Mr. Right?," Joe, September 1977, p. 13.

"The Last Word," The Daily Nation, 14 December 1977, p. 19 (A regular column until 1979).

"Do African Governments Care About Women?", IFDA Dossier, 16 (1980), 129-30.

"Female Circumcision," Africa Woman, No. 32 (1981), 20-2.

"Rural Women," Africa Woman, No. 33 (1981), 18-9.

MUTAI, CHELAGIT (Kenya)

"My Years in Prison," Viva, October 1978, pp. 15-9.

"What I Believe;" "The Events of the Month of November;" Viva, November 1978, pp. 31-2; 33, 71.

JOURNALISTIC ESSAYS

MWAURA, FLORENCE W. (Kenya)

"Kaguai's Death," Viva, October 1978, p. 88.

MWILU, KANE (Kenya)

with B. Conlon. "Intermarriage, Does It Work?," Viva, 1, 5 (1975), 20-1, 32.

"The Case for Abortion," Viva, 1, 5 (1975), 26-7, 48-9.

"Women, Property and Marriage Bill," Viva, 2, 8 (1976), 44-5.

"Letter from a Bourgeois Woman," Viva, 2, 11 (1976), 13-4.

NGULUBE, CLARA (Zambia)

"Marriage in Zambia," Africa Woman, No. 12 (1977), 62-3.

"Organiser, Hair-Dresser, Tailor, That's Joy Mecha, Zambia's Top Model," Africa Woman, No. 19 (1979), 13.

"Consumer Protection Zambia," Africa Woman, No. 32 (1981), 42.

"Veronica Zulu: Zambia Lawn Tennis Queen," Africa Woman, No. 36 (1981), 27, 39.

NKWAZEMA, EDITH (Nigeria)

"Janice Sawyerr: 'Mother' Of Nigerian Students in London," Africa Woman, No. 32 (1981), 13.

N'SKA, LECI (East Africa)

"Our Family's Christmas," Viva, 6, 12 (1980), 34-5.

"Mixed Children," Viva, 7, 1 (1981), 33-4, 49-50.

"The Discrimination Against Women in the Civil Service," Viva, 7, 2 (1981), 15-7, 45, 47.

JOURNALISTIC ESSAYS

NSUBUGA, EDITA (East Africa)

"And Justice for All - Profile of Ben Mukuria," Viva, 6, 12 (1980), 29.

"Never A Dull Moment," Viva, 7, 1 (1981), 24.

"Madagascar," Viva, 7, 3 (1981), 81, 83.

NTANTALA, PHYLLIS (South Africa)

"The Abyss of Bantus Education," Africa South, 4,2 (1960), 42-7.

"The Widows of the Reserve," An African Treasury. Ed. Langston Hughes. London: Gollancz, 1961, pp. 20-5.

"Five Years of Bantu Education," Fighting Talk, 15, 3 (1962).

An African Tragedy: The Black Woman Under Apartheid. Chicago: Agascha Productions, 1975.

NWAPA, FLORA (Nigeria)

"Women in African Politics," Africa Woman, No. 1 (1975), 35-6.

NWIGWE, NKUKU (Cameroon)

"Nchifua Kangkolo and the Co-operative Movement," Africa Woman, No. 21 (1979), 39-40.

"Folktales in a Camerounian Classroom," Africa Woman, No. 26 (1980), 16-7.

"Family Life in Cameroun," Africa Woman, No. 32 (1981), 41.

"To Cameroun for Leisure," Africa Woman, No. 33 (1981), 40.

"Problems of Cameroonian Youth," Africa Woman, No. 36 (1981), 53.

JOURNALISTIC ESSAYS

NYATE, FRANCES (East Africa)

"Love through a Sip," Viva, No. 1 (1974), 47-9.

NYAYWA, ROSE (Zambia)

"Fanni Shawa — Nursing Tutor Turned Director," Africa Woman, No. 27 (1980), 12.

"Village Industry Service in Zambia," Africa Woman, No. 32 (1981), 24.

OPONDO, DIANA (East Africa)

"The Mraru Bus," Viva, 6, 12 (1980), 55-7.

OTIENO, EVELYN (Kenya)

"Must It Always Be This?," Viva, 6, 4 (1980), 69-70.

RAHARIJAONA, BERTHE (Madagascar)

"Une grande figure malgache: Josefa Andrianaivoravelona," Bulletin de l'Academie Malgache, XLI (1971), 1-3.

SANGA, AMINATOU (Senegal)

"Senegalese Women," Africa Woman, No. 4 (1976), 32-3.

SEGUN, MABEL IMOUKHUEDE JOLAOSA (Nigeria)

"On Being a West African Writer," Ibadan, No. 12 (1961).

Friends, Nigerians, Countrymen. Ibadan: Oxford University Press, 1977.

SHEIKH, LELIA (Tanzania)

"Literacy in Tanzania," Africa Woman, No. 20 (1979), 42-4.

JOURNALISTIC ESSAYS

SIGWILI, NOKUGCINA (South Africa)

"Men Are Always Women's Children," Staffrider, 3, 1 (1980), 44.

SIKANETA, CLARA (Unidentified)

"Widows," Africa Woman, No. 7 (1976), 58.

SOW FALL, ANIMATA (Senegal)

with Rose Senghor. "The Educational Role of the African Woman in the Traditional Society," The Civilization of the Woman in African Tradition. Paris: Présence Africaine, 1975, pp. 232-41.

TLALI, MIRIAM (South Africa)

"Soweto Speaking," Staffrider, 1, 1 (1977) [A regular column].

UREY-NGARA, ABIGAIL (Unidentified)

"Marriage in Mozambique," Africa Woman, No. 11 (1977), 40-1.

"The Culture of South African Women;" "Zimbabwe's Beatrice Ndhlovu in Exile;" Africa Woman, No. 16 (1978), 8-9; 16.

"Sudan in Camera," Africa Woman, No. 17 (1978), 8-10.

"Modelling: All a Matter of Time, Patience and Hardwork," Africa Woman, No. 18 (1979), 8-9.

"Kenyan Women Forge Ahead," Africa Woman, No. 21 (1979), 8-10.

UWECHUE, AUSTUA (Nigeria)

"Interview - Lady Soames," Africa Woman, No. 29 (1980), 8-13.

"King Sobhuza II Still Going Strong," Africa Woman, No. 36 (1981), 24-5.

VIII. BROADCAST LITERATURE/INTERVIEWS

REFERENCES:

A. Afro-American Collection, Howard University, Washington, DC.

B. B.B.C. African Theatre, London, England

C. First Person Feminine, Radio Series, Iowa State University, Ames, Iowa

D. School of Communications, Howard University, Washington, DC.

E. Voice of America, English African Series on Writers

F. Ghana Broadcasting Corporation/Radio Ghana

G. Canadian Broadcasting Corporation

H. Ghana Broadcasting Corporation/TV

I. Voice of Kenya

ADDO, JOYCE (Ghana)

"The Observer," Hosted a one-hour public affairs show on current affairs in Toronto, Ontario Canada, Summer 1963 (G).

"Homemakers," A series on women's program, 1965-71 (F).

"Jobs for Women," Filmed series for Ghana Airways in London, England, 1969.

"Avenue A," A television series on family situations in Ghana, 1971-76 (H).

"Ghost Town," A television series, 1975-77 (H).

"Kalabule," A television series looking at smugglers, tax evaders, and the underground saboteurs, 1978-80 (H).

"Twenty-Four Hours," A television series for children, 1979-80 (H).

"Untitled Series," A television program to promote works on Ghanaian writers, review their works, and introduce new ideas to writers, 1981 (H).

BROADCAST LITERATURE/INTERVIEWS

AIDOO, CHRISTINA AMA ATA (Ghana)

"Reading of the short story, The Late Bud," from No Sweetness Here (1970), Tape III (C).

AMROUCHE, FADHMA AITH MANSOUR (Algeria)

"Reading of passages from the autobiography, Histoire de ma vie (1968), Tape XIV (C).

CHEDID, ANDREE (Egypt)

Reading of "La longue patience," from Les Corps et le temps, suivi de l'etroite peau (1978), Tape XVIII (C).

CLEMS, DARLENE (Ghana)

"The Prisoner, the Judge, and the Jailer (sic) [play]," 8-10 August 1971 (B).

"The Big Boss Cometh," 12 December 1971 (B).

DJEBAR, ASSIA (Algeria)

Reading of a chapter from the novel, Les impatients (1958), Tape XIII (C)

DOVE-DANQUAH, MABEL (Ghana)

Reading of the short story, "Anticipation," Tape I (C)

EMECHETA, BUCHI (Nigeria)

"A Kind of Marriage," Centre Play Commonwealth Season (Nigeria) - B.B.C TV Program, London.

"Tayan: The Modern Black Woman," B.B.C. TV Program, London.

"The Extraordinary People Show: Buchi Emecheta," B.B.C. TV Program, London, 1981.

"In the Light of Experience: Buchi Emecheta," B.B.C. TV, London, 1983.

BROADCAST LITERATURE/INTERVIEWS

GITHAE-MUGO, MICERE (Kenya)

Interviewed by the filmmaker Haile Gerima, August 1979 (D)

HEAD, BESSIE (South Africa/Botswana)

Interview recorded by Lee Nichols in Serowe, Botswana, 25 September 1976 (E)*

Book review of Bessie Head's The Collector of Treasures (1977) by Senda wa Kwayera on November 1978 (I)

Reading of the short story, "Snapshots of a Wedding" from A Collector of Treasures (1977), Tape XII (C).

KIMENYE, BARBARA (Uganda)

Reading of the short story, "The Winner" from Kalasandra (1965), Tape V (C).

KWAKU, ROSEMARY (Ghana)

"Korle Bu Service Canteen," forty-five minute taped interview recorded for a Charleston, West Virginia local radio station in September, 1973.

"Survival," A poem read on 16 February 1974 (H).

"Guinea Bissau:" "Freedom;" Poems read on 16 November 1974 (H).

"Ghana Moves Right," Play performed on 4 August 1974 (H).

"Blood Tears;" "For the Love of Odinga;" "Promise;" Poems read on 16 November 1974 (H).

"One Revolution;" "Sunshine and Rainbow;" "For Whom the New Year Dawns;" Poems read on 28 December 1974 (H).

"The Thrill of Being a Writer," A Youth Forum Program for the GBC External Service, 1974 (F).

"Mifoo Doo;" "The Bridge Between;" Poems read at the Greater Accra Festival of the Arts for 1975 on 16 August 1975 (F).

BROADCAST LITERATURE/INTERVIEWS

MLAMA, PENINA, also Penina Muhando (Tanzania)

Interviewed by Lee Nichols in Dar es Salaam on 9 September 1974 (E).

MUNTEMBA, MAUDE (Zambia)

Interviewed by the filmmaker Haile Gerima in August 1979 (D).

NWAPA, FLORA (Nigeria)

Interviewed by Lee Nichols in Claremont, California in April 1981 (E)*.

Reading of the short story. "This Is Lagos" from *This Is Lagos and Other Short Stories* (1971), Tape IV (C).

OGOT, GRACE (Kenya)

Interviewed by the filmmaker Haile Gerima (D).

Reading of the short story, "The Middle Door" from *The Other Woman* (1976), Tape VI (C).

Interviewed by Lee Nichols in Nairobi, Kenya on 28 August 1974 (E)*.

SOFOLA, ZULU (Nigeria)

Interviewed by Lee Nichols in Ibadan, Nigeria on 31 July 1974 (E)*.

SPIO-GARBRAH, ELIZABETH (Ghana)

"Poems and Sketches," Performed and read in 1961 (F).

SUTHERLAND, EFUA T. M. (Ghana)

Interviewed by Lee Nichols in Accra, Ghana on 21 July 1974 (E).

Reading of the short story, "New Life at Kyerefaso," Tape II (C).

BROADCAST LITERATURE/INTERVIEWS

TAOS-AMROUCHE, MARGUERITE (Algeria/Tunisia)

Reading of "Le Coffre" from Le Grain magique (1966), Tape XV (C).

Reading of "Le Grain magique" from Le Grain magique (1966), Tape XVI (C).

Reading of "Berber Songs" from Le Grain magique (1966), Tape XVII.

TLALI, MIRIAM (South Africa)

Reading of the short story, 'Soweto Hijack" from Staffrider, 1, 1 (1978), Tape XI (C).

ZIRIMU, ELVANIA N. (Uganda)

A memorial tribute to Mrs. Zirimu by Alex Tetteh-Lartey in 1979 for the B.B.C. African Service in London, England in 1979.

* Later published as Conversations with African Writers. Ed. Lee Nichols (Washington, DC: Voice of America, 1981) available to foreign readers and libraries only abroad.

IX. BIBLIOGRAPHY

BELINGA, THERESE BARATTE-ENO (Cameroon)

<u>Bibliographie: auteurs africains et malgaches de langue française</u>. 2nd edition. Paris: Office de Coopération Radiophonique, 1966, 1968.

<u>Ecrivains, cinéastes et artistes camerounais: bio-bibliographie</u>. Yaoundé: Ministère de l'information et de la Culture de la République Unie de Cameroun, 1978. 317 pages.

with Jacqueline Chauveau-Rabut and Mukala Kadima-Mzuji. <u>Bibliographie des auteurs africains de langue française</u>. Paris: Fernand Nathan, 1979. 245 pages.

HOUSE, AMELIA (South Africa)

<u>Black Women Writers from South Africa: A Preliminary Checklist</u>. Evanston: Northwestern University Program on Women, 1980.

X. INTERVIEWS

AIDOO, CHRISTINA AMA ATA (Ghana)

Lautré, Maxine. "An Interview with Ama Ata Aidoo," Cultural Events in Africa, 35 (1967), i-iv.

McGregor, Maxine Lautré. "Ama Ata Aidoo," African Writers Talking. Ed. Cosmo Pieterse and Dennis Duerden. New York: Africana Publishing Corporation, 1972, pp. 19-27.

BA, MARIAMA (Senegal)

Harrell-Bond, Barbara. "Interview: Mariama Bâ," The African Book Publishing Record, 6 (1980), 209-14.

BONNY, ANNE-MARIE (Cameroon)

Epee, Valere. "Anne-Marie Bonny, Poète de 17 ans," Abbia, No. 25 (1971). 160-61.

DANKYI, JANE (Ghana)

Kwaku, Rosemary. An Interview with Jane Dankyi," The Reporter, 2, 1 (1972) [Co-edited and transcribed with Dantun Idowu and Emmanuel Sarpey].

DE SHIELD, ANGELA (Liberia)

Anon. Angela DeShield," Africa Woman, No. 18 (1979), 20.

DIAKHATE, NDEYE COUMBA (Senegal)

Dia, Alioune Toure. "Ndeye Coumba Diakhaté la 'Césaire' sénégalaise," Mwasi, No. 96 (1980), 37-8.

DIKE, FATIMA (South Africa)

Amato, Rob. "A Xhosa Woman's Serious Optimism," Drum, October 1979, p. 14.

Heyns, Jackie. "Fatima Dike: The Queen of Our Stage," Drum, October 1979, p. 14.

INTERVIEWS

Gray, Stephen. "An Interview with Fatima Dike," Black South African Women Writers: A Preliminary Checklist. Ed. Amelia House. Evanston: Northwestern University Program on Women, 1980, pp. 22-32.

DJEBAR, ASSIA (Algeria)

"Assia Djebar," Dialogues, No. 39, (1967).

EMECHETA, BUCHI (Nigeria)

Anon. "Two Faces of Emancipation," Africa Woman, No. 2 (1976), 48-49.

Anon. "Matchet's Dairy: Buchi Emecheta," West Africa, 6 February 1978, pp. 238-39.

Baker, Jo. "Buchi Emecheta," Happy Home, March 1982, pp. 4-5, 10-1.

Kenall, Ena. "A Room of My Own: Buchi Emecheta," Observer, 25 March 1984, pp. 46-47.

FAIK-NZUJI, CLEMENTINE MADIYA (Zaire)

Anon. "Two Faces of Emancipation," Africa Woman, No. 2 (1976), 48.

FALL, KINE KIRAMA (Senegal)

Kamara, Jeannette. "Kiné Kirama Fall," Africa Woman, No. 7 (1976), 15-6.

FORSTER, RETTY (Sierra Leone)

"Retty Forster," Africa Woman, No. 12 (1977), 19.

GACHUKIA, EDDAH (Kenya)

Anon. "M.P. Eddah Gachukia," Africa Woman, No. 6 (1976), 50.

Anon. "Eddah Gachukia Speaks Up," Africa Woman, No. 12 (1977), 20.

INTERVIEWS

HEAD, BESSIE (South Africa/Botswana)

"Interview," MS, September 1975, pp. 72-3, 75.

Fradkin, Betty McGinnis. "Conversation with Bessie," World Literature Written in English, 17, 2 (1978), 427-34.

IFUDU, VERA (Nigeria)

"Vera Ifudu," West Africa, 5 May 1980, p. 775.

KING, DELPHINE (Sierra Leone)

Anon. "A Poetess of Freedom -- That's Delphine," Drum, October 1962, p. 13.

KUMAH, SYLVIE (Ghana)

Anon. "Sylvie Kumah," West Africa, 1 December 1980, p. 2411.

LEMSINE, AICHA (Algeria)

Algérie Actualité, No. 594 (1977), 16.

MAKWABARARA, ANGELINA (Zimbabwe)

Ngwire, Chiza. "Angelina Makwabarara — Breaking New Ground," Africa Woman, No. 36 (1981), 10.

M'BAYE, ANNETTE D'ERNEVILLE (Senegal)

Anon. "Annette M'Baye," Africa Woman, No. 4 (1976), 55.

INTERVIEWS

MUGO, MICERE GITHAE (Kenya)

Munene, Fibi. "Appraisals: Kenya Women 1975 Dr. Micere Mugo — The Quality of Our Leadership Is Disappointing," Viva, 1, 5 (1975), 46-47.

Owano, Nancy. "Dr. Micere Mugo, Kenya's Outspoken Intellectual and Academic Critic Talks to Nancy Owano," Africa Woman, No. 6 (1976), 14-15.

Berrian, Brenda F. "Interview with Micere Githae-Mugo," World Literature Written in English, 21, 3 (1982), 521-31.

MUNENE, FIBI (Kenya)

Mann, Roger. "Just Give Us a Little Time Viva-Focus: Fibi Munene," Viva, 2, 9 (1976), 13.

NDIAYE, OUMY (Senegal)

Aoulou, Yves. "La plus jeune journaliste du Sénégal," Amina, No. 75 (1979), 1.

NGU, MURSSA NASEKA (Zaire)

Anon. 'La solitude des femmes de travailleurs en France — Murssa Naseka Ngu, reporter photographe des sports zaïrois," Bingo, No. 240 (1973).

NJAU, REBEKA (Kenya)

"False Report on Girlfriends Saddened Us," Sunday Nation, 20 February 1977, pp. 14-5.

NWAPA, FLORA (Nigeria)

Anon. West Africa, 14 July 1972, p. 891.

Anon. West Africa, 9 October 1972, p. 1355.

Agetua, John. "Flora Nwakuche," Interviews with Six Nigerian Writers. Benin City: The Bendel Newspapers Corporation, 1974, pp. 22-7.

_____. Sunday Observer, 18 August 1975, p. 6.

Anon. "Flora Nwakuche," Africa Woman, No. 10 (1977), 8-10.

INTERVIEWS

Perry, Alistair. "Meeting Flora Nwapa," West Africa, 18 June 1984, p. 1262.

OGOT, GRACE AKINYI (Kenya)

Anon. " A Writer Prefers Pleasing to Preaching," Sunday Nation, 28 November 1971, pp. 15-6.

Anon. "Grace Ogot," Topic, No. 92 (1975), 5.

Stuphin, Gay. "Genuine Talent," Viva, 2, 11 (1976), 19.

Ganjuly, Shailaja. "An Afternoon with Grace Ogot," Femina, 8-22 September 1979, p. 39.

Lindfors, Bernth. "Interview with Grace Ogot," World Literature Written in English, 18, 1, (1979), 57-68.

Likimani, Muthoni. Women of Kenya. Nairobi: s.m. 1979, p. 27.

Lindfors, Bernth, ed. Mazungumza: Interviews with East African Writers, Publishers, Editors and Scholars. Athens: Ohio University Press, 1981.

INTERVIEWS

OGOT, PAMELA (Kenya)

Likimani, Muthoni. Women of Kenya. Nairobi: s.n., 1979, p. 28.

OGUNDIPE-LESLIE, OMOLARA (Nigeria)

"Women Under Discussion," West Africa, 16 April 1984, pp. 816-18.

"Aspects of Literature," West Africa, 23 April 1984, pp. 876-77.

SEGUN, MABEL IMOUKHUEDE JOLAOSA (Nigeria)

Anon. "Multi-Faceted Mabel," Africa Woman, No. 18 (1978), 14-5.

SIKAKANE, JOYCE (South Africa)

Ottah, Marilyn. "Joyce Sikakane," Africa Woman, No. 20 (1979), 16.

SOFOLA, ZULU (Nigeria)

Agetua, John. "Zulu Sofola," Interviews with Six Nigerian Writers. Benin City: The Bendel Newspapers Corporation, 1974, pp. 19-23.

Omotoso, Kole. "Interview with Playwright Zulu Sofola," Afriscope, 3, 12 (1973), 59-60.

Rwakaara, Beatrice. "A Nigerian Looks Twice at Tradition," The Daily Nation, 16 August 1981, p. 19.

SOW FALL, AMINATA (Senegal)

Hammond, Thomas H. "Entretien avec Aminata Sow Fall," Présence Francophone, No. 22 (1981), 191-95.

INTERVIEWS

SUTHERLAND, EFUA THEODORA MORGUE (Ghana)

Aidoo, Ama Ata. "An Interview," Cultural Events in Africa, 35 (1967)

Lautré, Maxine. "A Recorded Interview with Efua Sutherland on Current Theatre Movement in Ghana," Cultural Events in Africa, No. 42 (1968), i-iv.

_____. "Efua Sutherland," African Writers Talking. Ed. Cosmo Pieterse and Dennis Duerden. New York: Africana Publishing Corporation, 1972, pp. 183-95.

Woode, Kwesi. "Efua Sutherland: A Profile," Annual Writers' Congress. Accra: Ghana Association of Writers, 1973, pp. 16-8.

ULASI, ADAORA LILY (Nigeria)

Anon. "Adaora L. Ulasi," Topic, No. 92 (1975), 28.

Johnson, Thomas A. "African Women: Their Occupations Range from Magazine Editor to Fish Seller," The New York Times, 12 July 1975, p. 14.

ZIRIMU, ELVANIA NAMUKWAYA (Uganda)

Tetteh-Lartey, Alex. Arts and Africa, No. 315 (1979), 1-4 [B.B.C. African Service, London in memory of Mrs. Zirimu].

XI CRITICISM OF AUTHORS' WORKS

'ABD ALLAH, SUFI (Egypt)

Accad, Evelyne. Veil of Shame. Sherbrooke: Naaman, 1978, pp. 117-21; 135; 160.

ADDO, JOYCE (Ghana)

Nicol, Davidson. "West African Poetry," Africa South in Exile, 5, 3 (1961), 119.

ADDO, PATIENCE (Ghana)

Brown, Lloyd W. Women Writers in Black Africa. Westport: Greenwood Press, 1981, pp. 31-3.

ADEMOLA, FRANCES (Ghana)

Anon. "J. P. Clark and His Audience," African Forum, 1, 2 (1965), 84-6.

AFONSO, MARIA PERPETUA CANDEIAS DA SILVA

Hamilton, Russell. Voices from an Empire: A History of Afro-Portuguese Literature. Minneapolis: University of Minnesota Press, 1974, pp. 131-32.

AIDOO, AMA ATA (Ghana)

Adelugba, Dapo. "Language and Drama: Ama Ata Aidoo," African Literature Today, 8 (1976), 72-84.

_____. "No Sweetness Here: Literature as Social Criticism," Ba Shiru, 6, 1 (1974), 15-24.

Ansah, Paul. "The Situation of African Literature since 1960," Réflexions sur première décennie des Indépendances en Afrique noire/Reflections on the First Decade of Negro Independence. Paris: Presence Africaine, 1971, pp. 244-71.

Bamikunle, Aderemi. :The Two Plays of Aidoo — A Commentary," Work in Progress, Department of English, Ahmadu Bello University, Zaria, Nigeria (1972), 170-82.

Banham Martin and Clive Wake. African Theatre Today. London: Pitman Publishing, 1976, pp. 50-2, 55.

CRITICISM OF AUTHORS' WORKS

Bell, Roseann P. "The Absence of the African Woman Writer, CLA Journal, 21, 4 (1978), 496.

Berrian, Brenda F. "African Women As Seen in the Works of Flora Nwapa and Ama Ata Aidoo," CLA Journal, 25 , 3 (1982), 331-39.

_____. "The Afro-American West African Marriage Question: Literary and Historical Contexts," Paper presented at the African Studies Association, Los Angeles, California, 1 November, 1979, 13 pages.

_____. "There's a Lot to be Said: Female African Writers," Paper presented for the Women's Studies Speakers Series, University of Pittsburgh, Pittsburgh, Pennsylvania, 18 January, 1979, 20 pages.

Britwum, Atta. "New Trends," University of Cape Coast English Department Workpapers, 1 (1971), 15-21.

Brown, Lloyd W. "The African Woman as Writer," Canadian Journal of African Studies, 9, 3 (1975), 493-501.

_____. "Ama Ata Aidoo: The Art of the Short Story and Sexual Roles in Africa," World Literature Written in English, 13 (1974), 172-83.

_____. Women Writers in Black Africa. Westport: Greenwood Press, 1981, pp. 84-121.

Bruner, Charlotte. "Child Africa as Depicted by Bessie Head and Ama Ata Aidoo," Studies in the Humanities, 7, 2 (1979), 5-11.

Burness, Donald. "Womanhood in the Short Stories of Ama Ata Aidoo," Studies in Black Literature, 4, 2 (1973), 21-4.

Chapman, Karen. "Introduction," The Dilemma of A Ghost, Ama Ata Aidoo. New York:Collier-Macmillan, 1971, pp. 7-25; rpt. Sturdy Black Bridges: Visions of Black Women in Literature. Ed. Roseann P. Bell, Bettye J. Parker and Beverly Guy-Sheftall. New York: Doubleday, 1979, pp. 25-38.

Condé, Maryse. "Three Female Writers in Modern Africa: Flora Nwapa, Ama Ata Aidoo, Grace Ogot," Présence Africaine, No. 82 (1972), 136-39.

deGraft, Joseph C. 'Dramatic Question," Writers in East Africa. Ed. Andrew Gurr and Angus Calder. Nairobi: East African Literature Bureau, 1974, pp. 33-67.

Duah, Francis Bokaye. "Influence of Oral Folklore on Written Literature in Africa South of Sahara (as exemplified in Ghana)," The Art of the World of Culture of Sub-saharan Africa. Prague: Sbronik Studentskych Praci, Universita 17, Listopada V Praze, 1971, pp. 1-38.

CRITICISM OF AUTHORS' WORK

Duruaku, A. B. C. "Content and Form in Two Ghanaian Playwrights: Ama Ata Aidoo and Joe de Graft," B. A. Thesis, Department of English, University of Nigeria, Nsukka, 1979-1980.

Egejuru, Phanuel A. Black Writers: White Audience A Critical Approach to African Literature. Hicksville: Exposition Press, 1978, pp. 52-3, 139-40.

Eyah, Hansel. "The Treatment of Tragic Themes in African Theatre," Master's thesis, English Department, University of Leeds, 1976.

Graham-White, Anthony. 'Ama Ata Aidoo," Contemporary Dramatists. Ed. James Vinson. Pref. Ruby Cohn. London: St. James Press, 2nd edition; rpt. New York: St. Martin's Press, 1977, pp. 21-3.

──────. The Drama of Black Africa. New York: Samuel French, 1974, pp. 91, 98, 100, 104-6, 148, 172.

Hill, Mildred, "For Whom Things Did Not Change, Women as Workers in Ama Ata Aidoo's No Sweetness Here," Women and Work in Africa Symposium No. 6. University of Illinois at Urbana, Urbana, Illinois, 29 April, 1979.

Iyasere, Solomon O. "Modern African Literature: The Question of Ideological Commitment," West African Journal of Modern Languages, 2 (1976), 5-10.

Jahn, Janheinz. "Ghana's Written Literature," Ghanaian Writing: Ghana as Seen by Her Own Writers as well as by German Authors. Ed. A. W. Kayper-Mensah and Horst Wolff. Tubingen: Erdmann, 1972, pp. 234-340.

Kennedy, Scott. In Search of African Theatre. New York: Charles Scribner's Sons, 1973, p. 134.

Kilson, Marion. "Women and African Literature," Journal of African Studies, 4, 2 (1977), 161-66.

Lindfors, Bernth. "The Image of the Afro-American in African Literatuare," Literary Criterion, 12, 1 (1975), 36-45; prt. Association for Commonwealth Literature and Language Studies Bulletin, 4, 3 (1975), 19-26.

Lippert Anne, "Women Characters and African Literature," Afriscope, 3, 10 (1973), 45,49.

Little, Kenneth. "Mothers and Other Characters," West Africa, 24 September, 1979, p. 1759.

──────. The Sociology of Urban Women's Image in African Literature. London: Macmillan, 1980, pp. 14-5, 74-5, 121-25.

CRITICISM OF AUTHORS' WORK

Martin, Kristine L., "The Quest for Identity in West African Literature," Master's thesis, Iowa State University, Ames, Iowa, 1981.

McCaffrey, Kathleen. "Images of the Mother in the Stories of Ama Ata Aidoo," Africa Woman, No. 23 (1979), 40-1.

_____. "Images of Women in Literature of Selected Developing Countries (Ghana Senegal, Haiti, Jamaica)". Washington, DC: Pacific Consultants Contract afr-C-1197, Work Order 36, 1977.

_____. "Images of Women in West African Literature and Film: A Struggle against Dual Colonization," International Journal of Women's Studies, 3 (1980), 76-88.

Mensah, A. N. "Ama Ata Aidoo: Two Short Stories and Their Relevance to Modern Ghana," New Era, 3 (1968), 22-3.

Mphahlele, Ezekiel. "Introduction," No Sweetness Here, Ama Ata Aidoo. New York: Doubleday, 1972, pp. ix-xxiv.

_____. "Workshop II: More Guidelines for the Short Story," Staffrider, 2, 1 (1979), 50-2.

Nagenda, John. "Generations in Conflict: Ama Ata Aidoo, J. C. deGraft and R. Sharif Easmon," Protest and Conflict in African Literature. Ed. Cosmos Pieterse and Ian Munro. New York: Africana Publishing Corporation, 1970, pp. 101-8.

Nasidi, Yakubu. "A Study of Six West African Dramatists," Master's thesis, English Department, University of Leeds, 1976.

Nkosi, Lewis. "Women in Literature," Africa Woman, No. 6 (1976), 36-7.

Ogunba, Oyin. "Modern Drama in West Africa," Perspectives on African Literature: Selections from the Proceedings of the Conference on African Literature Held at the University of Ife. Ed. Christopher Heywood. New York: Africana Publishing Corporation, in association with the University of Ife Press, 1971, pp. 101-2.

Okonkwo, Juliet. "The Talented Woman in African Literataure," Africa Quarterly, 15 (1975), 35-47.

Omotoso, Kole. "End-of-the-Year Book Report," Afriscope, 4, 12 (1974), 39-40.

Rea, C. J. "The Culture Line: A Note on the Dilemma of a Ghost," African Forum, 1, 1 (1966), 11-3.

CRITICISM OF AUTHORS' WORKS

Ridden, Geoffrey. "Language and Social Status in Ama Ata Aidoo," Style, 9 (1974), 542-61.

Rushing, Andrea Benton. "Images of Black Women in Modern African Poetry: An Overview," Sturdy Black Bridges: Visions of Black Women in Literature. Ed. Roseanne P. Bell, Bettye J. Parker and Beverly Guy-Sheftall. New York: Doubleday, 1979, p. 24.

Schipper, Mineke. Theatre and Society in Africa. Johannesburg: Ravan Press, 1982, pp. 71-2.

Shoga, Yinka. "Women Writers and African Literature," Afriscope, 3, 10 (1973), 44-5.

Soyinka, Wole. "Modern Negro-African Theatre: The Nigerian Stage, A Study in Tyranny and Individual Survival," Anon. Colloquium: Function and Significance of African Negro Art in the Life of the People and for the People (March 30-April 8, 1966). Paris: Presence AFricaine, 1968, pp. 495-504.

Stewart, Daniele. "African Writing in Prose: A Critical Survey," Présence Africaine, No. 91 (1974), 99-103.

Vincent, Theo, "Form in the Nigerian Novel: An Examination of Aidoo's Our Sister Killjoy and Okpewho's The Last Duty," Paper presented at the African Studies Association Conference, Philadelphia Pennsylvania, 17 October 1980.

Warren, Lee. The Theatre in Africa: An Introduction. Englewood Cliffs: Prentice-Hall, 1975, pp. 51, 55.

AMROUCHE, FADHMA AITH MANSOUR (Algeria)

Chauvigné, Claude. "Fadhma Aïth Mansour, l'exilée: l'émouvant témoignage d'une femme kabyle," African Literature Conference, Appalachian State University, Boone, North Carolina, 6 April 1978.

BA, MARIAMA (Senegal)

Ojo-Ade, Femi. "Still a Victim? Mariama Bâ's Une si longue lettre," African Literature Today, Vo. 12. Ed. Eldred Jones London: Heinemann, 1982, pp. 71-87.

Gérard, Albert and Laurent, Jeannine. "Sembène's Progeny: A New Trend in the Senegalese Novel," Studies in Twentieth-Century Literature, 4, 2 (1980) 133-45.

CRITICISM OF AUTHORS' WORKS

Makward, Edris. "The Pursuit of Happiness in the Novels of Mariama Bâ," African Literature Association Conference, University of Maryland at Baltimore, Catonsville, Maryland, April 14, 1984.

CASELY-HAYFORD, ADELAIDE (Sierra Leone)

Okonkwo, Rina. "Adelaide Casely-Hayford; Cultural Nationlist and Feminist," Journal of History and Society of Sierra Leone, 2, 2 (1978). 10, 21.

CASELY-HAYFORD, GLADYS, pseudonym, Aquah Laluah (Sierra Leone and Ghana)

Cook, David. African Literature: A Critical Review. London: Longmans, 1977, p. 39.

Dathorne, O. R. The Black Mind: A History of African Literature. Minneapolis: University of Minnesota Press, 1974, pp. 251-52.

Jones, Eldred. "The Potentialities of Krio as a Literary Language," Sierra Leone Studies, 9 (1957), 40-8.

Nicol, Davidson. "West African Poetry," Africa South in Exile, 5, 3 (1961), 119.

Nwoga, Donatus. West African Verse. London: Longmans, 1967, pp. 125-30 [Introuductory Notes on selected poems].

Olafioye, Tayo. "Public Poetry of West Africa: A Survey," Ufahamu, 6, 1 (1975), 74-95.

Palmer, Eustace. "The Development of Sierra Leone Writing," A Celebration of Black and African Writing. Ed. Bruce King and Kolawole Ogungbesan. Zaria: Ahmadu Bello University Press and Oxford University Press, 1975, pp. 248-49.

CRITICISM OF AUTHORS' WORKS

CHEDID, ANDREE (Egypt)

Accad, Evelyne. "Andrée Chédid of Egypt: Female Poetics," African Studies Association, Philadelphia, Pennsylvania, October, 1980.

DEBECHE, DJAMILA (Algeria)

Accad, Evelyne. "The North African Woman's Conflict in Djamila Débêche's Aziza (1955) and Marguerite Taos-Amrouche's Rue des Tambourins (1960)," Folio, 11 (1978), 9-16.

DIKE, FATIMA (South Africa)

King, Val and Paul Alberts. "Fatima Dike: Lady of the Theatre," Bond, January, 1980, pp. 92-5.

DJEBAR, ASSIA (Algeria)

Accad, Evelyne. Veil of Shame: The Role of Women in Contemporary Fiction of North Africa and the Arab World. Sherbrooke: CELEF, 1978, pp. 58-9, 93-6, 100-101, 160-65.

Dejeux, Jean. Littérature magrébine de langue française. Ottawa: Naaman, 1973.

Khatibi, Abdelkebir. Le Roman magrébine. Paris: Maspero, 1968, pp. 61-65.

Mortimer, Mildred P. "La femme algérienne dans les romans d'Assia Djebar," The French Review, 49, 5 (1976), 759-63.

_____. "The Feminine Image in the Algerian Novel of French Expression," Ba Shiru, 8, 2 (1977), 51-62.

_____, "Evolution of Assia Djebar's Feminist Conscience: From La Soif to Femmes d'Algers," African Literature Association Conference, the Claremont Colleges, Claremont, California, April 9, 1981.

Zimra, Clarisse. "In Her Own Write: The Circular Structures of Linguistic Alienation in Assia Djebar's Early Novels," Research in African Literatures, (1980), 206-23.

EL SAADAWI, NAWAL (Egypt)

Perry, Alison."Third World Women's Book Fair," West Africa, 4 June 1984, pp. 1161-62.

CRITICISM OF AUTHORS' WORKS

EMECHETA, BUCHI (Nigeria)

Berrian, Brenda F. "The Image of the Woman in Buchi Emecheta's Novels," Western Association of Africanists, Arizona State University, Tempe, Arizona, March 16, 1979, 15 pages.

Brown, Lloyd W. Women Writers in Black Africa. Westport: Greenwood Press, 1981, pp. 35-60.

Chinweizu, "Time of Troubles," Times Literary Supplement, 26 February 1982, p. 228.

Little, Kenneth. The Sociology of the Urban Woman's Image in African Literature. London: Macmillan, 1980, pp. 40-3, 113-4, 151, 156-7.

Martini, Jurgen, "Linking Africa and the West — Buchi Emecheta," Images de l'Afrique en Occident: La Presse, Les Médits et la Littérature Conference, Université de Paris XI, le 20 novembre 1980.

Nkosi, Lewis. "Women in Literature," Africa Woman, No. 6 (1976), 36-7.

Ogunyemi, Chikwenye Okonjo, "From Buchi Emechea Onwordi to Buchi Emecheta," African Literature Association Conference, the Claremont Colleges, Claremont, California, April 9, 1981.

Perry, Alistair. "Buchi Emecheta - The Feminist Book Fair," West Africa. 18 June 1984, p. 1263.

Stevens, Andrew. "Ripe for Promotion," Sunday Times Magazine, 13 February 1983, pp. 30-3.

Ugwu, F. I. "Changing Images of Womanhood in Modern West African Fiction as portrayed by Cheikh Hamidou Kane, Sembene Ousmane and Buchi Emecheta," B.A. Thesis, Department of English, University of Nigeria, Nsukka, 1980-81.

Umeh, Marie. "Reintegration with the Lost Self: A Study of Buchi Emecheta's Double Yoke," African Literature Association Conference, University of Maryland at Baltimore, Catonsville, Maryland, April 12, 1984.

CRITICISM OF AUTHORS' WORKS

ESPIRITO SANTO, ALDA DO (São Tomé e Príncipe)

Hamilton, Russell. Voices from an Empire: A History of Afro-Portuguese Literature. Minneapolis: University of Minnesota Press, 1974, pp. 370-72, 375.

LaGuma, Alex. "Literature and Life," Lotus: Afro-Asian Writings, 1, 5 (1970), 239.

Moser, Gerald. Essays in Portuguese - African Literature. University Park: Pennsylvania State University, 1969, pp. 11, 24-5.

Preto-Rodas, Richard A Negritude as a Theme in the Poetry of the Portuguese-Speaking World. Gainesville: University Press of Florida, 1970, pp. 52-53.

FAIK-NZUJI, CLEMENTINE MADIYA (Zaire)

Allay, Jean. "Clémentine Nzuji et la Pléiade du Congo," Congo-Afrique, 6, 1 (1966), 28-33.

Goby, Beya Ngindu and Tshikumambila Nyembwe, "Deux nouvelles publications de C. Faik-Nzuji Madiya," Zaïre-Afrique, (1977), 55-8.

Malubungi, Lungenyi-Lumwe. "Langues et littératures zaïroises. Aspects actuels de la recherche," Zaïre-Afrique, 14, 83 (1974), 166-68.

Mukala, Kadima-Nzuji. "Littérature au Zaïre depuis l'indépendance: I. La poésie," Zaïre-Afrique, 12, 69 (1972), 551-53.

_____. "La Littérature au Zaïre depuis l'indépendance," Zaïre-Afrique, 12, 70 (1972), 166-68.

FALL, KINE KIRAMA (Senegal)

Sine, Babacar. "La poésie de Kiné Kirama Fall," Présence Africaine, 29 (1974), 174-75.

GEBRU, SENEDDU (Ethiopia)

Gérard, Albert S. Four African Literatures: Xhosa, Sotho, Zulu, Amharic. Los Angeles: University of California Press, 1971, pp. 335-36, 344.

CRITICISM OF AUTHORS' WORKS

GITHAE-MUGO, MICERE (Kenya)

Alot, Magaga. Kenya Prepares for FESTAC in Lagos," The Weekly Review, 27 December 1976, pp. 29-32.

Brown, Lloyd W. Women Writers in Black Africa. Westport: Greenwood Press, 1981, p. 24-5.

Chesaina, Jane C. "Who Is on Trial in The Trial of Dedan Kimathi? A Critical Essay on Ngugi wa Thiong'o and Micere Githae-Mugo's The Trial of Dedan Kimathi," Busara, 8, 2 (1976), 21-36.

Hirst, Terry. "The Trial of Dedan Kimathi," Joe, November 1976, pp. 27-8 [First performance of Kenyatta Day, 28 October 1976 in Nairobi].

James, O. "OK 'Book Worms', Unite " JOE, September 1977, p. 25-27

Kahiga, Miriam. "Women in the Theatre," JOE, September 1977, p. 30.

Maloba, O. W. "The Trial of Dedan Kimathi by Ngugi wa Thiong'o and Micere Githae-Mugo," Umma, 5 (1977), 19-20, 22.

Médjibodo, Nicole. "Dedan Kimathi, héros de la lutte de libération kenyanne," Présence Africaine, 3 (1979), 70-9.

Ouma, Hilary. "Another Look at the Kenya National Theatre," The Weekly Review, 15 November 1976, pp. 31-2.

Wanjala, Chris. "The Kenya National Theatre Revisited," The Weekly Review, 8 November 1976, p. 32.

_____. "Roadside Drama," The Weekly Review, 20 September 1976, p. 31.

GREKI, ANNA (Algeria)

Mortimer, Mildred. "Algerian Poetry of French Expression," African Literature Today, Vol. 6. Ed. Eldred Jones. London: Heinemann, 1973, pp. 71-3.

GUTU, LAETITIA (Zimbabwe)

Style, O-lan. "Africa: Southern," Journal of Commonwealth Literature, 14, 2 (1978), 10.

GWARAM, HAUWA (Nigeria)

Mack, Beverly. "Wake Daya Ba Ta Kare Nika - One Song will Not Finish the Grinding: Hausa Women's Oral Literature," Contemporary African Literature. Ed. Hal Wylie, Eileen Julien, and Russell J. Linneman. Washington, DC: Three Continents Press, 1983, pp. 15-20.

HEAD, BESSIE (South Africa and Botswana)

Abrahams, Cecil. "The Tyranny of Place: The Context of Bessie Head's Fiction," World Literature Written in English, 17, 1 (1978), 30-7.

Beard, Linda Susan. "Bessie Head's A Question of Power: The Journey through Disintegration to Wholeness," Colby Literary Journal, 15 (1979), 267-74.

_____, "Lessing and Head: A Question of Power," African Literature Association, Indiana University, Bloomington, Indiana, 24 March 1979.

Brown, Lloyd W. "Creating New Worlds in Southern Africa: Bessie Head and the Question of Power," Umoja, 3, 1 (1979), 43-53.

_____. Women Writers in Black Africa. Westport: Greenwood Press, 1981, pp. 158-85.

Bruner, Charlotte H. "Child Africa as Depicted by Bessie Head and Ama Ata Aidoo," Studies in the Humanities, 7, 2 (1979), 5-11.

_____. "Bessie Head: Restless in a Distant Land," When the Drumbeat Changes. Ed. Carolyn Parker and Stephen Arnold. Washington, DC: Three Continents Press, 1980, pp. 261-78.

Houchins, Sue E, "Bessie Head and Her Black American Sisters: A Comparison of Bessie Head to Alice Walker and Toni Morrison," African Literature Association Conference, Indiana University, Bloomington, Indiana, 21 March 1979.

Larson, Charles R. The Novel in the Third World. Washington, DC: Inscape, 1976.

Marquand, Jane. "In Exile and Community in Southern Africa: The Novels of Bessie Head," The London Magazine, 18, ix-x (1978), 48-61.

_____, "The Farm: A Concept in the Writing of Olive Schreiner, Pauline Smith, Doris Lessing, Nadine Gordimer and Bessie Head," African Literature Association Conference, Indiana University, Bloomington, Indiana, 24 March 1979.

Mitchison, Naomi. "Bessie Head," Contemporary Novelists. Ed. James Vinson. New York: St. Martin's PRess, 1972, pp. 580-82.

CRITICISM OF AUTHORS' WORKS

Moss, Rose, "The Censor: Repression and Evasions in the Fiction of Some South African Women Writers," African Literature Association, Indiana University, Bloomington, Indiana, 24 March 1979.

Mphahlele, Ezekiel. "The New Mood in African Literature," Africa Today, 19, 4 (1972), 54-70.

Nkosi, Lewis. Tasks and Masks: Styles and Themes in African Literature. London: Longman, 1981, pp. 100-2.

Ojo-Ade, Femi. "Bessie Head's Alienated Heroine: Victim or Villain?" Ba Shiru, 8, 2 (1977), 13-21.

Ravenscroft, Arthur. "The Novels of Bessie Head," Aspects of South African Literature. Ed. Christopher Heywood. New York: Africana Publishing Corporation, 1978, pp. 317-29.

Smith, Rowland, ed. Exile and Tradition: Studies in African and Caribbean Literature. London: Longman and Dalhousie, 1976.

JABAVU, NONI (South Africa)

Gérard, Albert S. "Les Lettres néo-africaines: Diversité de l'Afrique," La Revue Nouvelle, 36 (1962), 227-34.

Loeb, Harold. "The Literary Situation in South Africa," Southern Review, 8 (1972), 371-77.

Olney, James. Tell Me Africa: An Approach to African Literature. Princeton: Princeton University Press, 1973.

Visser, N. W. "South Africa: The Renaissance that Failed," Journal Of Commonwealth Literature, 11, 1 (1976), 42-57.

JOHN-ROWE, JULIANA (Sierra Leone)

Rowe, Slyvester, E. "Sierra Leone's Newly-Born Theatre," African Arts/Arts d'Afrique, 9, 1 (1975), 50, 56-9.

Warritay, Batillos I. "Cultural Misdirection and the Sierra Leone Theatre," Afriscope, 5, 8 (1975), 50, 52-3.

CRITICISM OF AUTHORS' WORKS

KASAHUN, ROMANA WORQ (Ethiopia)

Gérard, Albert S. Four African Literatures: Xhosa, Sotho, Zulu, Amharic. Los Angeles: University of California Press, 1971, p. 335-36.

KASESE, MEDARD (Zambia)

Brown, Lloyd W. Women Writers in Black Africa. Westport: Greenwood Press, 1981, p. 24.

KHUZWAYO, ELLEN (South Africa)

Perry, Alison. "Third World Women's Book Fair," West Africa, 4 June 1984, pp. 1161-62 (comments about the book Call Me a Woman).

KIMENYE, BARBARA (Uganda)

Brown, Lloyd, W. Women Writers in Black Africa. Westport: Greenwood Press, 1981, pp. 15-7.

Nazareth, Peter. "An Uncommitted Writer,: Literature and Society in Modern Africa: Essays on Literature. Nairobi: East African Literature Bureau, 1972, pp. 155-74; rpt. An African View of Literature. Evanston: Northwestern University Press, 1974, pp. 167-71.

_____. "Writing in East Africa," Afriscope, 4, 4 (1974), 56.

Schmidt, Nancy J. "Fiction about African Children for African Children: Books in Series," Bulletin of the Southern Association of Africanists, 4, 3 (1976), 2-5.

_____. "The Writer as Teacher: A Comparison of the African Adventure Stories of G. A. Henty, René Guillot, and Barbara Kimenye," African Studies Review, 19, 11 (1976), 69-80.

_____. "Children's Books by Well-Known African Authors," World Literature Written in English, 18, 1 (1979), 118-19.

CRITICISM OF AUTHORS' WORKS

KING, DELPHINE (Sierra Leone)

Palmer, Eustace. "The Development of Sierra Leone Writing," A Celebration of Black and African Writing. Ed. Bruce King and Kolawole Ogungbesan. Zaria: Ahmadu Bello University Press and Oxford University Press, 1975, pp. 245-57.

MME KOLIA (Ivory Coast)

Kiele, Gilbert Torou. "Mme Kolia: Le Théâtre une réalité," Eburnea, 116 (1977), 20-1.

LALUAH, ACQUAH also known as Gladys Casely-Hayford (Sierra Leone/Ghana)

Brown, Lloyd W. Women Writers in Black Africa. Westport: Greenwood Press, 1981, pp. 15, 24-5.

LARA, ALDA (Angola)

Hamilton, Russell. Voices from an Empire: A History of Afro-Portuguese Literature. Minneapolis: University of Minnesota Press, 1974, pp. 61-3.

Margarido, Alfredo. Estudos sobre literaturas das nacoes africanas de lingua portuguesa. Lisboa: Regra do jogo, 1980.

Moser, Gerald. Essays in Portuguese-African Literature. University Park: Pennsylvania State University, 1969, pp. 61-63.

LEMSINE, AICHA (Algeria)

Abdel-Sayed, Samiha. "Le drame du couple dans Les Impatients d'Assia Djebar, La Chrysalide d'Aïcha Lemsine et Le Sommeil délivré d'Andrée Chédid," African Literature Association Conference, Indiana University, Bloomington, Indiana, 22 March 1979.

Lippert, Anne, "Aïcha Lemsine's Algerian Woman: Fact or Fantasy?" African Literature Association Conference, Indiana University, Bloomington, Indiana, 22 March 1979.

CRITICISM OF AUTHORS' WORKS

LIKING, WEREWERE (Cameroon)

Anon. "In Search of a New Aesthetic Theatre: Liking Werewere," Afrika (Munich), 20, 5 (1979), 25-6.

MARGARIDO, MARIA MANUELA (São Tomé e Príncipe)

Hamilton, Russell. Voices from an Empire: A History of Afro-Portuguese Literature. Minneapolis: University of Minnesota Press, 1974, p. 375.

Preto-Rodas, Richard A. Negritude as a Theme in the Poetry of the Portuguese Speaking World. Gainesville: University Press of Florida, 1970, p. 52.

MPONGO, MARIE-EUGENIE (Zaire)

Nkashama, Ngandu. "La Littérature au Zaïre depuis l'indépendance: I. La poésie," Zaïre-Afrique, 12, 69 (1972), 560.

MSHAM, MWANA KUPONA BINTI (Kenya)

Werner, Alice. "The Utendi of Mwana Kupona," Harvard African Studies, 1 (1917), 147-81.

MUGOT, HAZEL DESILVA (Seychelles)

Bruner, Charoltte. "Hazel Mugot," Unwinding Theads Writing by Women in Africa. African Writers Series #256. London: Heinemann, 1983, pp. 86-7.

Shoga, Yinka. "Women Writers and African Literature," Afriscope, 3,10,(1973), 44-5.

MUHANDO, PENNINA (Tanzania)

Mbuhuni, L.A. "Old and New Drama from East Africa: A Review of the Works of Four Contemporary Dramatists: Rebecca Njau, Ebrahim Hussein, Penniah Muhando and Ngugi," African Literature Today, 8, (1976), 86.

Mollel, Jesse, "Towards A Genuine African Theatre: Tradition and Innovation in the Drama of Penina Muhando," Master's thesis, University of Alberta Edmonton, Canada, 1979.

CRITICISM OF AUTHORS' WORKS

MUNENE, FIBI (Kenya)

Alavo, Yves. "Le rôle de la femme au Kenya," Amina, No. 54 (1977), 10-11.

NJAU, REBEKA, pseudonym Marina Gashe (Kenya)

Beard, Linda Susan. "The Marriage Question in Novels by Black African Women," Western Association of Africanists, Arizona State University, Tempe, Arizona, 16 March 1979.

Bell, Roseann, P. "The Absence of the African Woman Writer," CLA Journal, 21, 4 (1978), 495.

Brown, Lloyd W. "The African Woman as Writer," Canadian Journal of African Studies, 9, 3, (1975), 496.

_____. Women Writers in Black Africa. Westport: Greenwood Press, 1981, pp. 24-5.

Kahiga, Miriam. "Women in the Theatre," JOE, September 1977, p. 30.

Little, Kenneth. The Sociology of the Urban Woman's Image in African Literature. London: Macmillan, 1980, pp. 19-23, 68-9, 126-27.

Litto, Frederic M., ed. Plays from Black Africa. New York: Hill and Wang, 1968, p. ix.

Porter, Abioseh, "Ideology and the Image of Women: Kenyan Women in Njau and Ngugi," Ariel, 12, 3 (1981), 61-74.

Schipper, Mineke. Theatre and Society in Africa. Johannesburg: Ravan Press, 1982, pp. 116-17.

NJOYA, RABIATOU (Cameroon)

Waters, Harold A. "Black French Theatre Update," World Literature Today, 57, 1 (1983), 47.

CRITICISM OF AUTHORS' WORKS

NWAPA, FLORA, Mrs. Nwakuche (Nigeria)

Abanobi, N. N. "Women: Role in the World of Flora Nwapa's Novels," B.A. Thesis. University of Nigeria, Nsukka, 1977-78.

Anozie, Sunday O, Sociologie du roman africain: Réalisme, structure et détermination dans le roman ouest-africain. Paris: Auber-Montaigne, 1970, pp. 26, 38, 103-9.

Bengu, Sibusiso M. E. "African Cultural Identity and International Relations: Analysis of Ghanaian and Nigerian Sources 1958-1974," Pref. Roy Preiswerk. Geneva, University of Geneva, 1976; doctoral dissertation; rpt. Gods Are Not Our Own. Pietermaritzburg: Shuster and Shuster, 1976.

Berrian, Brenda F. "African Women as Seen in the Works of Flora Nwapa and Ama Ata Aidoo," CLA Journal, 25, 3 (1982), 331-39.

_____. "There's a Lot To Be Said: Female African Writers," Women's Speakers Series, University of Pittsburgh, Pittsburgh, Pennsylvania, 18 January 1979, 20 pages.

Bottcher, Karl-Heinz. Tradition und Modernitat bei Amos Tutuola und Chinua Achebe: Grundzuge der Westafrinkanischen Erzahlliteratur Englischer Sprache. Bonn: Verlag Herbert Grundmann, 1974.

Brancaccio, Patrick, "The Dreams of Womanhood in Flora Nwapa's Efuru and Idu," African Literature Association Conference, the Claremont Colleges, Claremont, California, April 1981.

Brown, Lloyd W. "The African Woman as Writer," Canadian Journal of African Studies, 9, 3 (1975), 493-501.

_____. Women Writers in Black Africa. Westport: Greenwood Press, 1981, pp. 122-57.

Emenyonu, Ernest N. "African Literature Revisited: A Search for Critical Standards," Revue de Littérature Comparée, 48, 3-4 (1974), 390-91.

_____. "Post-War Writing in Nigeria," Issue, 3,2 (1973), 49-51.

_____. "Who Does Flora Nwapa Write For?" African Literature Today, 7, (1975), 28-33.

CRITICISM OF AUTHORS' WORKS

Fitzjohn, Amelia, "The Image of the Woman in the West African Novel in English: The Nigerian Views of Flora Nwapa," Unpublished essay, Washington, DC, Howard University, n.d., 31 pages.

Githaiga, A. Notes on Flora Nwapa's Efuru. Nairobi: Heinemann, 1978, 48 pages.

Gordimer, Nadine. "Themes and Attitudes in Modern African Writing," Michigan Quarterly Review, 9, (1970), 22; rpt. The Black Interpreters: Notes on African Writing. Johannesburg: Spro-Cas/Ravan, 1973, pp. 20-1.

Jarrett-Kerr, Martin. "Christian Faith and the African Imagination," Religion in Life, 41, 4 (1972), 559-60.

Klima, Valdimir. Modern Nigerian Novels. Dissertation Orientales, 18. Prague: Oriental Institute of Academic, Publishing House of Czezhoslovak Academy of Sciences, 1969.

Larson, Charles. "Whither the African Novel?" CLA Journal, 13 2 (1969), 146.

Laurence, Margaret. Long Drums and Cannons: Nigerian Dramatists and Novelists 1952-1966. London: Macmillan, 1968, pp. 187-91.

Leopold, Wanda. "Powiesci Ibo [Novels by Ibo Writers]," Przeglad Socjologiczny, 23 (1969), 370-87.

Lindfors, Bernth. "Achebe's Followers," Revue de Littérature Comparée, 48, 3 et 4 (1974), 577-78.

_____. "Nigerian Fiction in English, 1952-1967," DAI, 30 (1969), 2535A.

_____. "Nigerian Novels of 1966," Africa Today, 14, 5 (1967), 30-1.

Lippert, Anne. "The Changing role of Women as Viewed in the Literature of English and French Speaking Africa," Doctoral Dissertation, Indiana University, 1972, pp. 112-13.

Little, Kenneth. The Sociology of the Urban Woman's Image in African Literature. London: Macmillan, 1980, pp. 58, 135-35.

CRITICISM OF AUTHORS' WORKS

Mutiso, G.C.M. Socio-Political Thought in African Literature: Weusi? New York: Macmillan, 1974, pp. 57-8.

─────── . "Women in African Literature," East Africa Journal, 8, 3 (1971), 7.

Nandakumar, Prema. "An Image of African Womanhood: A Study of Flora Nwapa's Efuru," Africa Quarterly, 11, (1967), 136-46.

Nkosi, Lewis. "Women in Literature," Africa Woman, No. 6 (1976), 37.

Ofochebe, O. A. "Destiny and the Individual in Elechi Amadi's The Concubine. Flora Nwapa's Efuru, Onuora Nzekwu's Wand of Noble Wood," B. A. Thesis, University of Nigeria, Nsukka, 1977-1978.

Okonkwo, Juliet I. "The Talented Woman in African Literature," Africa Quarterly, 15, 1-2 (1975), 36-47.

O'Malley, P. "Recent Nigerian Fiction," Nigerian Opinion, 3, 4 (1967), 191.

Scheub, Harold. "Two African Women," Revue des Langues Vivantes, 37, 5 (1971).

Schmidt, Nancy J. "Children's Books by Well-Known African Authors," World Literature Written in English, 18, 1 (1979), 117-18.

Shoga, Yinka. "Women Writers and African Literature," Afriscope, 3, 10 (1973), 44-5.

Taiwo, Oladele. Culture and the Nigerian Novel. London: Macmillan; New York: St. Martin's Press, 1976, pp. ix, 5, 156, 183.

Vivilov, V. N. Proza Nigeri [Nigerian Prose]. Moscow: Nauka, 1973.

─────── . "Formirovania nigeriskai literatury (The Formation of Nigerian Literature)," Vzaimosviazi Afrikanskikh Literatur Mira: Cbornik Statel [Interrelationships of African Literatures and the Literatures of the World: A Collection of Articles]. Ed. Irina D. Nikiforova. Moscow: Nauka, 1975.

NZERIBE, GRACE NNENNA (Nigeria)

Lindfors, Bernth. "Postwar Popular Literature in Nigeria," Okike, 9 (1975), 52-64.

CRITICISM OF AUTHORS' WORKS

NZUJI, CAROLINE BALEKA BAMBA (Zaire)

Nkashama, Ngandu. "La Littérature au Zaïre depuis l'indépendance: I. La poésie," Zaïre-Afrique, 12, 69 (1972), 559.

_____. "La Littérature au Zaïre depuis l'indépendance," Zaïre-Afrique, 12, 70 (1972), 623-24.

ODAGA, ASENATH BOLE (Kenya)

Alot, Magaga. "Children Pose Major Challenge to Publishers," The Weekly Review, 6 September 1976, pp. 30-2.

Schmidt, Nancy J. "African Women Writers of Literature for Children," World Literature Written in English, 17, 1 (1978), 13-5.

OGOT, GRACE AKINYI (Kenya)

Anon. "Les Multiples Aspects de Grace Ogot," Bingo, août 1973, p. 54.

Beard, Linda Susan, "The Marriage Question in the Novels by Black African Women," Western Association of Africanists, Arizona State University, Tempe, Arizona, 16 March 1979.

_____, "The Self in the Writings of East African Women Writers," African Literature Association Conference, University of Florida, Gainesville, Florida, 10 April 1980.

Bede, Jacques. "La femme et le pays natal dans The Promised Land, de Grace Ogot," Mélanges africaines. Ed. Thomas Melone. Yaoundé: Equipe de Recherches en Littérature Comparée, n.d., pp. 373-443.

Bell, Roseann P. "The Absence of the African Woman Writer," CLA Journal, 21, 4 (1978), 497.

Berrian, Brenda F, " The Many Windows of Grace Ogot," Modern Language Association Conference, New York, New York, 28 December 1981.

Brown, Lloyd W. Women Writers in Black Africa. Westport: Greenwood Press, 1981, pp. 26-31, 183.

Condé, Maryse. "Three Female Writers in Modern Africa: Flora Nwapa, Ama Ata Aidoo and Grace Ogot," Présence Africaine, No. 82 (1972), 132-43.

Cook, David. In Black and White: Writings from East Africa with Broadcast Discussions and Commentary. Nairobi: East African Literature Bureau, 1976, pp. 145-48.

CRITICISM OF AUTHORS' WORKS

Dathorne, O. R. "Grace Ogot: Role of the Black Woman," African Literature in the Twentieth Century. Minneapolis: University of Minnesota Press, 1974, pp. 130-31.

Jarrett-Kerr, Martin. "Christian Faith and the African Imagination," Religion in Life, 41, 4, (1972), 559.

Killam, G. Douglas. "Kenya," Literature of the World in English. Ed. Bruce King. London and Boston: Routledge and Kegan Paul, 1974, pp. 126-27.

Kilson, Marion. "Women and African Literature," Journal of African Studies, 4, 2 (1977), 161-66.

Kimbugwe, Henry. "The African Lady," East Africa Journal, 6, 4 (1969), 23-4.

Little, Kenneth. The Sociology of the Urban Woman's Image in African Literature. London: Macmillan, 1980, pp. 24-7, 115-16.

Masolo, Dismas A. "Towards Authentic African Literature: Luo Oral Literature," Africa (Rome), 31, 1 (1976), 63-64.

Mazrui, Ali A. "Identity and the Novelist: An Iron Law of Individualism," Aspects of Africa's Identity: Five Essays. Ed. Paul E. Nursey-Bray. Kampala: Makerere Institute of Social Research, Makerere University, 1973, pp. 72, 74.

Mohr, Norma. "The Many Windows of Grace Ogot," African Review, 17, 7 (1976), 21-2.

Moore, Gerald. "The Language of Literature in East Africa," Dalhousie Review, 53, 4 (1973), 691-93.

Mphahlele, Ezekiel. "South Africa," Kenyon Review, 31, 4, (1969), 4777.

Mukayiranga, Callixta, "The African Woman in Grace Ogot's Work: The Promised Land (1966), Land Without Thunder (1968), The Other Woman (1976)," Thesis, Licence d'Enseignement en Lettres, University of Burundi, 1977. 108 pages.

Mutiso, G.C.M. Socio-Political Thought in African Literature: Weusi? New York: MacMillan, 1974, pp. 60-2.

_____. "Women in African Literature," East Africa Journal, 8, 3 (1971), 8.

Povey, John. "The Beginnings of an English Language Literature in East Africa," Books Abroad, 44, (1970, 380-86.

Roscoe, Adrian. Uhuru's Fire: African Literature East to South. Cambridge: Cambridge University Press, 1977, pp. 25-6.

CRITICISM OF AUTHORS' WORKS

Sharma, Veena. "In Search of a New Identity," <u>Eve's Weekly</u> (New Delhi), 12-18 July 1980, pp. 10-1.

Shoga, Yinka. "Women Writers and African Literature," <u>Afriscope</u>, 3, 10 (1973), 44-5.

Skurjat, Ernestyna. <u>Afryka W. Tworczosci Jej Pisarzy</u> [Africa Through the Works of Its Authors]. Studium Afrykanistyczne Uniwersytetu Worszowskiego, 14. Warsaw: Wydawnictwa Uniwersytetu Warszawskiego, 1973.

Tedjani, Bahadur. "Culture versus Literature," <u>Writers in East Africa: Papers From a Colloquium at the University of Nairobi.</u> Ed. Andrew Gurr and Angus Calder. Nairobi: East African Literature Bureau, 1974, pp. 140-41.

Wanjala, Chris. "Roadside Drama," <u>The Weekly Review</u>, 20 September 1976, p. 31.

OGOT, PAMELA, also known as Pamela Ogot Kola (Kenya)

Alot, Magaga. "Children Pose a Major Challenge to Publishers," <u>The Weekly Review</u>, 6 September 1976, pp. 30-2.

OLUDHE-MACGOYE, MARJORIE (Britain/Kenya)

Knight, Elizabeth. "Popular Literature in East Africa," <u>African Literature Today</u>, Vol. 10. Ed. Eldred Jones. London: Heinemann, 1979, pp. 185-86, 187.

OWUSU-NIMOH, MERCY (Ghana)

Anon. "First Noma Award Goes to Senegalese Woman Novelist," <u>The African Book Publishing Record</u>, 6 (1980), 95.

Zell, Hans, M. "The First Noma Award for Publishing in Africa," <u>The African Book Publishing Record</u>, 6 (1980), 200.

PEARCE, ESTHER TAYLOR (Sierra Leone)

Warritay, Batillos I. "Cultural Misdirection and the Sierra Leone Theatre," <u>Afriscope</u>, 5, 8 (1975), 50, 52-3.

CRITICISM OF AUTHORS' WORKS

PEREIRA-EMANUEL, FRANCESCA (Nigeria)

Brown, Lloyd W. "The African as Writer," Canadian Journal of African Studies, 9 (1975), 493-501.

_____. Women Writers in Black Africa. Westport: Greenwood Press, 1981, p.25.

RATSIMISETA, JASMINA (Madagascar)

Gerard, Albert. "The Birth of the Theatre in Madagascar," Educational Theatre Journal, 25 (1973), 362-65.

_____. African Language Literatures: An Introduction to the Literary History of Sub-Sahara Africa. London: Longman; Washington, DC: Three Continents Press, 1981, p. 87.

Rajemisa - Raolison, Régis. Dictionnaire historique et geographie de Madagascar. Fianarantsoa: Librairie Ambozontany, 1966.

RAZAFINIAINA, CHARLOTTE (Madagascar)

Gérard, Albert. "The Birth of Theatre in Madagascar," Educational Theatre Journal, 25 (1973), 362-65.

SAAD, SITI BINTI (Zanzibar)

Harries, Lyndon. "Swahili Literature in the National Context," Review of National Literatures, 2, 2 (1971), 42.

Roberts, Shaaban. Wasifu wa Siti Binti Saad (An account of Siti binti Saad). Tanga: Art and Literature, 1955, 1960, 1967, 1969. [Biographical account].

Sachs, Jurgen. "Swahili - Lieder aus Sansibar," Mitteilungen des Instituts Fur Orient - Forschung, 12 (1966), 221-40.

Suleiman, A. A. "Maisha ya Siti binti Saad, mwimbaji wa Unguya," Supplement to the East African Swahili Committee Journal (Arusha), 28, 1 (1958).

_____, "The Swahili Singing Star, Siti binti Saad, and the Tarab Tradition in Zanzibar," Swahili, 39 (1969), 87-90.

CRITICISM OF AUTHORS' WORKS

SETIDISHO, EDITH (South Africa)

Induku ayinamzi (A Stick has No Home). Cape Town: Oxford University Press, 1961. 107 pages, illus. [Xhosa].

Jahn, Janheinz. A Bibliography of Neo-African Literature from Africa, America and the Caribbean. New York: New York, Praeger, 1965, p. 124.

Kunene, Daniel. Review of National Literatures, 2, 2 (1971).

SIMMI, CHIMA (East Africa)

Tejani, Bahador. "Themes from Indian-English Literature from East Africa," Association for Commonwealth Literature and Language Studies Bulletin. (Mysore, India), 4, 3 (1975), 46-60.

SOFOLA, ZULU (Nigeria)

Medjigbodo, Nicole. "Zulu Sofola," Europe, 618 (1980), 59-64.

Nasiru, Akanji. "Folklore in Nigerian Drama: An Examination of the Works of Three Nigerian Dramatists," Literary Half-Yearly (Mysore, India), 19, 1 (1978), 51-63.

Schmidt, Nancy J. "African Women Writers of Literature for Children," World Literature Written in English, 17, 1 (1978), 7-8.

CRITICISM OF AUTHORS' WORKS

SOUSA, NOEMIA DE (Mozambique)

Anon. "Poetry in the Mozambican Revolution," Afriscope, 5, 4 (1975), 42-3.

Brown, Lloyd W. Women Writers in Black Africa. Westport: Greenwood Press, 1981, p. 24.

Hamilton, Russell. Voices from an Empire: A History of Afro-Portuguese Literature. Minneapolis: University of Minnesota Press, 1974, pp. 199-202.

Honwana, Luis Bernardo. "The Role of Poetry in the Mozambican Revolution," Lotus: Afro-Asian Writings, No. 8 (1971), 150-51, 152, 153.

Kesteloot, Lilyan. Anthologie négro-africaine. Panorama critique de prosateurs, poètes et dramaturges noirs du XXe siècle. Paris: Verviers, Gerard, 1967.

LaPin, Deirdre. "The Voices of Liberation: Poems of Portuguese Africa," Ba Shiru, 1, 1 (1970), 8-16.

Moser, Gerald. Essays in Portuguese-African Literature. University Park: Pennsylvania State University, 1969, pp. 11, 18-9, 28-9.

Nkosi, Lewis. "Women in Literature," Africa Women, No. 6 (1976), 36.

Preto-Rodas, Richard A. Négritude as a Theme in the Poetry of Portuguese-Speaking World. Gainesville: University Press of Florida, 1970, pp. 71-3.

SOW FALL, AMINATA (Senegal)

Gérard, Albert and Laurent, Jeannine. " Sembène's Progeny: A New Trend in the Senegalese Novel," Studies in Twentieth-Century Literature, 4, 2 (1980), 133-45.

Trinh, Minh-ha T. "Aminata Sow Fall et l'espace du don," Présence Africaine, No. 120 (1981), 70-81.

CRITICISM OF AUTHORS' WORKS

SUMBANE, NATALA (Mozambique)

Gerard, Albert. African Language Literatures: An Introduction to the Literary History of Sub-saharan Africa. Washington, DC: Three Continents Press, 1981, pp. 219-20.

SUTHERLAND, EFUA THEODORA MORGUE (Ghana)

Adedeji, Joel A. "Theatre and Ideology: An African Experience," Joliso, 2, 1 (1974), 72-82.

Anon. "Ghana's Living Theatre," West African Review, 32 (1962), 11-13.

Asgill, E. J. "African Adaptations of Greek Tragedies," African Literature today, 11 (1980), 175-89.

Bengu, Sibusiso M. E. Gods Not Our Own. Pietermaritzburg: Shuster & Shuster, 1976.

Berrian, Albert H. "African Literary Traditions," Journal of Human Relations, 8, (1960), 780-92.

Brown, Lloyd W. "The African Woman as Writer," Canadian Journal of African Studies, 9 (1975), 493-501.

_____. Women Writers in Black Africa. Westport: Greenwood Press, 1981, pp. 61-83.

Carpenter, Peter. "Theatre in East and West Africa," Drama, 68 (1963), 30-32.

Dathorne, O. R. The Black Mind: A History of African Literature. Minneapolis: University of Minnesota Press, 1974, pp. 259-60, 415, 419.

deGraft, Joseph C. "Dramatic Questions," Writers in East Africa. Ed. Andrew Gurr and Angus Calder. Nairobi: East African Literature Bureau, 1974, pp. 33-67.

Eyah, Hansel, 'The Treatment of Tragic Themes in African Theatre," Master's thesis, English Department, University of Leeds, 1976.

Graham-White, Anthony. The Drama of Black Africa. New York: Samuel French Inc., 1974, pp. 64, 74, 104, 106, 113-14.

_____. "Efua Sutherland," Contemporary Dramatists. Ed. James Vinson. Pref. Ruby Cohn. London: St. James Press: New York: St. Martins Press, 1977, pp. 768-70.

CRITICISM OF AUTHORS' WORKS

Hera, Janina. "Ghana: Teatr czyli zycie [Ghana Theatre Otherwise Life]," Dialog (Warsaw), 13, 6 (1968), 99-101.

Jahn, Janheinz. "Ghana's Written Literature," Ghanaian Writing: Ghana as Seen by Her Own Writers as Well as by German Authors. Tubingen: Horst Erdmann Verlag, 1972, pp. 235-36.

Kennedy, Scott. In Search of African Theatre. New York: Charles Scribner's 1973, pp. 19, 60-1, 117, 121-22, 126-28, 134, 168-71, 179-81, 186-90, 229.

Mphahlele, Ezekiel. "Trends in Present-Day African Literature," Penpoint, 15 (1963), 4-5; rpt. as "Who are the Writers of New Africa?" Drum, May 1963, p. 19, rpt. in UNESCO Courier, 20 (1967), 23-8; abridged from The Proceedings of the First International Congress of Africanists, Accra, 11th-18th December 1962. Ed. Lalage Brown and Michael Crowder. London: Longmans; Evanston, Northwestern University Press, 1964, pp. 220-32.

Nasidi, Yakubu, "A Study of Six West African Dramatists," Master's thesis, English Department, University of Leeds, 1976.

Nicol, Davidson. 'West African Poetry," Africa South in Exile, 5, 3 (1961), 118-19.

Nkosi, Lewis. Tasks and Masks: Styles and Themes in African Literature. London: Longman, 1981, pp. 178-80.

Ogunba, Oyin. "Modern Drama in West Africa," Perspectives on African Literature; Selections from the Proceedings of the Conference on African Literature Held at the University of Ife, 1968. Ed. Christopher Heywood. London: Heinemann; New York: Africana Publishing Corporation, in association with the University of Ife Press, 1971, pp. 97-8.

Okafor, M.B.C. "The Image and Role of Women as Portrayed by Two West African Female Playwrights: Zulu Sofola (Nigeria) and Efua Sutherland (Ghana) B.A. Thesis, Department of English, University of Nigeria, Nsukka, 1979-80.

Onukwufor, C. C. "Folklore and the Drama of Efua T. Sutherland," B.A. Thesis, Department of English, University of Nigeria, Nsukka, 1978-79.

Owusu, Martin, "The Impact of Greek Tragedy on Four West African Dramatists: Ola Rotimi, J. P. Clark, Efua Sutherland and Wole Soyinka," Master's Thesis, University of Bristol, 1974.

Schipper, Mineke. Theatre and Society in Africa. Johannesburg: Ravan Press, 1982, pp. 72-5.

CRITICISM OF AUTHORS' WORKS

Schmidt, Nancy J. 'African Women Writers of Literature for Children," World Literature Written in English, 17, 1 (1978), 8-9.

Schmidt, Nancy J. "Children's Books by Well-known African Authors," World Literature Written in English, 18, 1 (1980), 116-17.

Shoga, Yinka. "Women Writers and African Literature," Afriscope, 3, 10, (1973), 44-5.

Vavilov, V. N. "A Talented Poetess," Midwest Weekly, 2, 42 (1965), 22-3.

Warren, Lee. The Theater of Africa: An Introduction. Englewood Cliffs: Prentice-Hall, 1975, p. 45.

Zeitlin, Arnold. "Ghana's Young Theatre," Theatre Arts, 47, 11 (1963), 66-7, 71.

SWAARTBOOI, VICTORIA (South Africa)

Gérard, Albert S. Four African Literatures: Xhosa, Sotho, Zulu, Amharic. Los Angeles: University of California Press, 1971, p. 81.

Qangule, S. Z. "A Brief Survey of Modern Literature in the South African Bantu Languages," Limi, No. 6 (1968), 18.

Vilakazi, Benedict. "The Oral and Written Literature in Nguni," Ph.D. Dissertation, Johannesburg: University of Witwatersand, 1945, pp. 331-32.

TAOS-AMROUCHE, MARGUERITE (Tunisia)

Chauvigné, Claude, "L'Univers de Taos Amrouche," African Literature Association Conference, Indiana University, Bloomington, Indiana, 22 March 1979.

Yetiv, Issac. Le Thème de l'aliénation dans le roman maghrébin d'expression française de 1952 à 1956. Sherbrooke: CELEF, 1972, pp. 76; 77; 134.

TEAGE, HILARY (Liberia)

Banks-Henries, A. Doris. "Survey of Liberian Literature," Liberian Writing: Liberia as Seen by Her Own Writers as Well as German Authors. Tubingen: Horst Erdmann Verlag, 1970, pp. 14-6.

CRITICISM OF AUTHORS' WORKS

TOL'ANDE, ELISABETH MWEYA (Zaire)

Nkashama, Ngandu. "La littérature au Zaïre depuis l'indépendance: I. La poésie," Zaïre-Afrique, 12, 69 (1972), 556-57.

TUTU, MALAMAFUMA, MATILDA (Cameroon)

Kapumpa, Mumba. "Theatre: A New Challenge to Our Women," Africa Woman, 23 (1979), 52-3.

ULASI, ADAORA LILY (Nigeria)

Brown, Lloyd W. Women Writers in Black Africa. Westport: Greenwood Press, 1981, pp. 17-20, 93-4.

Dathorne, O. R. African Literature in the Twentieth Century. Minneapolis: University of Minnesota Press, 1974, p. 119.

Lindfors, Bernth. "New Trends in West and East African Fiction," Review of National Literatures, 11, 2 (1971), 24-5.

Shoga, Yinka. "Women Writers and African Literature," Afriscope, 3, 10 (1973), 44-5.

Taiwo, Oladele. "Social Criticism," Culture and the Nigerian Novel. New York: St. Martin's Press, 1976, pp. 34-73.

WACIUMA, CHARITY (Kenya)

Roscoe, Adrian. Uhuru's Fire: African Literature East to South. Cambridge; Cambridge University Press, 1977, p. 169.

WERE, MIRIAM KHAMADI (Kenya)

Calder, Angus. "The Kenyan Writer - Three Profiles," Writers in East Africa: Papers from a Colloquium at the University of Nairobi. Ed. Andrew Gurr and Angus Calder. Nairobi: East African Literature Bureau, 1975, pp. 17-8.

Schmidt, Nancy J. "African Women Writers of Literature for Children," World Literature Written in English, 17, 1 (1978), 12-3.

CRITICISM OF AUTHORS' WORKS

WHEATLEY, PHILLIS (Senegal/USA)

Burroughs, Margaret G. " Do Birds of a Feather Flock Together?" Jackson State Review, 6, 1 (1974), 61-73.

Giddings, Paula. "Critical Evaluation of Phillis Wheatley," Jackson State Review 6, 1 (1974), 74-81.

Isani, Mukhtar Ali. "The Original Version of Wheatley's 'On the Death of Dr. Samuel Marshall,'" Studies in Black Literature, 7, 3 (1976), 20.

Jamison, Angelene. "Analysis of Selected Poetry of Phillis Wheatley," Journal of Negro Education, 43, 3 (1974), 408-16.

Kake, I. B. "Phillis Wheatley: Une grande poétesse noire (1753-1787)," Bingo, 285 (1976), 34-5.

Ogunyemi, Chikwenye Okongo. "Phillis Wheatley: The Modest Beginning," Studies in Black Literature, 7, 3 (1976), 16-9.

Parks, Carole A. "Phillis Wheatley Comes Home." Black World, 23, 4 (1974), 92-7.

Richmond, M. A. Bid the Vassal: Interpretive Essays on the Life and Poetry of Phillis Wheatley and George Moses Horton. Washington, DC: Howard University Press, 1974. 216 pages.

Robinson, William H. Phillis Wheatley in the Black American Beginnings. Detroit: Broadside Press, 1975. 95 pages.

Robinson, William H. Phillis Wheatley: A Bio-Bibliography. Boston: G. K. Hall, 1981. 166 pages.

Shields, John C. "Phillis Wheatley and Mather Byles: A Study in Literary Relationship," CLA Journal, 23, 4 (1980), 377-90.

Sistrunk, Albertha. "Phillis Wheatley: An Eighteenth-Century Black American Poet Revisited," CLA Journal, 23, 4 (1980), 391-98.

Smith, Eleanor. "Phillis Wheatley: A Black Perspective," Journal of Negro Education, 43, 3 (1974), 401-7.

WILLIAMS, KATE NGOWO (Cameroon)

Keim, Karen. "Popular Fiction Publishing in Cameroon," The African Book Publishing Record, 9, 1 (1983), 7-11.

CRITICISM OF AUTHORS' WORKS

WILSON, BEVERLY R. (Liberia)

Banks-Henries, A. Doris. "Survey of Liberian Literature," Liberian Writing: Liberia as Seen by Her Own Writers as Well as German Authors. Tubingen: Horst Erdmann, 1970, p. 16.

ZIRIMU, ELVANIA NAMUKWAYA (Uganda)

Cook, David. African Literature: A Critical View. London: Longman, 1977, p. 25.

_____. In Black and White: Writings from East Africa with Broadcast Discussions and Commentary. Nairobi: East African Literature Bureau, 1976, pp. 37-8, 39.

_____. "In Solitary, The Submerged and the Undismayed: A Study in Western and African Literary Environments," Aspects of Africa's Identity: Five Essays. Ed. Paul Nursey-Bray. Kampala: Makerere Institute of Social Research, Makerere University, 1973, p. 60.

_____. "Theatre Goes to the People," Transition, 5, 25 (1966), 33.

Graham-White, Anthony. The Drama of Black Arica. New York: Samuel French Inc., 1974, p. 102.

Nazareth, Peter. "Writing in East Africa," Afriscope, 4, 4 (1974), 56.

BOOK REVIEWS OF AUTHORS' WORKS

ADEMOLA, FRANCES (Ghana)

Reflections: Nigerian Prose and Verse. Ezekiel Mphahlele. Lagos:
African Universities Press, 1962. 123 pages; rpt. Foreword Nnamdi Azikiwe.
Lagos: African Universities Press, 1965. 119 pages.

    Anon. Times Literary Supplement, 20 September 1963, p. 709.

    Banham, Martin, Books Abroad, 38, 2 (1964), 210-11.

    Eze, Mark N. Central African Examiner, 7, 8 (1964), 14.

    Izevoboye, D. S. Black Orpheus, 2, 7 (1971-1972), 53.

    Parkes, Frank. West Africa, 6 July 1963, pp. 755-57.

    Peterson, W. M. West African Journal of Education, 7, 3 (1963), 175.

ADIAFFI, ANNE-MARIE (Ivory Coast)

Une vie hypothèquée. Dakar: Les Nouvelles Editions Africaines, 1984. 128 pages.

    Paulus. Jeune Afrique, 10 mai 1984.

AIDOO, AMA ATA (Ghana)

The Dilemma of a Ghost. London: Longmans and Green, 1965. 50 pages; New York: Collier-Macmillan, 1971.

    Dipoko, Mbella Sonne. Présence Africaine, 30, 58 (1966), 254.

    Jones, Eldred. Bulletin of the Association for African Literature in English, 2 (1965), 33-4

    Lindfors, Bernth. Books Abroad, 40, 2 (1966), 358-59.

    Pieterse, Cosmo. The Journal of Commonwealth Literature, 2 (1966), 168-71.

    Rea, C. J. African Forum, 4, 1 (1968), 41-50.

Anowa. London: Longmans and Green, 1970. 66 pages: Washington, DC: Three Continents Press, 1979.

    Anon. Cultural Events in Africa, No. 62 (1970), 6.

    De Munbrun, Bo. Books Abroad, 45 (1971), 363.

    Jones, Eldred. African Literature Today, 8. New York: Africana Publishing Corporation, 1976, pp. 142-44.

    W. K. West Africa, 4 February 1971, p. 113.

BOOK REVIEWS OF AUTHORS' WORKS

No Sweetness Here. New York: Doubleday, 1971. 166 pages.

    Anon. Cultural Events in Africa, No. 62 (1970), 6.

    Gant, Liz. Black World, 23, 5 (1974), 96-97.

    Mensah, A. N. Legon Observer, February 1973, pp. 61-62.

    W. K. West Africa, 4 February 1971, p. 133.

Our Sister Killjoy or Reflections from a Black-Eyed Squint. London: Longmans and Green, 1978; New York: NOK Publishers, 1979.

    Anon. Ebony, 34 11 (1979), 31.

    Kern, Anita. World Literature Written in English, 17, 1(1978), 56-7.

    Larson, Charles. World Literature Today, 52, 2 (1978), 247.

    Ngara, John. Africa Woman, No. 12 (1977), 65-6.

    Randall-Tsuruta, Dorothy. Black Scholar, 11, 6 (1969), 74-5.

AKELLO, GRACE (Uganda)

My Barren Song. Asusha/Dar-es-Salaam: Eastern Africa Publications, Ltd., 1979. 140 pages.

    Okumu, Charles. Africa Woman. No. 38 (1982), 56.

ATTIK, MRIRIDA N'AIT (Morocco)

Songs of Mririda, Courtesan of the High Atlas. Trs. Daniel Halpern and Paula Paley. Greensboro: Unicorn, 1974. 54 pages.

    Accad, Evelyne. Books Abroad, 49 (1975), 837.

BA, MARIAMA (Senegal)

    Une si longue lettre. Dakar: Les Nouvelles Editions Africaines, 1980.

    Aire, Victor O. Canadian Journal of African Studies, 16, 3 (1982), 636-37.

    Emeka, Abanime. World Literature Today, 54, 2 (1980), 327.

BOOK REVIEWS OF AUTHORS' WORKS

    Irele, Abiola. West Africa, 14 April 1980, pp. 661-62; rpt. The African Book Publishing Record, 6 (1980), 107-8.

    Un chant écarlate. Dakar: Les Nouvelles Editions Africaines, 1981.
    Dunton, Chris. West Africa, 2 April 1984, pp. 725-26.

    White, Allan. London Review of Books, 4, 16 (1982), 19.

BAKALUBA, JANE JAGERS (Uganda)

Honeymoon for Three. African Secondary Readers. Nairobi: East African Publishing House, 1975. 183 pages, illus.

    Komolo, Ejiet. Dhana, 6, 2, (1976), 132-36.

BELINGA, THERESE BARATTE-ENO (Cameroon)

Bibliographie auteurs africains et malgaches de langue française. 2nd edition. Paris: Office de Coopération Radiophonique, 1968. 78 pages.

    Spackey, Gary. African Literature Today, Vol. 3. London: Heinemann, 1969.

Ecrivains, cinéastes et artistes camerounais; bio-bibliographie. Yaoundé: Ministère de l'Information et de la Culture de la République Unie de Cameroun 1978. 217 pages.

    Bruner, David K. World Literature Today, 53, 4 (1979), 732.

    Keim, Karen. Research in African Literatures, 11, 3 (1980), 418-20.

with Jacqueline Chauveau-Rabat and Mukala Kadima-Nzuji. Bibliographie des auteurs africains de langue française. Paris: Fernand Nathan, 1979. 245 pages.

    Cassirer, Thomas. Research in African Literatures, 13, 1 (1982), 96-8.

CHEDID, ANDREE (Egypt)

La Cité fertile. Paris: Flammarion, 1972. 171 pages.

    Knapp, Bettina. Books Abroad, 47 (1973), 601-2.

Nefertiti et le rêve d'Akhnaton. Paris: Flammarion, 1974. 230 pages.

    Knapp, Bettina. Books Abroad, 49 (1975), 378.

BOOK REVIEWS OF AUTHORS' WORKS

DIALLO, NAFISSATOU (Senegal)

A Dakar Childhood. Harlow/Essex: Longman Group Ltd, 1982. 134 pages [Translated Dorothy Blair].

    Bruner, Charlotte. World Literature Today, 57, 2 (1983), 330.

DOOH-BUNYA LYDIE (Cameroon)

La Brise du jour. Yaoundé: Editions CLE, 1977.

    Kern, Anita. The African Book Publishing Record, 7, 1 (1981), 14-5.

EGEJURU, PHANUEL A. (Nigeria)

Black Writers, White Audience: A Critical Approach to African Literature. Hicksville Exposition Press, 1978.

    Berrian, Brenda F. African Studies Review/Review of Books, Fal 1983, pp. 85-6.

EL SAADAWI, NAWAL (Egypt)

Woman at Point Zero. London: Zed Press, 1984.

    Perry Alison. West Africa, 30 April 1984, p. 932.

EMECHETA, BUCHI (Nigeria)

In the Ditch. London: Allison and Busby, 1972. 128 pages; New York: George Braziller, 1980.

    Blue, Adrianne. Book World (Washington Post), 13 May 1979, p. k8.

    Feuser, Willfried. Books Abroad, 49 (1975), 40-1.

    Larson, Charles. Books Abroad, 50 (1976), 87-90.

    W., D. West Africa, 8 September 1972, p. 1191.

BOOK REVIEWS OF AUTHORS' WORKS

Second-Class Citizen. London: Allison and Busby, 1975; New York: George Braziller, 1975. 175 pages.

Anon. Booklist, 1 December 1975, p. 499.

Anon. Choice, No. 13 (1976), 79.

Cunningham, Valentine. New Statesman, 22 June 1978, pp. 746-47.

Dailly, Christophe. Présence Africaine, 105-6 (1978), 288-89; rpt. Revue de Littérature et d'Esthétique Négro-Africaines, 2 (1979), 145-46.

Johnson, Marigold. Times Literary Supplement, 31 January 1975, p. 102.

Larson, Charles. Books Abroad, 50 (1976), 87-90.

_____. World Literature Today, 52 (1978), 247.

Levin, Martin. New York Times Book Review, 14 September 1975, p. 42.

Rubinstein, Roberta. World Literature Written in English, 15, 1 (1976), 71-2.

Simms, A. G. Library Journal, 1 September 1975, p. 1569.

Walker, Alice. Ms Magazine, 4, 7 (1976), 40, 106.

BOOK REVIEWS OF AUTHORS' WORKS

The Bride Price. London: Allison and Busby, 1976; New York: George Braziller, 1976. 168 pages.

    Adams, Pheobe Lou. Atlantic Monthly, 237 (May 1976), 111.

    Anon. Booklist, 15 March 1976, p. 1018.

    Anon. The New York Times Book Review, 27 January 1980, p. 35.

    Cima, Richard. Library Journal, 1 April 1976, p. 922.

    Clapp, Susannah. Times Literary Supplement, 11 June 1976, p. 1018.

    Collins, Harold. World Literature Today, 51 (197), 491.

    Cripwell, K. The Times Educational Supplement, 4 February 1977, p. 22

    Cunningham, Valentine. New Statesman, 25 June 1978, p. 856.

    _____. New Statesman, 2 June 1978, pp. 46-7.

    Dailly, Christophe. Présence Africaine, Nos. 105-6 (1978), 288-89; rpt. Revue de Littérature et d'Esthétique Négro-Africaines, 2 (1979), 145-46.

    Larson, Charles. World Literature Today, 51 (1977), 236.

    Lauer, Margaret. World Literature Written in English, 16, 2 (1977), 303-10.

    Morgan, Linda. Booklist, 15 March 1976, p. 1032.

    Ngara, John. Africa Woman, No. 5 (1976), 65.

    Oppenheim, Jane. Bestsellers, 36 (1976), 108.

    Robinson, Kathryn. School Library Journal, 23 (1976), 143.

The Slave Girl. London: Allison and Busby, 1977; New York: George Braziller, 1977. 179 pages.

BOOK REVIEWS OF AUTHORS' WORKS

    Anon. Choice, 15 (1978), 241-42.

    Anon. The Observer, 11 September 1977, p. 25.

    Anon. New Statesman, 14 October 1977, p. 515.

    Cima, Richard. Library Journal, 15 January 1978, pp. 191-92.

    Cunningham, Valentine. New Statesman, 2 June 1978, pp. 746-47.

    Fellows, Alice M. School Library Journal, No. 6 (1978), 69.

    Kern, Anita. World Literature Today, 53 (1979), 172.

    Larson, Charles. World Literature Today, 52 (1978), 247.

    Ngara, John. Africa Woman, No. 11 (1977), 66.

    Oppenheim, Jane. Bestsellers, 37 (1978), 301.

The Joys of Motherhood. London: Allison and Busby, 1979; New York: George Braziller, 1979. 224 pages.

    Anon. Booklist, 15 July 1979, p. 1606.

    Anon. Publishers Weekly, 9 April 1979, pp. 98-9.

    Bailey, Hilary. New Fiction, No. 19 (1979), 21.

    Blue, Adrianne. Book World, 13 May 1979, p. k8.

    Cima, Richard. Library Journal, 1 May 1979, p. 1076.

    Howard, Rhoda. Canadian Journal of African Studies, 15, 1 (1981), 133-35.

    Kemp, Peter. Listener, 102, 2620 (1979), 93-4.

    Lelyveld, Joseph. The New York Times Book Review, 11 November 1979, pp. 15, 39.

    Motion, Andrew. New Statesman, 27 April 1979, p. 600.

    Mullig, Angie. University Times (University of Pittsburgh), 10 May 1979, p. 5.

    Nabasuta, Helen. Christian Science Monitor, 5 July 1979, p. 15.

    Nicholl, Charles. Books and Bookmen, 24, 9 (1979), 41-2.

BOOK REVIEWS OF AUTHORS' WORKS

    Sachs, Sylvia. Pittsburgh Press, 14 May 1979, p. B18.

    Updike, John. New Yorker, 55, 20 (1979), 90-1.

    Wilson, A. N. The Observer, 6 May 1979, p. 36.

    Wilson, Judith. Essence, 10, 5 (1979), 17.

with Alice Emecheta. Titch the Cat. London: Allison and Busby, 1979.

    Lewis, Naomi. The Observer, 11 February 1979, p. 36.

    Rice, Miriam. Africa Woman, No. 27 (1980), 50-51.

Nowhere to Play. London: Allison and Busby, 1980.

    Anon. Book World, 11 (1981), 9.

    W., K. West Africa, 3 November 1980, pp. 2183-84.

Destination Biafra. London: Allison and Busby, 1982. 272 pages.

    Anon. British Book News, August 1982, p. 511.

    Baker, Jo. Happy Home, March 1982, p. 61.

    Berner, Robert L. World Literature Today, 57, 1 (1983), 160.

    Okri, Ben. West Africa, 15 March 1982, pp. 728-29.

Double Yoke. London: Ogwugwu Affor Co. Ltd., 1982.

    Anon. City Limits, 46, 20-26 (August 1982), 59-60.

    Perry Allison. West Africa, 4 June 1984, pp. 1161-62.

    Updike, John. The New Yorker, 23 April 1984, pp. 124-26.

Adah's Story (Comprises Second-Class Citizen and In the Ditch). London: Allison and Busby, 1983.

    Willis, Chris. West Africa, 11 June 1984, p. 1220.

BOOK REVIEWS OF ATUHORS' WORKS

FAIK-NZUJI, CLEMENTINE MADIYA (Zaire)

Les temps des amants. Kinshasa: Editions Mandore, 1969. 48 pages.

    Ayimpam, Théophile. Congo-Afrique, 9, 37 (1969), 383-71.

Kasala: poèmes. Kinshasa: Editions Mandore, 1969. 58 pages.

    Ayimpam, Théophile. Congo-Afrique, 9, 37 (1969), 368-71.

Enigmes Lubas. Nshinga. Etude Structurale. Kinshasa. Edition de l'Université Lovanium, 1970. 169 pages.

    Haring, Lee. Research in African Literatures, 3, 2 (1972), 215-20.

Kasala: chant héroique luba. Pref. Leo Stappers. Lubumbashi: Presses Universitaires Zaïre, 1974. 250 pages.

    Kalibwami, Justin. Présence Africaine, No. 96 (1975), III-IV.

Kasala: chant poétique luba. Lubumbashi: Presses Universitaires Zaïre, 1974.

    Maalu, Bungi. Zaïre-Afrique, 15, 94 (1975), 247-48.

Gestes interrompus. Lubumbashi: Editions Mandore, 1976.

    Goby, Beya Ngindu. Zaïre-Afrique, 17, 11 (1977), 55-7.

BOOK REVIEWS OF AUTHORS' WORKS

Lenga et autres contes d'inspiration traditionelle. Lubumbashi: Editions
St. Paul-Afrique, 1976. 78 pages.

   Tshikumambila, Myembwe. Zaïre-Afrique, 17, 11 (1977), 55-8.

La mère dévorante: essai sur la morphologie des contes africaines. Paris:
Editions Gallimard, 1976. 321 pages.

   Paulme, Denise Research in African Literatures, 9, 2 (1978), 290-94.

GACHUKIA, EDDAH (Kenya)

with S. Kichama Akivaga. Teaching African Literature in Schools. Vol. I.
Nairobi: Kenya Literature Bureau, 1978.

   Bishop, Rand. World Literature Written in English, 19, 1 (1980), 37-8.

GITHAE-MUGO, MICERE (Kenya)

The Long Illness of Ex-Chief Kiti. Nairobi: East African Literature Bureau, 1976.
61 pages.

   Wanjala, Chris. Africa, No. 71 (1977), 85.

Visions of Africa: The Fiction of Chinua Achebe, Margaret Laurence, Elspeth
Huxley and Ngugi wa Thiong'o. Nairobi: Kenya Literature Bureau, 1978. 198
pages.

   Johnson, Lemuel. The African Book Publishing Record, 5, 3 (1979), 169.

   Knipp, Thomas. Research in African Literatures, 12, 1 (1981).

BOOK REVIEWS OF AUTHORS' WORKS

HEAD, BESSIE (South Africa/Botswana)

When Rain Clouds Gather. London: Gollancz; New York: Simon and Schuster, 1969. 188 pages.

    Anon. Cultural Events in Africa, No. 61 (1969).

    Anon. Encore, 3, 7 (1974), 45.

    Anon. Today, 17, 2 (1970), 20-1.

    Brown, Joe C. West Africa, 23 August 1969, p. 995.

    Williams, Mark. The Gar, No. 33 (1979), 27.

    Wright, T. R. Books Abroad, 44 (1970), 362.

Maru. African Writers Series #101. London: New Heinemann; New York: McCall, 1971.

    Anon. Africa Report, 16, 8, (1971), 37.

A Question of Power. New York: Pantheon; New York: Humanities Press; London: Heinemann, 1977.

    Anon. Encore, 3, 7 (1974), 45.

    Anon. Today, 17, 2 (1970), 20-1.

    Berner, Robert L. Books Abroad, 49, 1 (1975), 176-77.

    Larson, Charles. Books Abroad, 48, 3 (1974), 521.

A Collector of Treasures. London: Heinemann, 1978. 109 pages.

    Cunningham, Valentine. New Statesman, 2 June 1978, p. 747.

    Kwayera, Senda Wa. "Voice of Kenya," November 1978.

Serowe, Village of the Rainland. London/Exeter: Heinemann, 1981. 200 pages.

    Kunene, Daniel P. World Literature Today, 57, 1 (1983), 160-61.

    Larson, Charles. World Literature Today, 56, 1 (1982), 66.

BOOK REVIEWS OF AUTHORS' WORKS

HOUSE, AMELIA (South Africa)

Black Women Writers from South Africa: A Preliminary Checklist. Evanston: Northwestern University Program on Women, 1980.

    Berrian, Brenda F. Research in African Literatures, 13, 2 (1982), 243-44.

    Dorsey, David. CLA Journal, 24, 3 (1981), 416-17.

JABAVU, NONI (South Africa)

The Ochre People: Scenes from South African Life. London: John Murray, 1963. 261 pages.

    Anon. Times Literary Supplement, 17 May 1963, p. 354.

    Bennett, Nicholas. Transition, 5, 1 (1965), 53-4.

    Coste, J. M. Présence Africaine, No. 60 (1966), 205-7.

KALIMUGOGO, G. (Kenya)

Trials and Tribulations in Sandu's Home. Nairobi: East African Literature Bureau, 1976. 164 pages.

    Arnold, Stephen. The African Book Publishing Record, 5, 1 (1979), 25.

KAYA, SIMONE (Ivory Coast)

Les danseuses d'Impe-Eya: jeunes filles à Abidjan. Abidjan: Inades, 1976. 120 pages.

    Dailly, Christophe. Revue de littérature et esthétique négro-africaines, 1 (1977), 185-87; rpt. World Literature Today, 51 (1977), 667-68.

KEITA, AOUA (Mali)

Femme d'Afrique: La Vie d'Aoua Keita racontée par elle-même. Paris: Presence Africaine, 1975. 397 pages.

    Guillou, Marik. Entente Africaine, (1978), 53.

BOOK REVIEWS OF AUTHORS' WORKS

KIMENYE, BARBARA (Uganda)

Kalasandra. London: Oxford University Press, 1965. 103 pages.

    Lindfors, Bernth. Books Abroad, 40, 4 (1966), 489.

    Thompson, David. The New African, 5, 3 (1966), 73.

    Welborn, Hebe. Transition, 5, 5 (1966), 56.

    Welbourn, F. B. Transition, 5, 6 (1966), 7-8.

LIKIMANI, MUTHONI (Kenya)

What Does A Man Want? Nairobi: East African Literature Bureau, 1974; rpt. 1977. 209 pages.

    Githae-Mugo, Micere. Viva, August 1975, p. 45.

MATENJWA, CHRISTINE (Kenya)

"Little Muya and Big Muya," The Cooking Pan and Other Plays. Ed. Margaret Macpherson. London: Heinemann, 1974.

    M., N. Africa, No. 95 (1979), 89.

MUHANDO, PENNINA (Tanzania)

Hatia. Nairobi: East African Publishing House, 1972. 41 pages.

    Githae-Mugo, Micere. African Literature Today, 8. Ed. Eldred Jones. New York: Africana Publishing Corporation, 1976, p. 139.

MVUNGI, MARTHA (Tanzania)

Three Solid Stones. London: Heinemann, 1975.

    Larson, Charles. Books Abroad, 50 (1976), 940.

    Osotoi. The Weekly Review, 9 February 1976, p. 31.

BOOK REVIEWS OF AUTHORS' WORKS

NJAU, REBEKA, pseudonym Marina Cashe (Kenya)

The Scar: A Tragedy in One-Act. Moshi: Kibo Art Gallery, 1965. 32 pages.

    Larson, Charles. Books Abroad, 15, 3 (1966), 360.

Ripples in the Pool. London: Heinemann, 1978. 152 pages.

    Birbalsingh, Frank. Canadian Journal of African Studies, 16, 1 (1982), 88-9.

    Bruner, Charlotte H. World Literature Today, 54, 1 (1980), 160.

    Chakava, Henry. Standard (Nairobi), February 1976.

    Kahiga, Sam. JOE, 29 February 1976, pp. 25-6.

NWAPA, FLORA, Mrs. Nwakuche (Nigeria)

Efuru. African Writers Series #26. London: Heinemann, 1966. 288 pages.

    Anon. Cultural Events in Africa, No. 61 (1969), 6.

    Anon. Times Literary Supplement, 7 April 1966, p. 281.

    Darnsborough, Anne. The New African, 7, 1 (1976), 10-1.

    Dipollo, Mbella Sonne. Présence Africaine, 30, 58 (1966), 249-50.

    Emenyonu, Ernest. Ba Shiru, Spring 1971, pp. 58-61.

    Ifeka, Caroline. Nigeria Magazine, No. 89 (1966), 131-32, 141.

    Jones, Eldred. Journal of Commonwealth Literature, 3 (1967), 127-31.

    Palmer, Eustace. African Literature Today, 1. Ed. Eldred Jones. New York: Africana Publishing Corporation, 1968, pp. 56-8; rpt. Journal of Commonwealth Literature, 3 (1968), 127-31.

Idu. African Writers Series #56. London: Heinemann, 1970. 218 pages.

    Adeola, James. African Literature Today, 5. Ed. Eldred Jones. New York: Africana Publishing Corporation, 1971, pp. 150-53.

    Anon. Cultural Events in Africa, No. 61 (1969), 6.

BOOK REVIEWS OF AUTHORS' WORKS

This Is Lagos and Other Stories. Enugu: Nwankwo-Ifejika & Company, 1971. 171 pages

    Anon. Cultural Events in Africa. No. 85 (1972), 6.

    Feuser, Willfried. Books Abroad, 49, 1 (1975), 48.

    Okoro, J. West Africa, 24 March 1979, pp. 353-54.

Never Again. Enugu: Nwamife Publishers, 1975. 80 pages.

    Kern, Anita. World Literature Written in English, 17, 1 (1978), 58-9.

    V., J. West Africa, 5 January 198, pp. 24-5.

OGOT, GRACE AKINYI (Kenya)

The Promised Land. Nairobi: East African Publishing House, 1966. 194 pages. Swahili translation: Nehi Bila Ngurumo. Nairobi: Longman Kenya, 1979. 143 pages.

    Anon. Cultural Events in Africa, No. 50 (1969), 6.

    Bjork, K. O. East Africa Journal, 4, 4 (1967), 39.

    Cook, David. Journal of Commonwealth Literature, No. 6 (1969), 9-10.

    Dossa, Shiraz. Nexus, 1, 2 (1967), 47.

    Knipp, Thomas. Books Abroad, 42, (1968), 327.

    Larson, Charles. Africa Report, 12, 9 (1967), 44-5.

    Moore, Gerald. Mawazo, 1, 2 (1967), 94-5.

Land without Thunder. Nairobi: East African Publishing House, 1968. 204 pages.

    Anon. Cultural Events in Africa, No. 50 (1969), 5-6; No. 54 (1969), 4.

    Cook, David and Austin S. Bukenya. Journal of Commonwealth Literature, No. 8 (1969), 14.

    Kent, Neera. Busara, 2, 1 (1969), 59-60.

    Welbourn, F. B. African Affairs, 69, 275 (1970), 197.

BOOK REVIEWS OF AUTHORS' WORKS

The Other Woman. Nairobi: Transafrica Publishers, 1977.

    Egudu, Romanus. World Literature Today, 52, 1 (1978), 165.

    Larson, Charles. World Literature Today, 51 (1977), 565.

    Mwagiru, Ciugi. JOE, October 1976, p. 25.

OWINO, ROSEMARIE (Kenya)

Sugar Daddy' Lover. Nairobi: Spear, 1975. 75 pages.

    Nyate, Frances. Viva, July 1975, p. 38.

OWUSU-NIMOH, MERCY (Ghana)

Rivers of Ghana. Kada: Monim Bookland, 1979.

    W., K. West Africa, 23 June 1980, pp. 1116-17.

POPPIE (South Africa)

Poppie (as told to Elsa Joubert). London: Hodder and Stoughton, 1980. 359 pages.

    Ramsey, Sally. Times Literary Supplement, 21 November 1980. p. 1342.

BOOK REVIEWS OF AUTHORS' WORKS

RAKOTOSON, MICHELE (Madagascar)

Dadabé. Paris: Edition Karthala, 1984. 100 pages.

    Fall, Elimane. Jeune Afrique Magazine, avril 1984.

SEBBAR, LEILA (Algeria)

Le Chinois Vert d'Afrique. Paris: Editions Stock, 1984.

    Shungu, Ekanga. Jeune Afrique Magazine, avril 1984.

SEGUN, MABEL IMOUKHUEDE JOLAOSA (Nigeria)

Friends, Nigerians, Countrymen. Ibadan: Oxford University Press, 1977.

    Anon. Africa Woman, No. 16 (1978), 66.

    Kern, Anita. World Literature Written in English, 17, 1 (1979), 60-61.

BOOK REVIEWS OF AUTHORS' WORKS

SIWUNDHLA, ALICE PRINCESS MSUMBA (South Africa)

Alice Princess: An Autobiography. Intro. Ralph Edwards. Mountain View: Pacific Press Publishing Association, 1965.

    Petty, Irene. Africa Report, 14, 5-6 (1969), 79.

SOFOLA, ZULU (Nigeria)

The Sweet Trap. Ibadan: Oxford University Press, 1977. 76 pages.

    Niven, Alistair. The African Book Publishing Record, No. 3-4 (1980), 262.

SOW FALL, AMINATA (Senegal)

La Grève des bàttu. Dakar: Les Editions Nouvelles, 1979.

    Abanime, Emeka. World Literature Today, 54, 2 (1980), 327.

    Azasu, Kwakuvi. West Africa, 17 May 1982, pp. 1329-31.

L'Appel des arènes. Dakar: Les Nouvelles Editions Africaines, 1982, 144 pages.

    Irele, Abiola. The African Book Publishing Record, 9, 2-3 (1983), 128.

SUTHERLAND, EFUA, THEODORA MORGUE (Ghana)

"New Life in Kyerefaso," An African Treasury. Ed. Langston Hughes. New York: Crown, 1960, pp. 111-17.

    Williams, Mark. The Gar, No. 33 (1979), 27.

Playtime in Africa. New York: Atheneum, 1962. 62 pages, illus.

    Bazzle, Lillie May. Freedomways, 2, 4 (1962), 496-97.

Foriwa. Accra: State Publishing Corporation, 1967. 67 pages.

    Banham, Martin. Journal of Commonwealth Literature, 7, 1 (1972), 106.

    Etherton, Michael. Books Abroad, 43 (1970), 305.

BOOK REVIEWS OF AUTHORS' WORKS

Edufa. London: Longmans and Green, 1969. 62 pages; Washington, DC: Three Continents Press, 1979.

    Amosu, Margaret. Journal of Commonwealth Literature, No. 6 (1969), 19-20.

    Anon. Cultural Events in Africa, No. 63 (1970), 7; No. 64 (1970), 3.

The Marriage of Anansewa. London: Longmans and Green, 1975. 86 pages; Washington, DC: Three Continents Press, 1980. 82 pages.

    Larson, Charles. Books Abroad, 50 (1976), 354.

TADJO, VERONIQUE (Ivory Coast)

Latérite. Collection Monde Noir Poche No. 24. Paris: Hatier/Agence, 1983. 94 pages.

    Kakou, Hyacinthe. Fraternité Matin, 15 juin 1984, p. 16.

THIAM, AWA (Mali)

La parole aux négresses. Paris: Denoel-Gonthier, 1978. 119 pages.

    Salim, Jay. L'Afrique littéraire et artistique, No. 51 (1979), 64-6.

ULASI, ADAORA LILY (Nigeria)

Many Things You No Understand. London: Michael Joseph, 1971. 190 pages.

    T., S. West Africa, 3 October 1970, pp 1155-56.

    Anon. Times Literary Supplement, 18 June 1970, p. 653.

    Cole, Barry. Spectator, 224, 7408 (1970), 822.

    Feuser, Willfried. Books Abroad, 49, 1 (1975), 48.

    Nwoga, Donatus. Journal of Commonwealth Literature, 6, 2 (1971), 17.

BOOK REVIEWS OF AUTHORS' WORKS

WACIUMA, CHARITY (Kenya)

The Golden Feather. Nairobi: East African Publishing House, 1966. 48 pages.

    Ojany, Agnes G. O. East Africa Journal, 4, 4 (1967), 38-9.

Daughter of Mumbi. Nairobi: East African Publishing House, 1969. 96 pages.

    Sentongo, Nuwa. Mawazo, 2, 3 (1970), 54-5.

Mweru, the Ostrich Girl. Nairobi: East African Publishing House, 1973. 23 pages.

    Ojany, Agnes G. O. East Africa Journal, 4, 4 (1967), 38-9.

WERE, MIRIAM KHAMADI (Kenya)

The Eighth Wife. Nairobi: East African Publishing House, 1972. 167 pages.

    Anon. Cultural Events in Africa, No. 56 (1969), 5.

    Anon. Books Abroad, 47 (1973), 816.

The High School Gent. Nairobi: East African Publishing House, 1972.

    Anon. Cultural Events in Africa, No. 88 (1972), 5.

ZIRIMU, ELVANIA NAMUKWAYA (Uganda)

When the Hunchback Made Rain and Snoring Strangers. Nairobi: East African Publishing House, 1975. 87 pages.

    Amuka, Peter. The Weekly Review, 5 April 1976, p. 31.

    Gibbs, James World Literature Today, 51 (1977), 149.

    Miyanja, D. K. Dhana, 6, 2 (1976), 138-40.

COMMENTARY

AIDOO, CHRISTINA AMA ATA (Ghana)

Anon. "The Education Front," West Africa, 14 June 1982, pp. 1572-73.

Wästberg, Per, ed. Afrikas moderna litteratur. Stockholm: Wahlstrom & Widstrand och Nordiska Afrikainstitutet, 1969, pp. 21; 58.

ASIBONG, ELIZABETH, E. (Nigeria)

Gérard, Albert. African Language Literatures: An Introduction to the Literary History of sub-saharan Africa. Washington DC: Three Continents Press; London: Longman, 1981, p. 264 [Comments about Hogan Kid Bassey-Eren owo akan eren owo].

BA, MARIAMA (Senegal)

Anon. "Prize for Publishing," West Africa, 9 June 1980, p. 1013.

Anon. "First Noma Goes to Senegalese Woman Novelist," The African Book Publishing Record, 6 (1980), 95.

Zell, Hans M. "The First Noma Award for Publishing in Africa," The African Book Publishing Record, 7 (1980), 199-200.

Anon. "Noma Book Prize Nominees," West Africa, 25 January 1982, p. 221.

BAETA, LILY (Ghana)

Gerard, Albert. African Language Literatures: An Introduction to the Literary History of Sub-Saharan Africa. Washington, DC: Three Continents Press; London: Longman, 1981, p. 272 [Comment about the Ewe tale Da to gli nam (Tell me a story, mother, 1952)].

BONNY, ANNE-MARIE (Cameroon)

Epee, Valere. "Anne-Marie Bonny, poète de 17 ans," Abbia, No. 25 (1971), 159.

CASELY-HAYFORD, ADELAIDE (Sierra Leone/Ghana)

Omostoso, Kole. Notes, Questions and Answers on Peter (sic) Edwards' West African Narrative. Ibadan: Onibonoje Press, 1968.

COMMENTARY

Walt, Vivienne. 'A Question of Language," West Africa, 21 June 1982, pp. 1654-55.

DIKE, FATIMA (South Africa)

Amato, Rob. "A Xhosa Woman's Serious Optimism," Speak (Cape Town), 1, 1 (1978), 14-7.

Heyns, Jackie. 'Fatima Dike: The Queen of Our Stage," Drum, October 1979, p. 4.

EMECHETA, BUCHI (Nigeria)

Oyovbaire, Sam. "Who is Lagging?", West Africa, 16 November 1981, pp. 2717-18 [A response to Emecheta's article which appeared in the 2 November 1981 edition of West Africa].

ENEM, EDITH (Nigeria)

Omotoso, Kole. "The Thriving Theatre Tradition in Nigeria," West Africa, 14 June 1982, p. 1583.

KAKAZA, LILLITH (South Africa)

Gérard, Albert. African Language Literatures: An Introduction to the Literary History of Sub-saharan Africa. Washington, DC: Three Continents Press; London: Longman, 1981, p. 198 [Comments about the novelette Intyatyambo yomzi (The Flower in the House) and the folk tale Utandiwe wakawa gcaleka (Tandiwe, a Damsel of Gaikaland)].

COMMENTARY

KUOH-MOUKOURY, THERESE (Cameroon)

Lagache, E. "Thérèse Kuoh-Moukoury, une vocation de femme," Jeune Afrique, ler décembre 1973, pp. 58-9.

KWAMI, MARTHE AFEWELE (Togo)

Olney, James. Tell Me Africa: An Approach to African Literature. Princeton: Princeton University Press, 1973, p. 44ff.

MAHUHUSI, M.A. (South Africa)

Gérard, Albert. African Language Literatures: An Introduction to the Literary History of Sub-saharan Africa. Washington, DC: Three Continents Press; London: Longman, 1981, p. 219 [Comments about the Tsonga novel, (Xikotikoti wa Matshotsho)].

MUGOT, HAZEL DESILVA (Seychelles)

Anon. Cultural Events in Africa, No. 56 (1969), 5.

Anon. Cultural Events in Africa, No. 77 (1971), 5.

Anon. Cultural Events in Africa, No. 84 (1972), 5.

MUHANDO, PENNINA (Tanzania)

Anon. Cultural Events in Africa, No. 56 (1969), 5 (Comment about the play, Hatia).

COMMENTARY

NANJALA, ELIZABETH (Kenya)

Knight, Elizabeth. "Popular Literature in East Africa," African Literature Today, Vol. 10 Ed. Eldred Jones. London: Heinemann, 1979, pp. 185; 188.

NSANZUBUHORO, VICTOIRE (Rwanda)

Gérard, Albert. African Language Literatures: An Introduction to the Literary History of Sub-saharan Africa. Washington, DC: Three Continents Press; London: Longman, 1981, p. 296 [Comment about the short stories, Nta byera (Nothing can be spotless)].

NWAPA, FLORA (Nigeria)

Wastberg, Per. Afrikas moderna litteratur. Stockholm: Wahlstrom & Widstrand och Nordiska Afrikainstitutet, 1969, p. 98.

Lindfors, Bernth. 'New Trends in West and East African Fiction," Review of National Literatures, 11, 2 (1971), 21; 26.

OGOT, GRACE A. (Kenya)

Lindfors, Bernth. "New Trends in West and East African Fiction," Review of National Literatures, 11, 2 (1971), 31.

OHENE, ELIZABETH (Ghana)

Anon. "PNDC's Purge of the Press," West Africa, 18 January 1982, pp. 142-43.

OWUSU-NIMOH, MERCY (Ghana)

Zell, Hans M. "Publishing in West Africa," West Africa, 27 August 1979, pp. 1553-56.

Anon. "Prize for Publishing," West Africa, 9 June 1980, p. 1013.

COMMENTARY

Anon. "First Noma Award Goes to Senegalese Woman Novelist," The African Book Publishing Record, 6 (1980), 95.

Zell, Hans M. "The First Noma Award for Publishing in Africa," The African Book Publishing Record, 7 (1980), 200 [Notes the fact that The Walking Calabash received honorable mention].

SEGUN, MABEL IMOUKHUEDE JOLASOA (Nigeria)

Anon. Women Today, 6, 5 (1965), 120 [Notes about My Father's Daughter].

Enie, Ibru. "What Should Our Children Read" Africa Woman, No. 18 (1978), 26.

DE SOUSA, NOEMIA (Mozambique)

Wästberg, Per. Afrikas moderna litteratur. Stockholm: Wahlström & Widstrand och Nordiska Afrikainstitutet, 1969, p. 90.

SUTHERLAND, EFUA T. M. (Ghana)

Wastberg, Per. Afrikas moderna litteratur. Stockholm: Wahlstrom & Widstrand och Nordiska Afrikainstitutet, 1969, p. 57.

TADJO, VERONIQUE (Ivory Coast)

Jusu, K. K. Man. "L'écriture féminine ivorienne," Fraternité Matin, 15 juin 1984, p. 16.

TELIKO, RAHMATULLAHI (Guinea)

Gerard, Albert. African Language Literatures: An Introduction to the Literary History of Sub-saharan Africa. Washington, DC: Three Continents Press; London: Longman, 1981, p. 56 (Notes that the poem, "Who Does Not Know God Is Lost" was translated by Christiane Seydou in 1966).

WACIUMA, CHARITY (Kenya)

Lindfors, Bernth. "New Trends in West and East African Fiction," Review of National Literatures, 11, 2 (1971), 33.

SYNOPSES OF AUTHORS' WORKS

CHIFAMBA, JANE (Zimbabwe)

King, E. W., ed. African Literature in Rhodesia. Salisbury: Mambo Pess,
  1966, pp. 139-41 [Synopsis of a children's book of folklore, Ngano Dzepasi Chigare (Tale of Old)].

CHRISTIE, PHILLIPA (Zimbabwe)

King, E. W., ed. African Literature in Rhodesia. Salisbury: Mambo Press, 1966,
  pp. 207-9 [Synopsis of the poem "Mhandu" (Enemy)].

NDONDO, LASSIE (Zimbabwe)

King, E. W. ed. African Literature in Rhodesia. Salisbury: Mambo Press, 1966,
  pp. 230-32 [Synopsis of the folk tale Qaphele Ingane].

TRANSLATION

AIDOO, CHRISTINA AMA ATA (Ghana)

"Ingen sødme her (No Sweetness Here)," Afrikansk Prosa. Comps. Pat Maddy og Ulla Ryum. Denmark: Stig Vendelkaers Farlag, n.d., pp. 58-75 [Transaltion into Danish by Paul Barum].

BA, MARIAMA (Senegal)

So Long A Long Letter (Une si longue lettre). London: Longman-Drumbeat Series, 1982. 89 pages. [Translation into English by Thomas Modupe].

DIALLO, NAFISSATOU (Senegal)

A Dakar Childhood (Une enfance dakaroise). London: Longman-Drumbeat Series, 1982, 134 pages. [Translation into English by Dorothy S. Blair].

EMECHETA, BUCHI (Nigeria)

    A. The Joys of Motherhood.

De zegeningen van het moedeschap. De Derdre Spreker-sene. Utrecht/Antwerpen: Aula, 1982 [Dutch translation].

Nnu Ego Zwanig Sacke Muschelgeld. Munchen: Frauenbuchverlag, 1983. 260 pages. [Translation into German by Helmi Martini-Honus and Jurgen Martini].

    B. The Moonlight Bride

Det Ukendte brudepar. Forlaget Hjulet, 1983. 93 pages. [Translation into Danish by Ritta Tejstø].

    C. Second-Class Citizen

Annenrangs Borger. Oslo: J. W. Cappelens Forlag A/S, 1983. 190 pages. [Translation into Norwegian by Jorunn Carlsen].

Másodrendü állampolgár. Budapest: Európa Könyukiadó, 1983. 233 pages. [Translation into Hungarian by Veres Julia].

    D. The Wrestling Match

Brottningsmatchen. Forlaget Hjulet, 1983. 80 pages. [Translation into Finnish by Ingrid Mjoberg].

TRANSLATION

Brydekampen. Forlaget Hjulet, 1983. 87 pages. [Translation into Finnish by Ritta Tejstø].

Det okanda brudparet. Forlaget Hjulet, 1983. [Translation into Finnish by Ingrid Mjoberg].

ESPIRITO, SANTO, ALDA DO (São Tomé e Príncipe)

" Donde están los hombres apesadas en este viento de locura?" <u>Poesia Africana de Hoy</u>. Eds. William Shand y Rodolfo Benasso. Buenos Aires:Editorial Sudamericana, 1968, pp. 156-67 [Translation into Spanish].

"Pa samma sida av Konoten," <u>Afrikansk Lyrik</u>. Ed. Per Wästberg. Stockholm: Albert Bonniers Förlag, 1970, pp. 104-6 [Translation into Swedish by Marianne Eyre].

"Huor er de maend der blev grebet af denne galskabens vind" <u>Afrikansk Lyrik i dag</u>. Eds. Uffe Harder and Jørgen Sonne. Copenhagen: Gylendal, 1970, pp. 189-91. [Translation into Danish].

GASHE, MARINA, pseudonym for Rebeka Njau (Kenya)

"Landsbyen (The Village)," <u>Afrikansk lyrik i dag</u>. Ed. Uffe Harder and Jørgen Sonne. Copnehagen: Gyldendal, 1970, p. 130 [Translation into Danish].

HEAD, BESSIE (Botswana/South Africa)

<u>Als er regen Komt</u> (When Rain Clouds Gather). De Derdre Spreker-Serie. Utrecht/Antwerpen: Aula, 1982 [Dutch translation].

ITAYEMI, PHEBEAN (Nigeria)

"Ingenting så underbart," <u>Afrika Berättar En Antologi sammanställd</u>. Ed. Per Wästberg. Stockholm: Boc-Serien, 1970, pp. 334-48 [Translation into Swedish].

TRANSLATION

JABAVU, NONI (South Africa)

Do ital. Il colore della pelle. Intr. Roberto Bosi. Milano: Mondadori, 1961. 208 pages. [Translation into Italian by Laura Grimaldi].

KUOH-MOUKOURY, THERESE (Cameroon)

La Danseuse d'Ivoire. Ed. Cyprian Ekwensi. Paris: Hatier, 1983.

OGOT, GRACE AKINYI (Kenya)

"Tekayo," Afrikansk Prosa. Comps. Pat Maddy og Ulla Ryum. Denmark: Stig Vendelk-RS Forlag, n.d., pp. 88-100 [Translation into Danish by Grethe Rasmussen].

DE SOUSA, NOEMIA (Mozambique)

"Ruego," Poesia Africana de Hoy. Ed. William Shand y Rodolfo Benasso. Buenos Aires: Editorial Sudamericana, 1968, pp. 155-57 [Spanish translation].

"Leve " Afrikansk Lyrik. Ed. Per Wastberg. Stockholm: Albert Bonniers Forlag, 1970, p. 101 [Translation into Swedish by Marianne Eyre].

"Appell," Afrika Berattar En Antologi sammanstalld. Ed. Per Wastberg. Stockholm: Boc-Serien, 1970, pp. 212-13 [Translation into Swedish].

"Appel," Afrikansk lyrik i dag. Eds. Uffe Harder and Jorgen Sonne. Copenhagen: Gyldendal, 1970, pp. 193-94 [Translation into Danish].

SOW FALL, AMINATA (Senegal)

A Beggar's Strike (Un greve si battu). London: Longmans-Drumbeat Series, 1980 [Translation into English by Dorothy Blair].

XII. BIBLIOGRAPHICAL/BIOGRAPHICAL INFORMATION

Alphabetical codes for the references cited frequently are as follows:

A. Abrash, Barbara. *Black African Literature in English since 1952*. New York: Johnson Reprint, 1967

B. Baldwin, Claudia. *Nigerian Literature: A Bibliography of Criticism, 1952-1976*. Boston: G. K. Hall, 1980.

C. Berrian, Brenda F. "Bibliographies of Nine Female African Writers," *Research in African Literatures*, 12, 2 (1981), 214-36.

D. Herdeck, Donald, ed. *African Authors: A Companion to Black African Writing 1300-1973*. Washington, DC: Three Continents Press, 1973.

E. House, Amelia. *Black Women Writers from South Africa: A Preliminary Checklist*. Evanston: Northwestern University Program on Women, 1980.

F. Jahn, Janheinz and Claus Dressler, comps. *Bibliography of Creative African Writing*. Nendeln: Krauss-Thomson, 1971.

G. Jahn, Janheinz, Ulla Schild and Almut Nordmann. *Who's Who in African Literature*. Tubingen: Horst Erdmann Verlag, 1972.

H. Lindfors, Bernth. *Black African Literature in English*. Detroit: Gale Research Company, 1979.

I. Ramsaran, J. M. *New Approaches to African Literature*. Ibadan: Ibadan University Press, 1970.

J. Saint-Andre-Utudjian, Eliane. *A Bibliography of West African Life and Literature*. New York: Africana Publishing Corporation, 1977.

K. Scheub, Harold. *African Oral Narratives, Proverbs, Riddles, Poetry and Songs*. Boston: G. K. Hall, 1977.

L. Schmidt, Nancy J. *Children's Books on Africa and Their Authors*. New York: Africana Publishing Corporation, 1975.

M. Schmidt, Nancy J. *Supplement to Children's Books on Africa and Their Authors*. New York: Africana Publishing Corporation, 1979.

N. Zell, Hans and Helene Silver, comps. *A Reader's Guide to African Literature*. New York: Africana Publishing Corporation, 1971.

O. Zell, Hans. *African Books in Print*, Vol I. London: Mansell Information, 1978.

BIBLIOGRAPHICAL/BIOGRAPHICAL INFORMATION

ACQUAH, BARBARA (Ghana)

L

ADDO, DORA (Ghana)

L

ADDO, JOYCE NAA ODOLE (Ghana)

Kay, Ernest, ed. International Who's Who of Authors and Writers. Cambridge: Cambridge University Press, 1976.

Mutiso, G. Socio-Political Thought in African Literature: Weusi? New York: Macmillan, 1974, p. 143.

ADEMOLA, FRANCES (Ghana)

A, B, D, F, J, N, O

AFONSO, MARIA PERPETUA CANDEIAS D SILVA (Angola)

F, G

AGADIZI, ANNA (Ghana)

L, M

AIDOO, CHRISTINA AMA ATA (Ghana)

Africa Year Book and Who's Who 1977. London: Africa Journal Ltd., 1976, p. 1045.

A, C, D, F, G, H, I, J, N

Omotoso, Kole. "End of the Year Book Report,: Afriscope, 4, 12 (1974), 40.

Sjurjat, Ernestyna. Afryka W. Toworosci Jej Pisarzy. [Africa Through the works of its authors]. Studium Afrykanistyczne Uniwersytetu Warsawskiego, 14. Warsaw: Wydawnictwa Uniwersytetu Warsawskigo, 1973.

BIBLIOGRAPHICAL/BIOGRAHICAL INFORMATION

AIGBOKHAI, JOSEPHINE (Nigeria)

    L

AJOSE, AUDREY (Nigeria)

    A, J, L, N

AKPABOT, ANNE (Nigeria)

    F, L, M

AL-HASAN, SUSAN (Ghana)

    K

AMROUCHE, MARIE-LOUISE also Marguerite Taos-Amrouche (Tunisia)

    K

ANDRIA, ANDREE (Madagascar)

    F

ANIZOBA, ROSE (Nigeria)

    F, L, N

ANKRAH, EFUA (Ghana)

    M

ANTHONY, MONICA (South Africa)

    E

ASHERI, JEDIDA (Cameroon)

    L

AVERY, GRETA (Sierra Leone)

    J

BIBLIOGRAPHICAL/BIOGRAPHICAL INFORMATION

BAKALUBA, JANE JAGERS (Uganda)

M

BLAINE-WILSON, CLARA (Liberia)

Cordor, Henry. A List of Liberian Authors and Aspiring Writers Arranged in Historical Order of the Republic of Liberia from 1820-1971. Monrovia: Liberian Literature Studies Programme, 1970.

BOITUMELO (South Africa)

E

CASELY-HAYFORD, ADELAIDE (Ghana/Sierra Leone)

D, H, J

CASELY-HAYFORD, GLADYS (Sierra Leone/Ghana)

C, D, F, G, H, J

Lang, D. M. and D. R. Dudley, eds. The Penguin Companion to Classical Oriental and African Literature. New York: McGraw-Hill, 1969, p. 336.

CLEMS, DARLENE (Ghana)

J

DAHAL, CHARITY (Kenya)

F, K

DANKWAH-SMITH, HANNAH

M

DANKYI, JOYCE

M

DIALLO, NAFISSATOU (Senegal)

O

BIBLIOGRAPHICAL/BIOGRAPHICAL INFORMATION

DIKE, FATIMA (South Africa)

    E

DOUTS, CHRISTINE (South Africa)

    E

DOVE-DANQUAH, MABEL (Ghana)

    A, D, J, M

DRONYI, JOYCE L. (Uganda)

    M

DUBE, VIOLET (South Africa)

    D

EMECHETA, BUCHI (Nigeria)

    B, C, H, J

ESAN, YETUNDE (Nigeria)

    A, B

ESPIRITO SANTO, ALDA DO (Sao Tome e Principe)

    D, G, I

ESSILFIE, NAA AFARLEY (Ghana)

    J

EYAKUZE, VALENTINE (Tanzania)

    A

Mutiso, G. C. M. Socio-Political Thought in African Literature: Weusi? New York: Macmillan, 1974, p. 149.

BIBLIOGRAPHICAL/BIOGRAPHICAL INFORMATION

FAIK-NZUJI, CLEMENTINE MADIYA (Zaire)

    G, K

FISH, MARY McCRITY (Liberia)

Cordor, S. Henry. A List of Liberian Authors and Aspiring Writers Arranged in Historical Order or the Republic of Liberia from 1820-1971. Monrovia: Liberian Literature Studies Programme, 1970.

FUTSHANE, ZORA T. (South Africa)

    D

GACHUKIA, EDDAH (Kenya)

    O

GATHII, HANNAH (Kenya)

    F

GICORU, NEREAS, Mrs. Hirst (Kenya)

    M

GITHAE-MUGO, MICERE (Kenya)

    H, O

Likimani, Muthoni. Women of Kenya. Nairobi: n. p., 1979, p. 25.

GITHUKU, MARY (Kenya)

    M

HEAD, BESSIE (South Africa/Botswana)

    D, E, H, N

BIBLIOGRAPHICAL/BIOGRAPHICAL INFORMATION

HLONGWANE, JANE (South Africa)

    E

HOUSE, AMELIA (South Africa)

    E

ITAYEMI-OGUNDIPE, PHEBEAN (Nigeria)

    D, J, M

IWUJI, VICTORIA B. C. (Nigeria)

    L

JABAVU, NONI (South Africa)

    D, E, G, I, N

Lang, D. M., ed. "African," The Penguin Companion to Literature. Harmondsworth: Penguin, 1969.

JOHNSON, RHODA OMOSUNLOLA (Nigeria)
    M

JOHNSON, VICTORIA (Liberia)

Cordor, S. Henry. A List of Liberian Authors and Aspiring Writers Arranged in Historical Order of the Republic of Liberia from 1820 to 1971. Monrovia: Liberian Literature Studies Programme, 1970.

JORDAN, NANDI (South Africa)

    E

KAKAZA, LILLITH OR LOTA G. (South Africa)

    D

BIBLIOGRAPHICAL/BIOGRAPHICAL INFORMATION

KAKHOKA, NTOMBIYAKHE KABIYELA (South Africa)

 E

KALIMUGOGO, G. (Kenya)

 O

KAVILA, ESTHER (Kenya)

 M, O

KAYA, SIMONE (Ivory Coast)

Anon. La femme africaine et malgache: éléments bibliographiques. Paris: Centre de documentation du Ministère de la Coopération, 1978, p. 24.

KEITA, AWA (Mali)

Anon. Le femme africaine et malgache: éléments bibliographiques. Paris: Centre de documentation du Ministère de la Coopération, 1978, pp. 10, 28.

KGOSITSILE, BALEKA (South Africa)

 E

KHAKETLE, CAROLINE N. M. R. (Lesotho)

 D, E

KHANGANYA, WILLMESS (Malawi)

 L

KIANGANA, KETA (West Africa)

Anon. La femme africaine et malgache: éléments bibliographiques. Paris: Centre de documentation du Ministère de la Coopération, 1978, p. 11.

KIMENYE, BARBARA (Uganda)

 A, D, F, G, H, L , M , N, O

Women and Women Writers in the Commonwealth. London: Commonwealth Institute and the National Book League, 1975, p. 31.

BIBLIOGRAPHICAL/BIOGRAPHICAL INFORMATION

KING, DELPHINE (Sierra Leone)

    A, F, H, N

KUOH-MOUKOURY, THERESE (Cameroon)

Anon. La femme africaine et malgache: éléments bibliographiques. Paris: Centre de documentation du Ministère de la Coopération, 1978, p. 15.

KURANKYI-TAYLOR, DOROTHY (Ghana)

    A, F, J

KWAKU, ROSEMARY (Ghana)

Anon. Dictionary of International Biography. Vol. 16. Cambridge: International Biographical Centre (I.B.C.), 1979.

Anon. The Who's Who of Women. Cambridge: International Biographical Centre (I.B.C.), 1976, p. 484.

Okike, No. 16 (1979), 70.

KYENDO, KALONDU (Kenya)

    K

LAMO, JANET (Uganda)

    M

LIKIMANI, MUTHONI (Kenya)

    M, O

Likimani, Muthoni. Women of Kenya. Nairobi: n.p., 1979.

MABUZA, LINDIWE (South Africa)

    E

MACAULEY, JEANNETTE (Sierra Leone)

    D, J

BIBLIOGRAPHICAL/BIOGRAPHICAL INFORMATION

MACKAY, ILVA (South Africa)

    E

MAI, JEANNE NGO (Cameroon)

    N

MAKEBA, MIRIAM (South Africa)

    K, L

MALAKA, MAUDE (South Africa)

    E

MALL, JASMINE (South Africa)

    E

MANDAO, MARTHA (Tanzania)

    O

MANDEBVU, STELLA (Zimbabwe)

    O

MANDELA, ZINDZI (South Africa)

    E

MARGARIDO, MARIE MANUELA (Sao Tomé e Príncipe)

    D

MASEKELA, BARBARA (South Africa)

    E

BIBLIOGRAPHICAL/BIOGRAPHICAL INFORMATION

MASHISHI, M. A. (South Africa)

    E

MASSAQUOI, PRINCESS FATIMA (Liberia)

    L

MATINDI, ANNE (Kenya)

    F, L, N. O

MATIP, MARIE-CLAIRE (Cameroon)

    F

MAURA, MARY (Kenya)

    L, N

M'BAYE, ANNETTE D'ERNEVILLE (Senegal)

Anon. La femme africaine et malgache: éléments bibliographiques. Paris: Centre de documentation du Ministère de la Coopération, 1978, p. 30.

    D, G

MDOE, JANET N. (Uganda)

    L

MENIRU, THERESA (Nigeria)

Anon. Women and Women Writers in the Commonwealth. London: Commonwealth Institute and the National Book League, 1975, p. 45.

    K, L

MENSAH, GRACE OSEI (Ghana)

    L, M

BIBLIOGRAPHICAL/BIOGRAPHICAL INFORMATION

MHLONGO, MAUREEN (South Africa)

    E

MITCHELL, ELIZABETH M. (Liberia)

Cordor, S. Henry. <u>A List of Liberian Authors and Aspiring Authors Arranged in Historical Order of the Republic of Liberia from 1820-971</u>. Monrovia: Liberian Literature Studies Programme, 1970.

MLAGOLA, MARTHA V. (Kenya)

    O

MOHAMEDALI, HAMIDA (Kenya)

Okola, Lennard, ed. <u>Drum Beat</u>. Nairobi: East African Publishing House, 1967.

MOREL, MARION (South Africa)

    D

MORITI, PALESA (South Africa)

    E

MOROLO, WINNIE (South Africa)

    E

MPHAHLELE, THERESA, K. (South Africa)

    E

MUGOT, HAZEL DE SILVA (Seychelles)

    O

MUHANDO, PENNINA (Tanzania)

    O

BIBLIOGRAPHICAL/BIOGRAPHICAL INFORMATION

MUTSILA, IRENE (South Africa)

    E

MWANA, KUPONA (Kenya)

    D

MWANGI, ROSE GECAU (Kenya)

    K, O

NAGENDA, SALA (Kenya)

    L

NAKACWA, THERESA (Uganda)

    F

NANJALA, ELIZABETH (Kenya)

    O

NCHWE, MANOKO (South Africa)

    E

NDORO, JOYCE (Kenya)

    F, L, N, O

NGONYAMA, SUSAN (South Africa)

    E

NGUBANE, HARRIET (South Africa)

    E

NGUYA, LYDIE MUMBI (Kenya)

    O

BIBLIOGRAPHICAL/BIOGRAPHICAL INFORMATION

NJAU, REBEKA (Kenya)

A, D, F, G, O

NTANTALA, PHYLLIS (South Africa)

D, E

NWAPA, FLORA (Nigeria)

Anon. Africa Year Book and Who's Who 1977. London: Africa Journal Ltd., 1976, p. 1272.

Anon. Women and Women Writers in the Commonwealth. London: Commonwealth Institute and the National Book League, 1975, p. 34.

B, C, F, G, H, I, J, M, N, O

Lang, D. M., ed. "African," The Penguin Companion to Literature. Harmondsworth: Penguin, 1969.

Skrujat, Ernestyna. Afryka W Tworczosci Jej Pisarzy (Africa through the works of its authors). Studium Afrykanistyczne, Uniwersytetu Warsawskiego, 14. Warsaw: Wydawnictwa Uniwersytetu Warsawskiego, 1973

NXUMALO, NATALIE VICTORIA (South Africa)

D

NYOKABI, SALLY (Kenya)

M

ODAGA, ASENATH BOLE (Kenya)

F, L, M, O

Likimani, Muthoni. Women of Kenya. Nairobi: n. p., 1979, p. 27.

ODOWELU, VICKI EZINMA (Nigeria)

F

BIBLIOGRAPHICAL/BIOGRAPHICAL INFORMATION

OGOT, GRACY AKINYI (Kenya)

Anon. La femme africaine et malgache: éléments bibliographiques. Paris: Centre de documentation du Ministère de la Coopération, 1978, p. 11.

    C, D, F, G, H, I, N, O

Killam, Douglas. "Kenya," Literatures of the World in English. Ed. Bruce King. London: Rouledge &Kegan Paul, 1974, pp. 126-27.

Lang, D. M., and D. R. Dudley, ed. "African," The Penguin Companion to Classical, Oriental and African Literature. Harmondsworth: Penguin, 1969, IV; New York: McGraw-Hill, 1969, pp. 349-50.

OGOT, PAMELA (Kenya)

    K, L, N

Likimani, Muthoni. Women of Kenya. Nairobi: N.p., 1979, p. 28.

OGUNDIPE-LESLIE, OMOLARA (Nigeria)

    F, J

OKONKWO, JULIET I. (Nigeria)

    J

OKOYE, IFEOMA (Nigeria)

    M

OMANGA, CLARE (Kenya)

    F, K, L, O

OMODING, ANNA (Uganda)

    M

BIBLIOGRAPHICAL/BIOGRAPHICAL INFORMATION

ONDITI, MARA (East Africa)

    M

OWINO, ROSEMARY (Kenya)

    O

OWUSU-NIMOH, MERCY (Ghana)

    M, O

PEREIRA-EMANUEL, FRANCESCA Y. (Nigeria)

    A

PHUMLU (South Africa)

    L

PHUNGULA, NOMUSA (South Africa)

    E

RATSIFANDRIHAMANANA, CLARISSE (Madagascar)

    F

RWAKYAKA, PROSCOVIA (Tanzania)

    D

SACKEY, JULIANA (Ghana)

    J, L

SEFORA, RITA (South Africa)

    E

SEGUN, MABEL IMOUKHEUEDE JOLAOSA (Nigeria)

    A, C, D, F, G, H, J, L, N, O

SELLO, DORIS (South Africa)

    E

BIBLIOGRAPHICAL/BIOGRAPHICAL INFORMATION

SHAFIK, LELIAH (Egypt)

Anon. Africa Year Book and Who's Who 1977. London: Africa Journal Ltd., 1976, p. 1324.

SIBANE, NONA (South Africa)

E

SIGWILI, NOKUGCINE (South Africa)

E

SIKAKANE, JOYCE (South Africa)

E

SOFOLA, ZULU (Nigeria)

Anon. Women and Women Writers in the Commonwealth. London: Commonwealth Institute and the National Book League, 1975, p. 38.

B, H, H, M, O

SOUSA, NOEMIA CAROLINA ABRANCHES DE (Mozambique)

D, G

SUTHERLAND, EFUA THEODORA MORGUE (Ghana)

A, C, D, F, G, H, I, J, L, N, O

Crane, Louise. MS Africa. New York: Lippincott, 1973, pp. 35-56.

SWAARTBOOI, VICTORIA (South Africa)

D

MacGregor, J. Mac. "The Late Miss Victoria Swaartbooi," South African Outlook, 68 (1937), 267.

BIBLIOGRAPHICAL/BIOGRAPHICAL INFORMATION

TAOS-AMROUCHE, MARGUERITE (Tunisia)

    K

THOMAS, GLADYS (South Africa)

    E

TLALI, MIRIAM (South Africa)

    E, O

ULASI, ADAORA LILY (Nigeria)

Anon. Africa Year Book and Who's Who 1977. London: Africa Journal Ltd., 1976, p. 1347.

    B, D, F, J, N

WACIUMA, CHARITY (Kenya)

    A, F, L, M, N, O

WERE, MIRIAM KHAMADI (Kenya)

    L, M

WHEATLEY, PHILLIS (Senegal and USA)

Baker, Houston A., ed. Black Literature in America. New York: McGraw-Hill, 1971, pp. 3-4.

Barksdale, Richard and Kenneth Kinnamon, ed. Black Writers of America. New York: Macmillan, 1972, pp. 38-44.

Graham, Shirley. The Story of Phillis Wheatley. New York: 1949.

Herdeck, Donald, ed. African Authors: A Companion to Black African Writing 1300-1973. Washington, DC: Black Orpheus Press, 1973, pp.

Robinson, William H. Phillis Wheatley: A Bio-Bibliography. Boston: G. K. Hall, 1981. 166 pages.

ZIRIMU, ELVANIA NAMUKWAYA (Uganda)

    A, C , F, H, J, O

A
AUTHORS GROUPED BY COUNTRIES

ALGERIA

Amrani, Danièle
Amrouche, Fadhma Aïth Mansour
Amrouche, Marie-Louise, also known as Marguerite Taos-Amrouche
Bittari, Zoubeida
Debeche, Djamila
Djabali, Leila
Djebar, Assia
Gréki, Anna
Guendouz, Nadia
Lemsine, Aicha
O'Lansen, Malika
Sebbar, Leila
Zerari, Zehor

ANGOLA

Abreu, Manuela da Conceicao
Afonso, María Perpétua Candeias da Silva
Almeida, Déolinda Rodriques de
Fonseca, Lília da
Lara, Alda
Lima, Maria Eugénia
*Neto, Maria Eugénia
Silva Maria de Jesus Nunes da
Veiga, Amélia
Xavier, Ermelinda Pereira

BOTSWANA

Buthelezi, Bafana
Mokorosi, Emely Selemeng
Selolwane, Onalenna

CAMEROON

Abada, Essomba Rose
Anyangwe, Gladys Ngwi
Asheri, Jedida
Belinga, Thérèse Baratte-Eno
Bonny, Anne-Marie
Dooh-Bunya, Lydie
Egbe, Pauline
Etoumba, Paule
Kuoh-Moukoury, Thérèse
*Libondo, Jeanne Ngo
Liking, Werewere
Mai, Jeanne Ngo
Malafa, Efosi
Matip, Maire-Claire
Njoya, Rabiatou
Norgah, Mary
Nwigwe, Nkuku
Tsogo, Delphine Zanga
Tutu Malamafuna, Matilda
Williams, Kate Ngowo
Yembe, Faustina

CAPE VERDE

Amarilis, Orlanda
Mascarenhas, Maria Margarida
Morazzo, Yolanda

EGYPT

'Abd Allāh, Sūfī
Bishai, Nadia
Chédid, Andrée
El Saadawi, Nawal
Loubna, Mama
Queen Hatshepsut
Qutb, Amīna

ETHIOPIA

Gebru, Seneddu
Kasahun, Romanä Wắrq
Zelleke, Serk-Addis

GABON

Kama-Bongo, Josephine

GHANA

Acquah, Barbara
Addo, Dora Yacoba
Addo, Joyce Naa Odole
Addo, Patience Henaku
Agadizi, Anna
Aidoo, Christina Ama Ata
Al Hasan, Susan
Allotey, Alice
Amegashie, Susan
Ankrah, Efua
Antiri, Janet Adwoa
*Appiah, Peggy
Baëta, Lily
Benskina, Princess Orelia
Boahemaa, Beatrice Yaa
Casely-Hayford, Adelaide
Casely-Hayford, Gladys, pseudonym Acquah Laluah
Clems, Darlene
Dankwah-Smith, Hannah
Dankyi, Jane Osafoa
Dove-Danquah, Mabel, pseudonym Marjorie Mensah
Essilfie, Naa Afarley
Griffin, Mary Abena
Kumah, Sylvie
Kurankyi-Taylor, Dorothy
Kwaku, Rosemary
Kyegyirba, Adwoa
Lokko, Sophia
Mensah, Grace Osei
Ohene, Oopokua
Owusu-Nimoh, Mercy
Sackey, Juliana
Spio-Garbrah, Elizabeth
Yeboah-Afari, Ajoa Victoria
Zagbede, Josephine

GUINEA

Télikô, Râhmatoullâhi

GUINEA-BISSAU

Ferreira, Ondina Maria Fonseca Rodriques
Ribeiro, Mariana Marques, pseudonym Ytchyana

IVORY COAST

Adiaffi, Anne-Marie
Cavally, Jeanne de
Kanie, Anoma
Kaya, Simone
Kolia (Mme)
Tadjo, Véronique
Wanne, Tegbo
Yaou, Regina

KENYA

Anyiko, Grace
Bobito, Jenifer
Chima, Simma
Dahal, Charity Kuguru
Gachukia, Eddah
Gashe, Marina, pseudonym for Rebeka Njau
Gathii, Hannah
Gicoru, Nereas
Githae, Madeleine, maiden name for Micere Githae-Mugo
Githae-Mugo, Micere
Githuku, Mary
Higiro, J.
*Hunter, Cynthia
Hunya, Janet
Ibingira, Grace
Kagondu, Agnes
Kahaku, Pauline W.
Kahiga, Hannah
Kalimugogo, G.
Karanja, Paula
Kavila, Esther
Khamadi, Miriam, maiden name for Miriam K. Were
Kimenyi, Luci W.
Kisangi, Esther
Kise, Mary
*Kitonga, Ellen
Kuria, R. Lucy
Kyendo, Kalondu
Likimani, Muthoni
Marva, Ravi

Matenjwa, Christine
Matindi, Anne
Maura, Mary
Mboni, Sarah
Messenga (Miss), pseudonym
Mlagola, Martha V.
Mohamedali, Hamida
Msham, Mwana Kupona Binti
Muli, Anne Keeru
*Muthoni, Susie
Mwangi, Beatrice
Mwangi, Rose Gecau
Nagenda, Sala
Nanjala, Elizabeth
Ndegwa, Catherine D.
Ndele, Serena
Ndele, Susan
Ndoro, Joyce
Ngatho, Stella
Nguya, Lydie Mumbi
Njau, Rebeka
Njoroge, Lizzie Nyambura
Odaga, Asenath Bole
Ogada, Penniah A.
Ogot, Grace Akinyi
Ogot, Pamela
Olimba, Maude
*Oludhe-Macgoye, Marjorie
Omanga, Clare
Owino, Rosemarie
Rosemary, pseudonym
Siganga, Jenifer
Waciuma, Charity
Wangeci, Agatha
Wanjiru, L. Mumbi
Wanjiru, Pauline
Waruhiu, Doris May
Were, Jane
Were, Miriam Khamadi

LESOTHO

Khaketla, Caroline, N.M.R.

Ramala, Maggie
Tlali, Sophia

LIBERIA

*Banks-Henries, A. Doris
Blaine-Wilson, Claire
Brown Mitchell, Elizabeth M.
Fish, Mary McCrity
Jabbeh, Patricia D. M.
Johnson, Victoria
Massaquoi, Fatima Fahnbulleh
Teage, Hilary
Tulay, Elizabeth Lovo Jallah
Ware, Rebecca J. N.
Wilson, Beverly R.

MADAGASCAR

Andria, Aimée
Dreo, Pelandrova
Nirina, Esther
Rakotoson, Michèle
Ratisifandrihamanana, Clarisse
Ratsimiseta, Jasmina

MALAWI

Chirwa, Nellie
Kaphwiyo, Josephine
Khanganya, Willmess

MALI

Kéita, Awa (or Aoua)

MOROCCO

Attik, Mririda N'Ait
Bannuna, Khanata

MOZAMBIQUE

Flora
Lobo, Maria Manuela de Sousa
Machel, Josina
Morais, Desi
Mucavale, Joana Mateus
Mwakala, Maria
Nachale, Joana
Roby, Maria Emilia
Sousa, Noémia Carolina Abranches Soares de
Tembe, Rosaria
Zinondo, Tokozile

NIGERIA

Achebe, Christie Chinwe
Acholonu, Catherine
Aigbokhai, Josephine
Ajose, Audrey
Akpabot, Anna
Anizoba, Rose
Asibong, Elizabeth E.
Chukwuma, Helen
Coge, Maimuna Barmani
Egejuru, Phanuel A.
Emecheta, Buchi
Enem, Edith
Eronini, Faustina Nwachi
Esan, Yetunde
Fakunle-Onadeko, Olufumilayo
Gwaram, Hauwa
Ifudu, Theodora
Ifudu, Vera
Itayemi-Ogundipe, Phebean
Iwuji, Victoria B. C.
Johnson, Rhoda Omosunlola
Karibo, Minji
Katsina, Binta
Meniru, Theresa
Moneke, Obiora
Nwagboso, Rosaline
Nwapa, Flora
Nzeribe, Ejine
Nzeribe, Grace Nnenna
Obi, Dorothy
Odowelu, Vicki Ezinma

Ogundipe-Leslie, Omolara
Okonkwo, Juliet I.
Okoye, Ifeoma
Ovbiagele, Helen
Pereira-Emanuel, Francesca Yetunde
Sa'adu, A. B.
Segun, Mabel Imoukhuede Jolaosa
Shuaib, Yinka
Sikuade, Yemi
Sofola, Zulu
Udensi, Uwa
Ulasi, Adaora Lily
*Uwemedimo, Rosemary

RWANDA

Nsanzubuhoro, Victoire

SAO TOME E PRINCIPE

Espírito Santo, Alda do
Margarido, Maria Manuela Conceicao Carvalho da

SENEGAL

Bâ, Mariama
Bâ, Oumar (Mlle)
Diakhaté, Ndeye Coumba
Diallo, Nafissatou
Dogbe, Anne
Fall, Kiné Kirama
M'Baye, Annette D'Erneville
Sow Fall, Aminata
*Wheatley, Phillis

SEYCHELLES

Mugot, Hazel DeSilva

SIERRA LEONE

Atarrah, Christine
Avery, Greta
Casely-Hayford, Adelaide
Casely-Hayford, Gladys

John-Rowe, Juliana
King, Delphine
Macauley, Jeannettte
Pearce, Esther Taylor
Williams, Daphne B. E.

SOUTH AFRICA

Anthony, Monica
Boitumelo
Dike, Fatima
Dlovu, Nandi
Douts, Christine
Dube, Violet
Futshane, Zora Z.T.
Head, Bessie
Hlongwane, Jane
House, Amelia
Jabavu, Noni Helen Nontando
Jordan, Nandi
Kakaza, Lillith (or Lota G.)
kaXhoba, Ntombiyakhe kaBiyela
Kgositsile, Beleka
Khuzwayo, Ellen
Kichwa, Morena Halim
Mabuza, Lindiwe
Mackay, Ilva
Magidi, Dora Thizwilandi
Mahuhusi, M. A.
Makeba, Miriam
Malaka, Maude
Mall, Jasmine
Mandela, Zindzi
Maoka, Shimane
Masekela, Barbara
Mashishi, Kedisaletse
Matlou, Rebecca
Mhlongo, Maureen
Mkhomo, Joy Florence Chrestophene
Mokhomo, Makhokolotso
Mokwena, Joan
Morel, Marion
Moriti, Palesa
Morolo, Winnie
Mphahlele, Theresa Kefilwe
Mtungwa, Gloria
Mutsila, Irene
Mvemve, Lindiwe
Nchwe, Manoko
Ngcobo, Lauretta
Ngonyama, Susan

Ngubane, Harriet
Nxumalo, Natalie Victoria
Phumla
Phungula, Nomusa Cynthia
Sefora, Rita
Sello, Doris
Setidisho, Edith
Sibane, Nona
Sigwili, Nokugcina
Sikakane, Joyce N.
Siwundhla, Alice Princess
Swaartbooi, Victoria
Thomas, Gladys
Tlali, Miriam

SUDAN

Ponti-Lako, Agnes

TANZANIA

Babisidya, M.
Chogo-Wapakabulo, Angelina
Lihamba, Amandina
Mandao, Martha
*Mbilinyi, Marjorie, J.
Mhando, Blandina
Muhando, Pennina
Mvungi, Martha
Pala, O.
*Pierce, Jacqueline

TOGO

Akafia, Wotsa
Kwami, Marthe Aféwélé

TUNISIA

Chaibi, Aicha
Taos-Amrouche, Marguerite, a.k.a Marie-Louise Amrouche

UGANDA

Akello, Grace
Anselm Sister
Apoko, Anna

Bakaluba, Jane Jagers
Datta, Soroj
Dronyi, Joyce L.
El-Miskery, Sheikha
Kalebu, Betty
Kayanja, Lydie
Kimenya, Barbara
Kokunda, Violet
Lamo, Janet
Mbowa, Rose
Mdoe, Janet N.
Nabwire, Constance
Nagenda, Sarah
Nakacwa, Theresa
Omoding, Anna
Princess Elizabeth of Toro
Rwakyaka, Proscovia
Zirimu, Elvania Namukwaya

ZAIRE

Faik-Nzuji, Clémentine Madiya
Mpongo, Marie-Eugénie
Mudimbe-Boyi, Elisabeth Mbulamwanza
Ndaaya, Citeku
Nzuji, Caroline Baleka Bamba
Tol'Ande, Elisabeth Françoise Mweya

ZAMBIA

Kasese, Medard
Muntemba, Maude
Phiri, Irene

ZANZIBAR

Saad, Siti Binti

ZIMBABWE

Chifamba, Jane
Christie, Phillipa
Dube, Hope
Gutu, Laetitia
Makura, Tendai
Mandebvu, Stella

Ndondo, Lassie

EAST AFRICA

Abdullah, Nuru Binti
Achola
Alifaijo, Margaret
Amooti, Beatrice Tinkamanyire
Apio, Lydie M.
Bateyo, Juliet M.
Damani, Charu
Jetha, Nazara
Kagoda, Namuluuta
Kiyingi, Elizabeth
Lehai, Joy
Lusinde, Ruth
Lwanga, Susan
Masembe, Harriet
Mhelema, Marjorie
Mukwaya, Jean B.
Nakitwe, Angela Nashakoma
Namubiru, Margaret
Noronha, Lydie
Olisa, Margaret
Onditi, Mara

NORTH AFRICA

Olivesi, Djamila

WEST AFRICA

Seydou Amadu, Christiane
Thiam, Awa

UNIDENTIFIED

Nene, Amélia
Rush, Brenda Utamu
Tookoram, Meryl
Umelo, Rosina
Urey-Ngara, Abigail

*Non-African women married to African men who are counted among the African writers within the respective African countries.

B

AUTHORS GROUPED BY GENRE

AUTOBIOGRAPHY/BIOGRAPHY

Amrouche, Fadhma Aïth Mansour
Apoko, Anna
Casely-Hayford, Adelaide
Diallo, Nafissatou
Emecheta, Buchi
Jabavu, Noni Helen Nontando
Keita, Aoua
Kwami, Marthe Aféwélé
Magidi, Doro Thizwilandi
Nwapa, Flora
Princess Elizabeth of Toro
Segun, Mabel Imoukhuede Jolaosa
Sikakane, Joyce
Siwundhla, Alice Princess Msumba
Swaartbooi, Victoria
Waciuma, Charity
Were, Miriam Khamadi

CHILDREN'S LITERATUARE

'Abd Allâh, Sûfi
Acquah, Barbara
Addo, Dora Yacoba
Addo, Joyce
Agadizi, Anna
Ajose, Audrey
Akapbot, Anne
Anizoba, Rose
Ankrah, Efua
Apoko, Anna
Asheri, Jedida
Casely-Hayford, Adelaide
Cavally, Jeanne de
Chifamba, Jane
Dahal, Charity Kuguru
Dankwah-Smith, Hannah
Dankyi, Jane Osafoa
Dogbe, Anne
Dronyi, Joyce L.
Emecheta, Buchi
Fakunle-Onadeko, Olufunmilayo
Gicoru, Nereas
Githuku, Mary
Gutu, Laetitia
Iwuji, Victoria B. C.

Johnson, Rhoda Omosunloloa
Kalimugogo, G.
Kavila, Esther
Khanganya, Willmess
Kimenye, Barbara
Kyendo, Kalondu
Lamo, Janet
Likimani, Muthoni
Loubna, Mama
Mandoa, Martha
Massaaquoi, Princess Fatima
Matindi, Anne
Maura, Mary
M'Baye, Annette d'Erneville
Mdoe, Janet N.
Meniru, Theresa
Mfodwo, Esther Bekoe
Mlagola, Martha V.
Moneke, Obiora
Nagenda, Sala
Ndoro, Joyce
Ntabagoba, Jenniah
Nwapa, Flora
Nyokabi, Sally
Odaga, Asenath Bole
Odowelu, Vicki Ezinma
Ogot, Pamela
Ohene, Oopokua
Okoye, Ifeoma
Omanga, Clare
Omoding, Anna
Onditi, Mara
Owusu-Nimoh, Mercy
Phumla
Sackey, Juliana
Segun, Mabel
Sofola, Zulu
Sutherland, Efua T. M.
Umelo, Rosina
Waciuma, Charity
Wanne, Tebgo

DRAMA: PUBLISHED PLAYS

Acquah, Barbara
Addo, Patience
Aidoo, Christina Ama Ata
Chédid, Andrée

Chogo-Wapakabulo, Angelina
Clems, Darlene
Djebar, Assia
Dike, Fatima
Kama-Bongo, Joséphine
Kasahun, Romana Warq
Khaketla, Caroline N.M.R
Kwaku, Rosemary
Liking, Werewere
Matenjwa, Christine
Matindi, Anne
Mugo, Micere Githae
Muhando, Pennina
Njau, Rebeka
Njoya, Rabiatou
Ogot, Grace
Rakotoson, Michèle
Ramala, Maggie
Sofola, Zulu
Sutherland, Efua T. M.
Udensi, Uwa
Zirimu, Elvania Namukwaya

DRAMA: PERFORMED PLAYS

Addo, Joyce
Addo, Patience
Clems, Darlene
Dike, Fatima
Emecheta, Buchi
Enem, Edith
Gathii, Hannah
John-Rowe, Juliana
Khaketla, Caroline N.M.R.
Kwaku, Rosemary
Lokko, Sophia
Nakacwa, Theresa
Njau, Rebeka
Pearce, Esther Taylor
Sutherland, Efua T.M.
Zirimu, Elvania N.

FOLKLORE

Al-Hasan, Susan
Amooti, Beatrice Tinkamanyire
Amrouche, Marie-Louise

Antiri, Janet Adwoa
Anyangwe, Gladys Ngwi
Attik, Mririda n'Ait
Baëta, Lily
Chifamba, Jane
Dahal, Charity Kuguru
Dankwah-Smith, Hannah
Dankyi, Jane Osafoa
Faik-Nzuji, Clémentine M.
Kagoda, Namuluuta
Kakaza, Lillith or Lota G.
Meniru, Theresa
Messenga, (pseudonym)
Mfodowo, Esther B.
Mvungi, Martha
Mwangi, Rose G.
Ndoro, Joyce
Njoroge, Lizzie N.
Nzeribe, Ejine
Nzuji, Caroline B. B.
Odaga, Asenath Bole
Ogot, Pamela
Omanga, Clare
Seydou Amadu, Christiane
Sumbane, Natala
Taos-Amrouche, Marguerite
Tookaram, Meryl
Ulasi, Adora L.
Waciuma, Charity
Zirimu, Elvania N.

JUVENILE LITERATURE

Aigbokhai, Josephine
Bakaluba, Jane Jagers
Bobito, Jenifer
Emecheta, Buchi
Kagondu, Agnes
Kimenye, Barbara
Kisangi, Esther
Kise, Mary
Kuria, R. Lucy
Magidi, Dora Thizwilandi
Makeba, Miriam
Mwangi, Beatrice
Ndondo, Lassie
Nguya, Lizzie Mumbi
Odaga, Asenath Bole
Odowelu, Vicki Ezinma

Sofola, Zulu
Waciuma, Charity
Wanjiru, Pauline
Waruhiu, Doris May
Were, Miriam Khamadi
Yaou, Regina

MISCELLANEOUS PROSE

Abada, Essomba Rose
Addo, Joyce
Ademola, Frances
Aidoo, Christina Ama Ata
Alifaijo, Margaret
Anselm (Sister)
Avery, Greta
Boitumelo
Casely-Hayford, Gladys May
Chite, Helen
Chukuma, Helen
Damani, Charu
Egejuru, Phanuel A.
Emecheta, Buchi
Espírito Santo, Alda do
Essilfie, Naa Afarley
Faik-Nzuji, Clémentine Madiya
Gachukia, Eddah
Gicoru, Nereas
Githae-Mugo, Micere
Head, Bessie
House, Amelia
Hunya, Janet
Ifudu, Theodora
Itayemi-Ogundipe, Phebean
Jabavu, Noni
Jetha, Nazara
Kagondu, Agnes
Kahiga, Hannah
Kahiga, Miriam
Kayanja, Lydie
Kisangi, Esther
Kuria, R. Lucy
Lehai, Joy
Lusinde, Ruth
Macauley, Jeannette
Matenjwa, Christine
Mlama, Pennina

Mohamedali, Hamida
Mudimbe-Boyi, Elisabeth M.
Mwangi, Beatrice
Namubiru, Margaret
Njau, Rebeka
Nzuji, Caroline B. B.
Odaga, Asenath Bole
Ogot, Grace
Ogundipe-Leslie, Omolara
Okonkwo, Juliet I.
Pala, O.
Sackey, Juliana A.
Segun, Mabel I. J.
Sofola, Zulu
Sutherland, Efua T. M
Taos-Amrouche, Marguerite
Thiam, Awa
Tlali, Miriam
Wanjiru, Pauline
Waruhiu, Doris May
Yeboah-Afari, Ajoa V.

NOVELS/NOVELETTES

Adiaffi, Anne-Marie
Afonso, María Perpétua Candeias da Silva
Aidoo, Christina Ama Ata
Andria, Aimée
Bá, Mariama
Benskina, Princess Orelia
Bittari, Zoubeida
Boahemaa, Beatrice Yaa
Chaibi, Aïcha
Chédid Andrée
Dlovu, Nandi
Djebar, Assia
Dooh-Bunya, Lydie
Dreo, Pelandrova
Dube, Hope
El Saadawi, Nawal
Emecheta, Buchi
Fakunle-Onadeko, Olufunmilayo
Fonseca, Lília da
Futshane, Zora Z. T.
Gebru, Seneddn
Head, Bessie
Higiro, J.
Kakaza, Lillith
Kalimugogo, G.
Kaya, Simone
Kuoh-Moukoury, Thérèse
Lemsine, Aïcha

Likimani, Muthoni
Liking, Werewere
Mahuhusi, M. A.
Makura, Tendai
Mitchell, Elizabeth M.
Mkhombo, Joy Florence Chrestephene
Mugot, Hazel deSilva
Ncgcobo, Lauretta
Njau, Rebeka
Nwapa, Flora
Ogot, Grace A.
Okoye, Ifeoma
Olivesi, Djamila
Ovbiagele, Helen
Owino, Rosemarie
Rakotoson, Michele
Ramala, Maggie
Ratisfandrihamanana, Clarisse
Sebbar, Leila
Sikuade, Yemi
Sow Fall, Aminata
Taos-Amrouche, Marguerite
Tlali, Miriam
Tsogo, Delphine Zanya
Ulasi, Adoara Lily
Umelo, Rosina

POETRY

Abdullah, Nuru Binti
Abreu, Manuela de
Achebe, Christie Chinwe
Acholonu, Catherine
Addo, Joyce
Ademola, Frances
Aidoo, Christina Ama Ata
Akafia, Wotsa
Akello, Grace
Allotey, Alice
Almeida, Deolinda Rodriques de
Amegashie, Susan
Amrani, Daniele
Apio, Lydie M.
Asibong, Elizabeth E.
Attik, Mririda n'Ait
Avery, Greta
Ba, Oumar
Babukika, Justine
Bateyo, Juliet M.
Bishai, Nadia
Boitumelo
Bonny, Anne-Marie
Chedid, Andree
Chima, Simma
Chirwa, Nellie

Christie, Phillipa
Chukwuma, Helen
Coge, Maimuna Barmani
Datta, Soroj
Diakhate, Ndeye Coumba
Diamoneke, Cécile -Ivelyse
Djabali, Lelia
Djebar, Assia
Douts, Christine
Egbe, Pauline
Emecheta, Buchi
Eronini, Faustina Nwachi
Esan, Yetunde
Espírito Santo, Alda do
Faik-Nzuji, Clémentine Madiya
Fall, Kiné Kirama
Flora
Gashe, Marina
Githae, Madeleine
Githae-Mugo, Micere
Greki, Anna
Griffin, Mary Abena
Guendouz, Nadia
Gwaram, Hauwa
House, Amelia
Ibingira, Grace
Jordan, Nandi
Kahaku, Pauline W.
Kanie, Amona
Kaphwiyo, Josephine
Karanja, Paula
Karibo, Minji
Katsina, Binta
KaXhoba, Ntombiyakhe kaBiyela
Kgositsile, Baleka
Khaketla, Caroline N.M.R.
Khamadi, Miriam
Kichwa, Morena Halim
Kimenyi, Luci W.
King, Delphine
Kumah, Sylvie
Kurankyi-Taylor, Dorothy
Kwaku, Rosemary
Laluah, Acquah
Lara, Alda
Lima, Marie Eugénia
Lwanga, Susan
Mabuza, Lindiwe
Machel, Josina

Mackay, Ilva
Mai, Jeanne Ngo
Malafa, Efosi
Mall, Jasmine
Mandela, Zindzi
Maoka, Shimane
Margarido, Maria Manuela Conceicao Carvalho da
Marva, Ravi
Masekela, Barbara
Masembe, Harriet
Mashishi, Kedisaletse
Matenjwa, Christine
Matip, Marie-Claire
Matlou, Rebecca
M'Baye, Annette d'Erneville
Mbowa, Rose
Mhando, Blandina
Mhlongo, Maureen
Mohamedali, Hamida
Mokhoma, Makhokolotso
Mokorosi, Emely Semeleng
Morais, Dési
Morazzo, Yolanda
Moriti, Palesa
Morolo, Winnie
Mphahlele, Teresa K.
Mpongo, Marie-Eugénie
Mtungwa, Gloria
Mucavale, Joana Mateus
Mukwaya, Jean B.
Muntemba, Maude
Mutsila, Irene
Mvemve, Lindiwe
Mwakala, Maria
Nachale, Joana
Nakitwe, Angela N.
Nchwe, Manoko
Ndaaya, Citekù
Nene, Amélia
Ngatho, Stella
Nirina, Esther
Njau, Rebeka
Noronha, Lydie
Obi, Dorothy
Ogundipe-Leslie, Omolara
O'Lansen, Malika
Pererira-Emanuel, Francesca Yetunde
Phiri, Irene
Phungula, Nomusa Cynthia
Queen Hatshepsut

Riberiro, Mariana Marques
Roby, Maria Emilia
Rush, Brenda Utamu
Rwakyaya, Proscovia
Saad, Siti Binti
Sa'adu, A. B.
Schuaib, Yinka
Segun, Mabel I. J.
Sigwili, Nokugcina
Sousa, Noémia Carolina Abranches Soares de
Sutherland, Efua T. M.
Taos-Amrouche, Marguerite
Teage, Hilary
Télikò, Râhmatoullâhi
Tembe, Rosaria
Thomas, Gladys
Tlali, Sophia
Tol'Ande, Elisabeth Françoise Mweya
Veiga, Amelia
Wangeci, Agatha
Ware, Rebecca J. N.
Wheatley, Phillis
Williams, Daphne B. E.
Wilson, Beverly R.
Xavier, Emelinda Pereira
Zagbede, Josephine
Zelleke, Serk-Addis
Zinondo, Tokozile
Zirimu, Elvania N.

SHORT STORIES

'Abd Allāh, Sūfī
Achola
Ademola, Frances
Afonso, María Perpétua Candeias da Silva
Aidoo, Christina Ama Ata
Akello, Grace
Amarilis, Orlanda
Anthony, Monica
Attarah, Christina
Bunnūna, Khanāta
Casely-Hayford, Adelaide
Casely-Hayford, Gladys
Chédid, Andrée
Djebar, Assia
Dove-Danquah, Mabel
Dube, Violet

Faïk-Nzuji, Clémentine M.
Fonseca, Lília da
Githae, Madeleine
Head, Bessie
House, Amelia
Itayemi-Ogundipe, Phebean
Jabbeh, Patricia D. M.
Kalebu, Betty
Kalimugogo, G.
Kimenye, Barbara
Kiyingi, Elizabeth
Kokunda, Violet
Kwaku, Rosemary
Lara, Alda
Lobo, María Manuela de Sousa
Malaka, Maud
Mascarenhas, María Margarida
Mboni, Sarah
Mensah, Grace Osei
Mhelma, Marjorie
Mitchell, Elizabeth M.
Mokwena, Joan
Muli, Anne Keeru
Nabwire, Constance
Nakitwe, Angela Nashakoma
Ndegwa, Catherine D.
Ndele, Serena
Ndele, Susan
Njau, Rebeka
Noronha, Lydie
Nsanzubuhoro, Victoire
Nwagboso, Rosaline
Nwapa, Flora
Ogada, Penniah a.
Ogot, Grace A.
Olimba, Maude
Ponti-Lako, Agnes
Qutb, Amīna
Roberts, Maima
Rosemary, (pseudonym)
Segun, Mabel I. J.
Sello, Doris
Setidisho, Edith
Sibane, Nona
Siganga, Jenifer
Silva, María de Jesus Nunes da
Sumbane, Natala
Sutherland, Efua, T. M.
Thomas, Gladys
Tlali, Miriam
Tulay, Elizabeth Lovo Jallah

Urey-Ngara, Abigail
Wanjiru, L. Mumbi
Were, Jane
Were, Miriam Khamadi
Yeboah-Afari, Adjoa V.
Zirimu, Elvania N.

C

JOURNALISTS GROUPED BY COUNTRIES

CAMEROON

Kuoh-Moukoury, Thérèse
Nwigwe, Nkuku

EGYPT

Shafik, Doria

GHANA

Addo, Joyce Naa Odole
Amegashie, Susan
Dove-Danquah, Mabel, pseudonym Marjorie Mensah
Kwaku, Rosemary
Ohene, Elizabeth
Yeboah-Afari, Ajoa Victoria

GUINEA

Diallo, Assiatou

KENYA

Charles, Mou
Gethi, Angelina
Gitonga, Birgita
Kahiga, Miriam
Kiarie, Miriam
Majale, Irene
Matenjwa, Christine
Munene, Fibi
Mutai, Chelegit
Mwaura, Florence W.
Mwilu, Jane
Otieno, Evelyn
*Owano, Nancy
*Reggi, Mae Alice

LIBERIA

De Shield, Angela

MADAGASCAR

Raharijaona, Berthe

NIGERIA

Segun, Mabel Imoukhuede Jolaosa
Ulasi, Adaora Lily
Uwechue, Austua

SENEGAL

Kiangana, Keita
Kamara, Sylviane Diouf
Kutta, Sarah Kala-Lobe
M'Baye, Annette d'Erneville
Sanga, Aminatou

SIERRA LEONE

Ademu-John, Cecilia
Cole, Bernadette

SOUTH AFRICA

Morel, Marion
Ntantala, Phyllis
Tlali, Miriam

TANZANIA

Sheikh, Lelia

UGANDA

Katumba, Rebecca
Mbugua, Isabel

ZAIRE

Ngu, Murssa Naseka

ZAMBIA

Chite, Helen, pseudonym for Enid S. Sibajene
Ngulube, Clara

ZIMBABWE

Makwabarara, Angelina

EAST AFRICA

N'ska, Leci
Nsubuga, Edita
Nyate, Frances
Opondo, Diana
Urey-Ngara, Abigail

UNIDENTIFIED

Diamoneke, Cécile-Ivelyse
Gabba, Anna
Ibru, Emie
Sikaneta, Clara

D

FORTHCOMING WORKS

ADDO, JOYCE (Ghana)

"The Villa Kakalika" (novel)

EMECHETA, BUCHI (Nigeria)

"Head Above Water" (autobiography)

"Gwendolyn" (novel)

GITHAE-MUGO, MICERE (Kenya)

"Me Kitili" (play based upon the life of the Kenyan woman, Me Kitili)

with L. Wasambo Were. "A New Approach to The Teaching of Literature in Schools in Kenya," Nairobi: East African Publishing House,

M'BAYE, ANNETTTE D'ERNEVILLE (Senegal)

"La vaine pâture" (novel)

"La bague de cuivre et d'argent" (short story which won a prize by <u>Jeune Afrique</u>)

MUGOT, HAZEL DESLIVA (Seychelles)

"Sega of the Seychelles," Nairobi: East African Publishing House, (collection of folk poems).

NGATHO, STELLA (Kenya)

"Foresight Is Better Than Hindsight" (play based upon the author's experiences as a Speech Therapist in the Atlanta, Georgia Public School System)

"In Exile and Nostalgia" (poetry)

NWAPA, FLORA (Nigeria)

"Ona" (novel)

"She Died Laughing" (novel)

ODAGA, ASENATH BOLE (Kenya)

The Teaching of Oral Literature in Schools. Nairobi: East African Publishing House (critical work)

OGOT, GRACE AKINYI (Kenya)

"Ber Wat" [Luo novel].

"A loo kod Apol Apol" [Luo novel based on Luo myths and legends].

"Simbi Nyayima" [Luo novel based on Luo myths and legends].

OGUNDIPE-LESLIE, OMOLARA (Nigeria)

"Four Poems," An Anthology of Poetry by Nigerian Women Writers. Ed. Nina Mba.

"Soyinka's Ogun Abibimain," Critical Essays on Wole Soyinka, Ed. James Gibbs.

E

NON-AFRICAN WOMEN MARRIED TO AFRICAN MEN

AMOSU, MARGARET (Britain/Nigeria)

Bibliography

A Preliminary Bibliography of Creative Writing in the European Languages.
Ibadan: Institute of African Studies, University of Ibadan, 1964.

Creative African Writing in the European Langauges: A Preliminary Bibliography.
Ibadan: Bulletin of African Studies, University of Ibadan, 1965. 35 pages.

with O. Soyinka and E. O. Osunlana. 25 Years of Medical Research, 1948-1973.
A List of Papers Published by Past and Present Members of the Faculty of Medicine at the University of Ibadan and Its Foundation to November 1973.
Ibadan: Medical Library, University of Ibadan, 1973. 184 pages.

APPIAH, PEGGY (Britain/Ghana)

Children's Literature

Ananse the Spider: Tales from an Ashanti Village. New York: Pantheon,
1966. 152 pages, illus.

Tales of an Ashanti Father. London: Deutsch, 1967. 157 pages, illus.

The Children of Ananse. Evans Children's Library. London: Evans, 1968.
176 pages, illus.

The Pineapple Child and Other Tales from the Ashanti. London: Deutsch,
1969. 137 pages, illus.

The Lost Ear-Ring. Evans English Readers. London: Evans, 1971. 14 pages, illus.

A Smell of Onions. London: Longman, 1971. 84 pages; rpt. Washington, DC: Three
Continents Press, 1979.

Gift of the Mmoatia. Accra: Ghana Publishing Corporation, 1972. 110 pages, illus.

Why There Are So Many Roads. African Junior Series. Lagos: Pilgrim, 1972.
62 pages, illus.

Ring of Gold. London: Deutsch, 1976. 157 pages.

A Dirge Too Soon. Tema: Ghana Publishing Corporation, 1976. 181 pages.

Why The Hyena Does Not Care for Fish, and Other Tales from the Ashanti Gold Weights. London: Deutsch, 1977. 77 pages, illus.

Critical Essay

"Akan Symbolism," African Arts, 13, 1 (1979), 64-7.

BANKS-HENRIES, A. DORIS (USA/Liberia)

Biography

Heroes and Heroines of Liberia. New York: Macmillan, 1962. 42 pages, illus.

More about Heroes and Heroines of Liberia. Monrovia: n. p., n.d. 66 pages, illus.

Presidents of the First African Republic. London: Macmillan, 1963. 102 pages.

A Biography of President William V. S. Tubman. London: Macmillan, 1967. 180 pages.

Critical Essays/Works

Civics for Liberian Schools. London: John Corah & Son, 1954. 120 pages.

Africa: Our History. New York: Colilier-Macmillan International, 1969. 180 pages.

Liberia's Fulfillment: Achievements of the Republic of Liberia during the Twenty-Five Years under the Administration of President William V. S. Tubman, 1944-1969. Monrovia: Banks, 1969. 213 pages.

The Role of the Woman in Africa's Evolution. Monrovia: Henries, 1971. 36 pages.

Higher Education in Liberia. Monrovia: Curriculum and Materials Center, Department of Education, 1971. 49 pages.

"Survey of Liberian Literature," Liberian Writing: Liberia as Seen by Her Own Writers as well as by German Authors. Tubingen: Erdmann, 1970, pp. 7-42.

"Message from the President of the Society of Liberian Authors," KAAFA, 1, 1 (1971), 7-16.

"Liberian Poets and Their Poems," Towards the Study of Liberian Literature: An Anthology of Critical Essays on the Literature of Liberia. Ed. S. Henry Cordor. Monrovia: Liberian Literature Studies Programme, 1972, pp. 73-5.

"One Hundred and Fifty Years of Liberian Literature," <u>KAAFA</u>, 2, 1 (1972), 13-21; rpt. <u>Towards the Study of Liberian Literature: An Anthology of Critical Essays on the Literatue of Liberia.</u> Ed. S. Henry Cordor. Monrovia: Liberian Literature Studies Programme, 1972, pp. 53-60.

"Writing and Problems of Writers in Liberia;" "Some Aspects of Liberian Literature;" <u>Towards the Study of Liberian Literature: An Anthology of Critical Essays on the Literature of Liberia.</u> Ed. S. Henry Cordor. Monrovia: Liberian Literature Studies Programme, 1972, pp. 135-38, 141-43.

<u>Writing of A. Doris Banks Henries.</u> Bedford, New York: African Imprint Library Services, 1973 (one reel).

"Liberian Literature," <u>KAAFA</u>, 4, 1 (1974), 1-9.

"Black Cultural Identity," <u>Présence Africaine</u>, (1977), 101-2, 119-28.

Folklore

<u>Liberian Folklore: A Compilation of Ninety-Nine Folktales with Some Proverbs.</u> London: Macmillan, 1966. 152 pages.

Poetry

<u>Poems of Liberia (1838-1961).</u> London: Macmillan, 1963. 113 pages ,Editor..

"Poems," <u>Poems of Liberia 1838-1961).</u> London: Macmillan, 1963, pp. 86-114.

"Pageant of Modern Africa," <u>Présence Africaine</u>, No. 57 (1966), 335-36.

KITONGA, ELLEN (USA/Kenya)

with Jonathan Kariara. <u>An Introduction to East African Poetry.</u> Nairobi: Oxford University Press, 1976.

<u>A Study Guide to John Ruganda's Play "The Burdens."</u> London: Heinemann, 1980.

LIBONDO, JEANNE NGO (USA/Cameroon)

Children's Literature

<u>Joseph, Haven't You Got Your Bicycle Yet?</u> Heinemann Secondary Reading Scheme. London: Heinemann, 1973. 57 pages, illus. (a play).

Published Play

"Oh, How Dearly I Detest Three," Nine African Plays for Radio. Ed. Gwyneth Henderson and Cosmo Pieterse. London: Heinemann, 1973, pp. 87-104.

MBA, NINA (Australia/Nigeria)

Poetry

"Turn Again," Okike, No. 17 (1980), 34.

"An Anthology of Poetry by Nigerian Women Writers," (A forthcoming edited collection of poetry).

MBILINYI, MARJORIE (USA/Tanzania)

Critical Essay

"The 'New Woman' and Traditional Norms in Tanzania," Journal of Modern African Studies, 10, 1 (1972), 57-72.

Short Story

"A Woman's Life," Ghala, 9, 1 (1972), 31-5; rpt. Fragment from a Lost Diary and Other Stories: Women of Asia, Africa, and Latin America. Ed. Naomi Katz and Nancy Milton. Boston: Beacon Press, 1973, pp. 254-64.

NETO, MARIA EUGENIA (Portugal/Angola)

Children's Literature

E nas Florestas os Bichos Falaram. 3rd. edition. Luanda: União dos Escritos Angolanos, 1978 (Collection of short stories for children).

A Formaçao de uma Estrela e Outras Históricas na Terra. Lisboa: Edicoes 70, 1979. 68 pages (Collection of short stories for children).

As Nossas Mãos Constroem a Liberdade. Lisboa: Edicoes 70, 1979. 66 pages (collection of short stories for children).

A Lenda das Asas da Menina Mestiça-Flor. Luanda: Cadernos Lavra & Oficina, 35, 1981. 45 pages.

Poetry

"Jinga Mbandi, Primeira Guerrilheiro," Angola, Cultura e Revolução, caderno no. 3 Algers: Centro de Estudos Angolanos, 1966.

Foi Esperanca e Foi Certeza. Lisboa: Edicoes 70, 1979. 73 pages

Short Story

"Ngangula," Femmes du monde entier

OLUDHE-MACGOYE, MARJORIE (Britain/Kenya)

Children's Literature

Growing Up at Lima School. East Africa Senior Library. Nairobi: East African Publishing House, 1971. 77 pages, illus.

Journalistic Essay

"It Still Has A Meaning," Viva, 6, 12 (1980), 26.

Letter

"Family Planning for African Women," East Africa Journal, 4, 6 (1967), 5-6 (Letter in response to a Grace Ogot article on family planning).

Novel

Murder in Majengo. Nairobi: Oxford University Press, 1972. 138 pages.

Poetry

"A Song of Advent;" "Sleeping Beauty;" East Africa Journal, 5, 7 (1968), 36.

"Ultimatum," East Africa Journal, 6, 1 (1969), 43-7.

"Freedom Song," East Africa Journal, 6, 1 (1969), 14; rpt. Poems from East Africa. Ed. David Cook and David Rubadiri. London: Heinemann, 1976, pp. 134-45; rpt. Aftermath: An Anthology of Poems in English from Africa Asia and the Caribbean. Ed. Robert Weaver and Joseph Bruchac. Greenfield: Greenfield Review Press, 1977, pp. 28-9; rpt. Attachments to the Sun. Ed. Douglas Blackburn, Alfred Horsfall and Chris Wanjala. London: Edward Arnold, 1978, p. 28.

"Barn Dance-Kenya Style;" "Apollo 13: or No Getting Away from It;" Zuka, 5 (1970), 39-41.

"Letter to a Friend;" "Song of Kisumu;" <u>Ghala</u>, 8, 1 (1970), 17-20.

"A Working Sonnet;" "Why?;" "Home;" <u>Zuka</u>, 6 (1972), 17-8.

"For Miriam;" "A Freedom Song;" "Letter to A Friend;" <u>An Introduction to East African Poetry</u>. Ed. Jonathan Kariara and Ellen Kitonga. Nairobi: Oxford University Press, 1976, pp. 39-44, 49-51, 76-86 (with notes).

<u>Song of Nyarloka and Other Poems</u>. Naiobi: Oxford University Press, 1977.

Short Stories

"Homecoming," <u>East Africa Journal</u>, 3, 10 (1967), 23-5.

"The Day of the Year," <u>Zuka</u>, No. 4 (1969), 12-7.

"Ultimatum," <u>East Africa Journal</u>, 6, 1 (1969), 43-7.

"The Frontier," <u>JOE</u>, June 1976, pp. 14-5.

UWEMEDIMO, ROSEMARY (USA/Nigeria)

Children's Literature

<u>Mammy-Wagon Marriage</u>. London: Hurst & Blackett, 1961.

<u>Akpan and the Smugglers</u>. Lagos: African Universities Press, 1965. 78 pages.

F

NON-AFRICAN WOMEN JOURNALISTS MARRIED TO KENYAN MEN

OWANO, NANCY (USA/Kenya)

"Marriage Bill Stirs Up Storm in Kenya," Africa Woman, No. 7 (1976), 54-5.

"Music and Drama," Africa Woman, No. 8 (1977), 54-5.

"Mini Debate on a Maxi Issue," Africa Woman, No. 12 (1977), 45.

"Listening to the Problems," Sunday Nation, 16 August 1981, p. 19.

REGGI, MAE ALICE (USA/Kenya)

"Are You a Week-End Wife?," The Daily Nation, 4 July 1979, p. 13.

Both women write for the newspaper, "The Daily Nation" in Nairobi, Kenya.

G

NON-AFRICAN WOMEN WRITERS PUBLISHED BY AFRICAN PUBLISHERS

HUNTER, CYNTHIA (Britain)

Children's Literature

Truphena, City Nurse. Nairobi: East African Publishing House, 1974. 20 pages, illus.

Anna the Air Hostess. East Africa Senior Library. Nairobi: East African Publishing House, 1967. 109 pages.

The Speck of Gold and Other Stories. East African Readers Library. Nairobi: East African Publishing House, 1968. 52 pages, illus.

Truphena, Student Nurse. East African Senior Library. Nairobi: East African Publishing House, 117 pges, illus.

Pamela the Probation Officer. Nairobi: East African Publishing House, 1971. 144 pages.

Animal Families. Nairobi: East African Publishing House, n.d. 95 pages.

"The Fairy Wedding," The Standard, 7 August 1981, p. 14.

MUTHONI, SUSIE (Britain)

Children's Literature

Florence, the Blue Flamingo. Nairobi: East African Publishing House, 1973. 18 pages.

The Hippo Who Couldn't Stop Crying. Nairobi: East African Publishing House, n.d. 15 pages; Swahili translation: Kiboko Mlizi. Nairobi: East African Publishing House, n.d. 24 pages.

PIERCE, JACQUELINE (USA/Tanzania)

Novel

bamanga. Nairobi: East African Publishing House, 1974. 166 pages.

Leopard in a Cage. Nairobi: East African Publishing House, 1976. 232 pages.

H

BIOGRAPHICAL BOOKS ON AFRICAN WOMEN

BABA OF KORO (Nigeria)

Smith, Mary K. Baba of Koro: A Woman of the Muslim Hausa. Intr. M. G. Smith. London: Faber and Faber, 1954. 254 pages; French Translation: Baba de Koro: l'autobiographie d'une musulmane Hausa du Nigeria. Paris: Plon, 1969. 354 pages.

"Baba of Koro," Growing Up. Ed. Deborah Manley. Lagos: African Universities Press, 1967.

POPPIE (South Africa)

Joubert, Elsa. Poppie. London: Hodder and Stroughton, 1980. 359 pages.

MARIA THOLO (South Africa)

Hermer, Carol. The Diary of Maria Tholo. Johannesburg: Ravan Press, 1979. 200 pages.

———. "The Diary of Maria Tholo — Friday, September 17," Staffrider, 3, 3 (1980), 26-7.

I

AFRICAN WOMEN'S MAGAZINES

AFRICA WOMAN (London)

AFRICAN WOMAN (London, now defunct)

AMINA, le magazine de la femme sénégalaise (Dakar)

AWA, la revue de la femme noire, now defunct and formerly edited by Annette M'Baye

LA FEMME EGYYPTIENNE, now defunct (Cairo)

LA FEMME ET L'ISLAM (Cairo)

LE FEMME NOUVELLE (Cairo)

MARIEMOU, revue de le jeune fille et de la femme mauritaniennes (Nouachott)

MWASI (Lomé)

VIVA (Nairobi)

WOMEN'S WORLD (Lagos, formerly edited by Adaora Lily Ulasi)

Special Note:

NEW AFRICAN (London) now has a special section on African women since 1980.

STAFFRIDER (Johannesburg) now has a special section for African women since 1979.

ADDENDUM

CHILDREN'S LITERATURE

ADDO, JOYCE (Ghana)

The Kube Family: The New House. Accra: Educational Press, 1981. 32 pages.

The Kube Family: Rikki and Toli. Accra: Educational Press, 1981. 32 pages.

CAVALLY, JEANNE DE (Ivory Coast)

Papi. Abidjan: Les Nouvelles Editions Africaines, 1978. 32 pages.

Pouê-Pouê le petit cabri. Abidjan: Les Nouvelles Editions Africaines, 1981. 24 pages.

Le Réveillon de Boubacar. Abidjan: Les Nouvelles Editions Africaines, 1981. 16 pages.

FAKUNLE - ONADEKO, OLUFUNMILAYO (Nigeria)

Where is the Princess? Lagos: Heinemann Educational Books, 1980. 36 pages.

MENIRU, THERESA (Nigeria)

The Drums of Joy. London: Macmillan, 1982. 96 pages.

NWAPA, FLORA (Nigeria)

Journey to Space. Enugu: Tana Press, 1980. 20 pages.

OWUSU - NIMOH, MERCY (Ghana)

The Walking Calabash. Accra: Ghana Publishing Corporation, 1977. 70 pages.

Stories of Kafizee. Accra: Ghana Publishing Corporation, 1979. 55 pages.

NOVELS

DLOVU, NANDI (South Africa)

Angel of Death. Macmillan Pacesetters. London: Macmillan Education, 1982. 124 pages.

DREO, PELANDROVA (Madagascar)

Pelandrova. Paris: L'Harmattan, 1976. 400 pages.

DUBE, HOPE (Zimbabwe)

State Secret. Macmillan Pacesetters. London: Macmillan Education, 1981. 138 pages.

EMECHETA, BUCHI (Nigeria)

Naira Power. Macmillan Pacesetters. London: Macmillan Education, 1982. 108 pages.

The Rape of Shavi. London: Ogwugwu Afor Co., Ltd., 1984.

KALIMUGOGO, G. T. (Kenya)

The Prodigal Chairman. Nairobi: Uzima Press, 1980. 195 pages.

Pilgrimage to Nowhere. Nairobi: Uzima Press, 1982. 160 pages.

OVBIAGELE, HELEN (Nigeria)

Evbu My Love. Macmillan Pacesetters. London: Macmillan Education, 1982. 180 pages.

You Never Know. Macmillan Pacesetters. London: Macmillan Education, 1982. 116 pages.

A Fresh Start. Macmillan Pacesetters. London: Macmillan Education, n.d.

NOVELS

SIKUADE, YEMI (Nigeria)

Sisi. Macmillan Pacesetters. London: Macmillan Education, n.d.

UMELO, ROSINA (West Africa)

Felicia. Macmillan Pacesetters. London: Macmillan Education, 1978.
    128 pages.

WEREWERE, LIKING (Cameroon)

Elle sera de Jaspe et de Corail. (Journal d'une Misovire). Abidjan: n.p.,
    n.d. 144 pages.

A la rencontre de... Abidjan: Les Nouvelles Editions Africaines, 1981.
    146 pages.

PUBLISHED PLAYS

WEREWERE, LIKING (Cameroon)

La Puissance d'um. Abidjan: CEDA, 1980. 63 pages.

Une Nouvelle terre. Abidjan: Nouvelles Editions Africaines, 1980. 92 pages.

POETRY

OGUNDIPE-LESLIE, OMOLARA (Nigeria)

Sew the Old Days and Other Poems. Lagos: Evans, 1982. 44 pages.

FOLKLORE

ODAGA, ASENATH BOLE (Kenya)

The Tindai: Stories from Kenya. Nairobi: Uzima Press, 1980. 137 pages.

SEYDOU AMADU, CHRISTIANE (West Africa)

La Geste de Ham-Bodêdio ou Hama le Rouge. Classiques Africains, 18. Paris: Armand Colin, 1975.

Contes et fables des vieillées. Paris: Nubia, 1976. 300 pages.

JUVENILE LITERATURE

KIMENYE, BARBARA (Uganda)

The Gemstone Affair. London: Oxford University Press, n.d.

The Scoop. London: Oxford University Press, n.d.

CRITICAL ESSAYS/WORKS

EMECHETA, BUCHI (Nigeria)

"Introduction and Comments," Our Own Freedom. London: Sheba Feminist Publishers, 1981. 111 pages.

"That First Novel," Kunapipi, 3, 2 (1981), 115-23.

"A Nigerian Writer Living in London," Kunapipi, 4, 1 (1982), 114-23.

POST-ADDENDUM*

AUTOBIOGRAPHY/BIOGRAPHY

NYONDO, FLORENCE   (ZAMBI)

The Cold Hand of Death. Lusaka: Multimedia Publications, 1982. 79 pages.

CHILDREN'S LITERATURE

VORMAWOR, PATIENCE O.   (GHANA)

Afua and the Magic Calabash. Accra: Adwinsa Publications, 1983. 14 pages.

WIREDU, ANOKYE   (GHANA)

The Adventures of Dabodabo Akosua. Accra: Adwinsa Publications, 1981. 16 pages.

JUVENILE LITERATURE

KIMENYE, BARBARA   (UGANDA)

The Gemstone Affair. Nairobi: Thomas Nelson, 1978. 72 pages.

The Scoop. Nairobi: Thomas Nelson, 1978. 69 pages.

NOVELS/NOVELETTES

BERTHELOT, LILIAN   (MAURITIUS)

Le participe futur. Port-Louis: Père Vaval, n.d.

CHEYNET, ANNE   (MAURITIUS)

Les muselés. Paris: L'Harmattan, 1977. 159 pages.

DIALLO, NAFISSATOU   (SENEGAL)

Le fort maudit. Monde noir poche, 6. Paris: Hatier, 1980. 125 pages.

FAKUNLE-ONADEKO, FUNMILAYO   (NIGERIA)

Chasing the Shadow. Oshogbo: Fakunle Major Press, 1980. 151 pages.

*The citations for the post-addendum are not included in the index

HUMBERT, MARIE-THERESE   (MAURITIUS)

A l'autre bout de moi.   Paris: Stock, 1979. 468 pages.

JACQUEMARD, SIMONNE   (MOROCCO)

Lalla Zahra. Paris: Seuil, 1983. 187 pages.

JOHNEVI, ETA   (GHANA)

Roses for Sondia.   Accra: Johnevi Publishers, 1973. 208 pages.

KUOH-MOUKOURI, THERESE   (CAMEROON)

Rencontres essentielles: roman. Adamawa, Cameroon: Imprimerie Edgar, 1969. 127 pages.

NDIAYE, ADJA NDEYE BOURY   (SENEGAL)

Collier de cheville. Dakar: Les Nouvelles Editions Africaines, 1983. 159 pages

NWAKOBY, MARTINA AWELE   (NIGERIA)

A Lucky Chance. Ibadan: Macmillan, 1980. 96 pages.

A House Divided. Enugu: Fourth Dimensions, 1981. 184 pages.

OKOLO, EMMA   (NIGERIA)

The Blood of Zimbabwe. Enugu: Fourth Dimension Publishing Company, 1979. 160 pages.

No Easier Road. Enugu: Fourth Dimensions Publishing Company, 1981. 176 pages.

RATSITOHAINA, HARISATA   (MADAGASCAR)

Je ne savais pas...Paris: T.M.T., 1969. 140 pages.

SHORT STORIES

GITHAE-MUGO, MICERE   (KENYA)

"A Self-Help Campaign," Busara, 7, 1 (1975), 1-11.

HEAD, BESSIE   (SOUTH AFRICA/BOTSWANA)

"Tao," Freedomways, 7, 1 (1967), 26-32.

MAMI, LAYLA (TUNISIA)

Saw-ma'a Tahtariq (The Minaret in Flames). Tunis: Dar Al-Kutub Al-Sharkiyyah 1968.

SIGWILI, NOKUNGCINA (SOUTH AFRICA)

"My Dear Madam...," Staffrider, 3, 1 (1980), 44.

THAMIR, NAJIA (SYRIA/TUNISIA)

Aradnā Al-Hayāt (We Wanted Life). Tunis: Dār Al-Kutub As-Sharquiyya, n.d.

Samar Wa 'Ibar (Oral and Moral Evening Tales). Tunis: Dar Al-Kutub As-Sharquiyya, 1972.

PUBLISHED PLAYS

DUBE, HOPE (SOUTH AFRICA)

The Great Flood. Cape Town: Maskew Miller, 1982. 39 pages.

LIKING, WEREWERE (CAMEROON)

Une nouvelle terre. Du sommeil d'injuste. Théâtre-Rituel. Dakar: Les Nouvelles Editions Africaines, 1980, pp. 15-49; 50-92.

NJOYA, RABIATOU (CAMEROON)

Toute la rente y passe. Ange noir, angle blanc. CLE Theatre, 13. Yaoundé: C.L. n.d. 11 pages et 24 pages.

PERFORMED PLAYS

LEMOINE, JOY (NIGERIA)

"Spring '81 A One Woman Play," London, 1982

OGOT, GRACE AKINYI (KENYA)

"Miahe," Reunion Cultural Group, Kisumu, Kenya, 28 December 1981-1 January 198 (A play adapted by Asenath Odaga in Luo from The Promised Land)

POETRY

ANDRIA, AIMEE   (MADAGASCAR)

L'Année en fleurs. Paris: Edition de la Revue Moderne, 1973. 55 pages.

BACHIR, ZOUBEIDA   (TUNISIA)

Hanĭn (Nostalgia). Tunis: MTE, 1968.

BERTHELOT, LILIAN   (MAURITIUS)

Intemporelles. Port-Louis: Edition Chien de Plomb, 1973.

DJOUPE, MARTINE   (CAMEROON)

Terre dessechée. Bofoussam, Cameroon: La Librairie Populaire, 1979. 28 pages.

KANGETHE, NJERI   (KENYA)

"A Boss's Prayer," Viva, March 1983, p. 32.

LIKING, WEREWERE   (CAMEROON)

On ne raisonne pas avec le venin-poèmes. Paris: St. Germain-des-Près, 1977. 64 pages.

NWANODI, GRACE OKOGBULE   (NIGERIA)

Icheke and Other Poems. Ibadan: Mbari Publications, 1964.

FOLKLORE

ODAGA, ASENATH   (KENYA)

The Tinda. Nairobi: Uzima Press, 1980. 137 pages.

BOOK REVIEWS BY AUTHORS

OGOT, GRACE AKINYI (KENYA)

"Flora Nwapa's Efuru," East Africa Journal, 3, 7 (1966), 38-9.

CONFERENCE PAPERS/SPEECHES

ODAGA, ASENATH (KENYA)

"Writing for Children: A Personal Observation," East African Community, Nairobi, Kenya, 5 December 1982.

CRITICAL ESSAYS/WORKS

BA, MARIAMA (SENEGAL)

"La fonction politique des littératures africaines écrites," Ecriture française, 3, 5 (1981), 5.

CHABAKU, MOTLALEPULA (SOUTH AFRICA)

"Growing Up in the Era of the Pass Laws," MS, November 1982, pp. 67-8.

GACHUKIA, EDDAH (KENYA)

Notes on Ngugi wa Thiong'o "The River Between." Nairobi: Heinemann Educational Books, 1976. 32 pages.

"Chinua Achebe and Tradition," Standpoints on African Literature: A Critical Anthology. Ed. Chris Wanjala . Nairobi: East African Literature Bureau, 1973, pp. 172-87.

GITHAE-MUGO, MICERE (KENYA)

"Children's Literature in Kenya," East African Literature: An Anthology. Ed. Arne Zettersten. London: Longman, 1983, pp. 206-11.

KITAMBI, BERNADETTE (TANZANIA)

Hadithi Zetu. Dar-es-Salaam: Tanzania Publishing House, n.d.

MUDIMBE-BOYI, MBULAMWANZA   (ZAIRE)

L'Oeuvre romanesque de Jacques-Stephen Alexis. Ecrivain haitien. Lubumbashi: Editions du Mont-Noir, 1975. 128 pages.

OLUDHE-MACGOYE, MARJORIE   (BRITAIN/KENYA)

"Socialism in the Kitchen," East Africa Journal, 3, 7 (1966), 17-21.

JOURNALISTIC ESSAYS

KGOSITSILE, BALEKA   (SOUTH AFRICA)

"Women's Struggle in South Africa," Viva, April 1983, pp. 16-9.

MATENJWA, WANJIKU   (KENYA)

"Why Women Allow Themselves To Be Used," Viva, June 1982, pp. 8, 11-2.

MBUGUA, ISABEL   (KENYA)

"The World Should Know the Incredible Contribution Our Race Has Made to History --An Exclusive Interview with Cicely Tyson-Davis," Viva, February 1982, pp. 14-7.

"Why Abortions Take Tragic Tolls," Viva, April 1982, pp. 16-8.

"Men and Women on 'Liberation'," Viva, May 1982, pp. 12-5.

"What It Means To Be Fat," Viva, June 1982, pp. 22-3.

MUNENE, FIBI   (KENYA)

"Feelings on Family Planning," Africa Woman, January/February 1982, pp. 48-9.

INTERVIEWS

Kiba, Simon. "Aminata Sow Fall: son second roman est présélectionné pour le Goncourt," Awoura, octobre 1979, pp. 16-7.

CRITICISM OF AUTHORS' WORKS

BA, MARIAMA (SENEGAL)

Anon. "Mariama Bâ prix Noma 1980: écho des voix féminines de détresse," Le Soleil, 13 juin 1980, p. 2.

Dia, Alioune Toure. "Succès littéraire de Mariama Bâ pour son livre: Une si longue lettre," Amina, janvier 1979.

Makward, Edris. "The Pursuit of Happiness in the Novels of Mariama Bâ," African Literature Association Conference, University of Maryland at Baltimore, Catonsville, Maryland, April 14, 1984. 18 pages.

BACHIR, ZOUBEIDA (TUNISIA)

Samir, Ayadi. "Une Alice au pays des poèmes," La Presse, 30 June 1968.

DIKE, FATIMA (SOUTH AFRICA)

Barnett, Ursula A. A Vision of Order. A Study of Black South African Literature in English (1914-1980). Amherst: University of Massachusetts, 1983, pp. 240, 242-43, 246.

DJEBAR, ASSIA (ALGERIA)

Mortimer, Mildred P. "Female Space in African Fiction: Assia Djebar and Mariama Bâ," African Literature Association Conference, University of Maryland at Baltimore, Catonsville, Maryland, April 13, 1984.

Dejeux, Jean. Assia Djebar, romancière algérienne, cinéaste arabe. Sherbrooke: Editions Naaman, 1984. 120 pages.

EMECHETA, BUCHI (NIGERIA)

Bazin, Nancy Topping. "Feminist Perspectives in African Fiction: Bessie Head and Buchi Emecheta," African Literature Association Conference, University of Maryland at Baltimore, Catonsville, Maryland, April 12, 1984.

Davies, Wendy. "Two Nigerian Women Writers," Centrepoint," 3, 9 (1981).

Umeh, Marie. "Reintegration with the Lost Self: A Study of Buchi Emecheta's Double Yoke," African Literature Association Conference, University of Maryland at Baltimore, Catonsville, Maryland, April 12, 1984.

HEAD, BESSIE (SOUTH AFRICA)

Barnett, Ursula A. A Vision of Order. A Study of Black South African Literature in English (1914-1980). Amherst: University of Massachusetts, 1983, pp. 25, 26, 39, 119-26, 191, 198-203, 269.

Imfeld, Al. "Portraits of African Writers," Deutsche Welle Transcript No. 3 (1979), 9.

Moorsam, Sarah. "No Bars to Expression," New Society, 19 February 1981, p. 35.

LIKING, WEREWERE (CAMEROON)

Anon. "In Search of a New Aesthetic Theatre: Liking Werewere," Afrika (Munich), 20, 5 (1979), 25-6.

Hourantier, Marie-José. "Introduction," Une nouvelle terre. Du sommeil d'injuste. Dakar: Les Nouvelles Editions Africaines, 1980, pp. 7-12.

SOW FALL, AMINATA (SENEGAL)

Anon. "Aminata Sow Fall: La grève des battu," Afrique-Nouvelle, 1-7 août 1979.

Anon. "Huit questions à Aminata Sow Fall," Le Soleil, 20 juin 1979.

Gérard, Albert and Jeannine Laurent. "Sembène's Progeny: A New Trend in the Senegalese Novel," Studies in Twentieth Century Literature, 4, 2 (1980), 135-45.

TLALI, MIRIAM (SOUTH AFRICA)

Barnett, Ursula A. A Vision of Order. A Study of Black South African Literature in English (1914-1980). Amherst: University of Massachusetts, 1983, pp. 39, 157-63, 191.

ULASI, ADORA LILY (NIGERIA)

Taiwo, Oladele. Culture and the Nigerian Novel. New York: St. Martin's Press, 1976, pp. 45-52.

BOOK REVIEWS OF AUTHORS' WORKS

CAVALLY, JEANNE DE (IVORY COAST)

Pouê-Pouê le petit cabri. Abidjan: Les Nouvelles Editions Africaines, n.d.

    Nancy Schmidt. The African Book Publishing Record, 2-3 (1983), 119-20.

Le reveillon de Boubacar. Abidjan: Les Nouvelles Editions Africaines, n.d.

    Nancy Schmidt. The African Book Publishing Record, 2-3 (1983), 120.

DUBE, HOPE (SOUTH AFRICA)

The Great Flood. Cape Town: Maskew Miller, 1982. 39 pages.

    Josette C. Hollenbeck. The African Book Publishing Record, 4 (1983), 192.

JACQUEMARD, SIMONNE (MOROCCO)

Lalla Zahra. Paris: Seuil, 1983. 187 pages.

    J.D. Gauthier. World Literature Today, 58, 2 (1984), 312-13.

KIMENYE, BARBARA (UGANDA)

The Gemstone Affair. Nairobi: Thomas Nelson, 1978. 72 pages.

    Esther Y. Smith. The African Book Publishing Record, 8, 1 (1982), 11.

The Scoop. Nairobi: Thomas Nelson, 1978. 69 pages.

    Esther Y. Smith. The African Book Publishing Record, 8, 1 (1982), 11.

OGOT, GRACE AKINYI (KENYA)

The Graduate. Nairobi: Uzima Press, 1980. 58 pages.

    Ursula Edmonds. The African Book Publishing Record, 8, 3 (1982), 132.

SOFOLA, ZULU (NIGERIA)

Old Wines Are Tasty: A Play. Ibadan: Ibadan University Press, 1981. 58 pages.

Patrick Greig Scott. The African Book Publishing Record, 8, 2 (1982), 64-5.

SOW FALL, AMINATA   (SENEGAL)

L'Appel des arènes. Dakar: Les Nouvelles Editions Africaines, 1982. 144 pages.

Frederic Michelman. World Literature Today, 58, 1 (1984), 153-54.

COMMENTARY

JORDAN, NONTANDI   (SOUTH AFRICA)

Barnett, Ursula A. A Vision of Order. A Study of Black South African Literature in English (1914-1980). Amherst: University of Amherst Press, 1983, pp. 218, 220, 222.

ODAGA, ASENATH   (KENYA)

Alot, Magaga. "What Children Are Reading," Viva, March 1982, pp. 53-4.

TRANSLATION

ATTIK, MRIRIDA N'AIT   (MOROCCO)

Fernea, Elizabeth Warnock. "Women's Songs from the Berber Mountains of Morocco," Middle Eastern Women Speak Out. Eds. Elizabeth Warnack Fernea and Basima Qattan Bezirgan. Austin: University of Texas Press, 1977, pp. 127-35.

M'RABET, FADELA   (ALGERIA)

Fernea, Elizabeth Warnock. "Excerpts from Les Algériennes by Fadēla M'rabet, Modern Algerian Journalist," in Middle Eastern Muslim Women Speak Out. Eds. Elizabeth Warnock Fernea and Basima Qattan Bezirgan. Austin: The University of Texas Press, 1977, pp. 319-58.

INDEX

A

'AFD ALLAH SUFI   4, 26, 126, 205, 225

ABADA, ESSOMBA ROSE   89, 205, 220

ABDULLAH, NURU BINTI   49, 204, 222

ABREU, MANUELA DE CONCEICAO   49, 215, 222

ACHEBE, CHRISTIE CHINWE   49, 89, 210, 222

ACHOLA   26, 215, 225

ACHOLONU, CATHERINE   49, 210, 222

ACQUAH, BARBARA   4, 40, 187, 206, 217

ADDO, DORA YACOBA   4, 187, 206

ADDO, JOYCE NAA ODOLE   46, 49, 86, 112, 126, 187, 206, 218, 220, 222, 228, 231, 244

ADDO, PATIENCE HENAKU   40, 46, 126, 206, 217, 218

ADEMOLA, FRANCES   26, 49, 89, 126, 157, 187, 220, 222, 225

ADEMU-JOHN, CECILIA   104, 229

ADIAFFI, ANNE-MARIE   157, 207, 221

AFONSO, MARIA PERPETUA CANDEIAS DE SILVA   18, 26, 126, 187, 204, 221, 225

AGADIZI, ANNA   4, 187, 206

AIDOO, CHRISTINA AMA ATA   18, 26-7, 40, 49-50, 86, 89, 101, 113, 119, 126-30, 157-58, 177, 183, 187, 206, 217, 220, 221, 222, 225

AIGGOKHAI, JOSEPHINE   14, 188, 210, 219

AJOSE, AUDREY   4, 188, 210

AKAFIA, WOTSA   50, 213, 222

AKELLO, GRACE   27, 50, 158, 213, 222, 225

AKPABOT, ANNE   4, 188, 209

AL-HASAN, SUSAN   77, 188, 206, 218

ALIFAIJO, MARGARET   97, 215, 220

ALLOTEY, ALICE   51, 206, 222

ALMEIDA, DEOLINDA RODRIQUES FRANCISCO DE   51, 204, 222

AMARILIS, ORLANDA   27-8, 205, 225

AMEGASHIE, SUSAN   51, 104, 206, 222, 228

AMOOTI, BEATRICE TINKAMANYIRE   77, 215, 218

AMOSU, MARGARET   233

AMRANI, DANIELE   51, 204, 222

AMROUCHE, FADHMA AITH MANSOUR   1, 113, 130, 204

AMROUCHE, MARIE-LOUISE or MARGUERITE AMROUCHE TAOS   77, 188, 204, 218

ANDRIA, AIMEE   18, 188, 209, 221

ANIZOBA, ROSE   4, 188, 210

ANKRAH, EFUA   4, 188, 206

ANSELM (SISTER)   97, 213, 220

ANTHONY, MONICA   28, 188, 212, 225

ANTIRI, JANET ADWOA   77, 206, 219

ANYANGWE, GLADYS NGWI   79, 205, 219

ANYIKO, GRACE   104, 207

APIO, LYDIE M.   51, 215, 222

APOKO, ANNA   1, 5, 213

APPIAH, PEGGY   77, 206, 233-34

ASHERI, JEDIDA   5, 188, 205

ASIBONG, ELIZABETH   51, 177, 210, 222

ATTARAH, CHRISTINE   28, 211, 225

ATTIK, MRIRIDA N'AIT 51, 78, 158, 209, 219, 222

AVERY, GRETA 52, 89, 188, 211, 220, 222

B

BA, MARIAMA 18, 119, 130-31, 158-59, 177, 183, 211, 221

BA, OUMAR 52, 211, 222

BABA OF KORO 242

BABISIDYA, M. 18, 213

BABUKIIKA, JUSTINE 14, 222

BAETA, LILY 78, 177, 206, 219

BAKALUBA, JANE JAGERS 14, 159, 189, 214, 219

BANKS-HENRIES, A. DORIS 78, 209, 234-35

BANNUNA, KHANATA 28, 209, 225

BATEYO, JULIET M. 52, 215, 222

BELINGA, THERESE BARATTE-ENO 117, 159, 205

BENSKINA, PRINCESS ORELIA 18, 206, 221

BISHAI, NADIA 52, 205, 222

BITTARI, ZOUBEIDA 18, 204, 221

BLAINE-WILSON, CLARA 189, 209

BOAHEMAA, BEATRICE YAA 18, 206, 221

BOBITO, JENIFER 14, 207, 219

BOITUMELO 52, 89, 189, 212, 220, 222

BONNY, ANNE-MARIE 52, 119, 177, 205, 222

BROWN, ELIZABETH MITCHELL also known as Elizabeth Mitchell 18, 209

BUTHELEZI, BAFANA 204

C

CASELY-HAYFORD, ADELAIDE   1, 5, 28, 131, 177-78, 189, 206, 211, 225

CASELY-HAYFORD, GLADYS   28, 90, 131, 189, 206, 211, 220, 225

CAVALLY, JEANNE DE   207, 216, 244

CHAIBI, AICHA   19, 213, 221

CHARLES, MOU   104, 228

CHEDID, ANDREE   19, 29, 40, 53, 113, 132, 159, 205, 217, 221, 222, 225

CHIFAMBA, JANE   5, 78, 182, 214, 219

CHIMA, SIMMA   53, 149, 207, 222

CHIRWA, NELLIE   53, 209, 222

CHISHIBA, DOROTHY   104

CHITE, HELEN   pseudonym for Enid S. Sibajene   102, 220, 230

CHOGO-WAPAKUBULO, ANGELINA   40, 213, 218

CHRISTIE, PHILLIPA   53, 182, 214, 223

CHUKWUMA, HELEN   54, 86, 210, 220, 223

CLEMS, DARLENE   41, 46, 113, 189, 206, 218

COGE, MAIMUNA BARMANI   54, 210, 223

COLE, BERNADETTE   104, 229

D

DAHAL, CHARITY KUGURU   5, 78, 189, 207, 219

DAMANI, CHARU   97, 215, 220

DANKWAH-SMITH, HANNAH   5, 78, 189, 206, 219

DANKYI, JANE OSAFOA   5, 78. 119, 189, 206, 219

DATTA, SOROJ   54, 214, 223

DEBECHE, DJAMILA   19, 132, 204

DE SHIELD, ANGELA   119, 228

DIAKHATE, NDEYE COUMBA   54, 119, 211, 223, 248

DIALLO, ASSIATOU   104, 105

DIALLO, NAIFSSATOU   1, 160, 183, 189, 211

DIAMONEKE, CECILE-IVELYSE   54, 223, 230

THE DIARY OF MARIA THOLO   242

DIKE, FATIMA   41, 46, 119, 120, 132, 178, 212, 218

DJABALI, LEILA   54, 204, 223

DJEBAR, ASSIA   19, 27-8, 41, 120, 132, 204, 218, 221, 223, 225

DLOVU, NANDI   212, 221, 247

DOGBE, ANNE   5, 211, 248

DOOH-BUNYA, LYDIE   19, 160, 205, 221

DOUTS, CHRISTINE   55, 212, 223

DOVE-DANQUAH, MABEL   28, 113, 206, 225, 228

DREO, PELANDROVA   209, 221, 246

DRONYI, JOYCE L.   51, 214

DUBE, HOPE   214, 221, 247

DUBE, VIOLET   29, 78, 212, 225

E

EGBE, PAULINE   55, 205, 223

EGEJURU, PHANUEL   83, 90, 160, 210, 220

EL-MISKERY, SHEIKHA   55, 214

EL SAADAWI, NAWAL   132, 160, 205, 221

EMECHETA, BUCHI   2, 6, 14, 19, 46, 55, 83, 86, 97-8, 113, 120, 133, 160-64, 178, 183-84, 210, 218, 219, 220, 221, 223, 231, 245, 246

ENEM, EDITH   46, 90, 178, 210, 218

ERONINI, FAUSTINA NWACHI   55, 210, 223

ESAN, YETUNDE   46, 55, 210, 223

ESPIRITO SANTO, ALDA DO   55-6, 90, 134, 184, 211, 220, 223

ESSILFIE, NAA AFARLEY   90, 206, 220

EYAKUZE, VALENTINE   205

F

FAIK-NZUJI, CLEMENTINE MADIYA   30, 56-7, 79, 90-1, 120, 134, 165-66, 191, 214, 219, 220, 223, 226

FAKUNLE-ONADEKO, OLUFUNMILAYO   19, 210, 221, 244

FALL, KINE KIRAMA   57, 117, 120, 134, 211, 223, 248

FERREIRA, ONDINA   207

FISH, MARY McCRITY   191, 209

FLORA   57, 210, 223

FONSECA, LILIA DA   30, 204, 221, 226

FORSTER, RETTY   117, 120

FUTSHANE, ZORA   20, 191, 212, 221

G

GABBA, ANNA   105, 230

GACHUKIA, EDDAH   91-2, 120, 166, 191, 207, 220

GASHE, MARINA or Rebeka Njau   57, 184, 207, 223

GATHII, HANNAH   47, 191, 207, 218

GEBRU, SENEDDU   20, 57, 134, 205, 221

GETHI, ANGELINA   105, 228

GICORU, NEREAS   6, 83, 102, 191, 207, 220

GITHAE, MADELINE, also Micere Githae-Mugo   30, 57, 84, 87, 92, 114, 135, 166, 191, 207, 220, 223, 226, 231

GITHUKU, MARY 6, 191, 207

GITONGA, BIRGITA 105, 228

GREKI, ANNA 57, 129, 135, 204, 223

GRIFFIN, MARY ABENA 57, 206, 223

GUENDOUZ, NADIA 58, 204, 223

GUTU, LAETITIA 6, 135, 214

GWARAM, HAUWA 58, 136, 210, 223

H

HEAD, BESSIE 20-1, 30, 101, 114, 121, 136-37, 167, 184, 191, 212, 220, 221, 226

HIGIRO, J. 21, 207, 221

HLONGWANE, JANE 192, 212

HOUSE, AMELIA 31, 58, 105, 117, 168, 192, 212, 220, 223, 226

HUNYA, JANET 83, 207, 220

HUNTER, CYNTHIA 207, 240

I

IBINGIRA, GRACE 58, 207, 223

IBRU, EMIE 105, 230

IFUDU, THEODORA 99, 210, 220

IFUDU, VERA 117, 121, 210

IKPEAZU, NGOZI 105

ITAYEMI-OGUNDIPE, PHEBEAN 31, 84, 184, 192, 210, 220, 226

IWUJI, VICTORIA B.C. 6, 192, 210

J

JABAVU, NONI HELEN NONTANDO   2, 84, 131, 137, 168, 185, 192, 212, 220

JABBEH, PATRICIA D. M.   31, 209, 226

JETHA, NAZARA   99, 215, 220

JOHN-ROWE, JULIANA   47, 137, 212

JOHNSON, RHODA OMOSUNLOLA   6, 192, 210, 217

JOHNSON, VICTORIA   192, 209

JORDAN, NANDI   59, 192, 212, 223

K

KAGODA, NAMULUUTA   79, 215

KAGONDU, AGNES   14, 99, 207, 219, 220

KAHAKU, PAULINE W.   59, 207, 223

KAHIGA, HANNAH   9, 220

KAHIGA, MIRIAM   84, 105-6, 207, 228

KAKAZA, LILLITH OR LOTA G.   21, 79, 178, 192, 212, 219, 221

KALEBU, BETTY   31, 214, 226

KALIMUGOGO, G. T.   6, 21, 31, 168, 193, 207, 217, 221, 226, 246

KAMA-BONGO, JOSEPHINE   41, 206, 218

KAMARA, SYLVIANE DIOUF   229

KANIE, ANOMA   59, 207, 223

KAPHWIYO, JOSEPHINE   59, 209, 223

KARANJA, PAULA   59, 207, 223

KARIBO, MINJI   59, 210, 223

KASAHUN, ROMANA WARQ, OR Romaneywork   41, 138, 205

KASESE, MEDARD   59, 138, 214

KATSINA, BINTA   60, 210, 223

KATUMBA, REBECCA   106, 229

KAVILA, ESTHER   6, 193, 217

kaXHOBA, NTOMBIYAKHE kaBIYELA   60, 193, 212, 223

KAYA, SIMONE   21, 168, 193, 207, 221

KAYANJA, LYDIE   95, 214, 220

KEITA, AWA OR AOUA   2, 168, 193, 209

KGOSITSILE, BALEKA   60, 193, 212, 223

KHAKETLA, CAROLINE N. M. R.   41, 47, 60, 193, 208, 218, 223

KHAMADI, MIRIAM   also Miriam Khamadi Were   60, 207, 223

KHANGANYA, WILLMESS   6, 193, 209, 217

KHUZWAYO, ELLEN   138, 212

KIANGANA, KEITA or Keta   193, 229

KIARIE, MIRIAM   106, 228

KICHWA, MORENA HALIM   57, 212, 223

KIMENYE, BARBARA   7, 31, 114, 138, 169, 193, 214, 217, 219, 226, 245

KIMENYI, LUCI W.   60, 207, 223

KING, DELPHINE   61, 117, 121, 194, 212, 223

KISANGI, ESTHER   14, 99, 207, 219, 220

KISE, MARY   14, 207, 219

KITAMBI, BERNADETTE   92

KITONGA, ELLEN   207, 235

KIYINGI, ELIZABETH   31, 215, 226

KOKUNDA, VIOLET   32, 214, 226

KOLIA (Mme)   207

KUMAH, SYLVIE   61, 121, 206, 223

KUOH-MOUKOURY, THERESE   21, 106, 179, 185, 194, 205, 221, 228, 246

KURANKYI-TAYLOR, DOROTHY   61, 194, 206, 223

KURIA, R. LUCY   15, 99, 207, 219, 220

KUTTA, SARAH KALA-LOBE   107, 229

KWAKU, ROSEMARY   32, 41, 47, 61, 107, 114, 194, 206, 218, 223, 226, 228

KWAMI, MARTHE AFEWELE   2, 179, 213

KYEGYIRBA, ADWOA   206

KYENDO, KALONDU   9, 194, 207, 217

L

LALUAH, ACQUAH   62, 223

LAMO, JANET   7, 194, 214, 217

LARA, ALDA   32, 62, 204, 223, 226

LEHAI, JOY   99, 215, 220

LEMSINE, AICHA   121, 204, 221

LIBONDO, JEANNE NGO   42, 205, 235-36

LIHAMBA, AMANDINA   42, 213

LIKING, WEREWERE   42, 140, 205, 218, 222, 245, 246

LIKIMANI, MUTHONI   7, 21, 169, 194, 207, 217, 222

LIMA, MARIA EUGENIA   62, 204, 223

LOBO, MARIA MANUELA DE SOUSA   32, 226

LOKKO, SOPHIA   47, 206, 218

LOUBNA, MAMA   8, 205, 217

LUSINDE, RUTH   96, 102, 215, 220

LWANGA, SUSAN   62-3, 215, 223

M

MABUZA, LINDIWE   62, 194, 212, 223

MACAULEY, JEANNETTE   194, 212, 220

MACHEL, JOSINA   63, 210, 223

MACKAY, ILVA   63, 195, 212, 224

MAGIDI, DORA THIZWILANDI   2, 15, 212, 219

MAHUHUSHI, M. A.   22, 179, 212, 222

MAI, JEANNE NGO   63, 195, 205, 224

MAJALE, IRENE   107, 228

MAKEBA, MIRIAM   15, 195, 212, 219

MAKURA, TENDAI   21, 214, 222

MAKWABARARA, ANGELINA   121, 230

MALAFA, EFOSI   64, 205, 224

MALAKA, MAUDE   32, 195, 212, 226

MALL, JASMINE   64, 195, 212

MANDAO, MARTHA   8, 195, 213, 217

MANDEBVU, STELLA   22, 195, 214

MANDELA, ZINDZI   64, 195, 212, 224

MAOKA, SHIMANE   64, 212, 224

MARGARIDO, MARIA MANUELA CONCEICAO CARVALHO DA   64, 140, 195, 211, 224

MARVA, RAVI   65, 207, 224

MASCARENHAS, MARIA MARGARIDA   32, 132, 205, 226

MASEKELA, BARBARA   65, 107, 195, 212, 224

MASEMBE, HARRIET   65, 215, 224

MASHISHI, KEDISALETSE   65, 212, 224

MASSAQUOI, FATIMA FAHNBULLEH   8, 196, 209, 217

MATENJWA, CHRISTINE   42, 65, 103, 169, 208, 218, 220, 224, 228

MATINDI, ANNE   8, 42, 196, 208, 217, 218

MATIP, MARIE-CLAIRE   65, 196, 205, 224

MATLOU, REBECCA   65, 212, 224

MAURA, MARY   8, 196, 208, 217

MBA, NINA   236

M'BAYE, ANNETTE D'ERNEVILLE   65-6, 107-8, 121, 196, 211, 217, 224, 229, 231

MBILINYI, MARJORIE J.   213, 236

MBONI, SARAH   32, 208, 226

MBOWA, ROSE   66, 214, 224

MBUGUA, ISABEL   66, 108, 229

MDOE, JANET N.   8, 214, 217

MENIRU, THERESA   9, 79, 210, 217, 219, 244

MENSAH, GRACE OSEI   32, 206, 226

MESSENGA   79, 208, 219

MFODWO, ESTHER BEKOE   9, 79, 217, 219

MHANDO, BLANDINA   66, 213, 224

MHELEMA, MARJORIE   33, 215, 226

MHLONGO, MAUREEN   66, 197, 212, 224

MITCHELL, ELIZABETH M.   22, 33, 197, 222, 226

MKHOMO, JOY FLORENCE CHRESTEPHENE   22, 212, 222

MLAGOLA, MARTHA V.   9, 197, 208, 217

MLAMA, PENNINA   also Penina Muhando   92, 115, 220

MOHAMEDALI, HAMIDA   66, 85, 197, 208, 221, 224

MOKHOMO, MAKHOKOLOTSO A.   67, 224

MOKOROSI, EMELY SEMELENG   67, 204, 224

MOKWENA, JOAN   33, 212, 226

MONEKE, OBIORA   9, 210, 217

MORAIS, DESI   67, 210, 224

MORAZZO, YOLANDA   67, 205, 224

MOREL, MARION   108, 197, 212, 229

MORITI, PALESA   67, 197, 212, 224

MOROLO, WINNIE   67, 197, 212, 224

MPHAHLELE, THERESA KEFILWE   67, 197, 212, 224

MPONGO, MARIE-EUGENIE   68, 140, 214, 224

MSHAM, MWANA KUPONA BINTI   140, 198, 208

MTUNGWA, GLORIA   68, 212, 224

MUCAVALE, JOANA MATEUS   210, 224

MUDIMBE-BOYI, ELISABETH M.   92, 214, 221

MUGO, MICERE GITHAE   42, 68, 122, 218

MUGOT, HAZEL DESILVA   22, 140, 179, 197, 211, 222, 231

MUHANDO, PENNINA   42-3, 140, 169, 179, 197, 213, 218

MUKWAYA, JEAN B.   68, 215, 224

MULI, ANNE KEERU   33, 208, 226

MUNENE, FIBI   108, 122, 141, 228

MUNTEMBA, MAUDE   68, 115, 214, 224

MUTAI, CHELAGIT   108, 228

MUTHONI, SUSIE   208, 240

MUTSILA, IRENE   68, 198, 212, 224

MVEMVE, LINDIWE   69, 212, 224

MVUNGI, MARTHA   80, 169, 213, 219

MWAKALA, MARIA   69, 210, 224

MWANGI, BEATRICE   15, 100, 208, 219, 221

MWANGI, ROSE GECAU   80, 198, 208, 219

MWAURA, FLORENCE W.   108, 228

MWILU, JANE   108, 228

N

NABWIRE, CONSTANCE 214, 226

NACHALE, JOANA 69, 210, 224

NAGENDA, SALA 91, 198, 208, 214, 217

NAKACWA, THERESA 47, 198, 214, 218

NAKITWE, ANGELA NASHAKHOMA 33, 69, 215, 224, 226

NAMUBIRU, MARGARET 96, 215, 221

NANJALA, ELIZABETH 180, 198, 208

NCGCOBO, LAURETTA 22, 222

NCHWE, MANOKO 69, 198, 212, 224

NDAAYA, CITEKU 69, 214, 224

NDEGWA, CATHERINE 33, 208, 226

NDELE, SERENA 34, 208, 226

NDELE, SUSAN 34, 208, 226

NDIAYE, OUMY 118, 122

NDONDO, LASSIE 15, 182, 215, 219

NDORO, JOYCE 9, 80, 198, 208, 217, 219

NENE, AMELIA 69, 215, 224

NETO, MARIA EUGENIA 204, 236-37

NGATHO, STELLA 69, 208, 224, 231

NGCOBO, LAURETTA 22, 212

NGONYAMA, SUSAN 198, 212

NGU, MURSSA NASEKA 122, 230

NGUBANE, HARRIET 198, 213

NGULUBE, CLARA 108, 230

NGUYA, LYDIE MUMBI   15, 198, 208, 219

NIRINA, ESTHER   70, 209, 224

NJAU, REBEKA   22, 34, 43, 47, 70, 85, 122, 141, 170, 199, 208, 218, 221, 222, 224, 226

NJOROGE, LIZZIE NYAMBURA   80, 208, 219

NJOYA, RABIATOU   43, 141, 205, 218

NKWAZEMA, EDITH   108

NORGAH, MARY   205

NORONHA, LYDIE   34, 70, 215, 224, 226

NSANZUBUHORO, VICTOIRE   33, 180, 211, 226

N'SKA, LECI   230

NSUBUGA, EDITA   109, 230

NTABGOBA, JENNINAH   9, 217

NTANTALA, PHYLLIS   109, 199, 229

NWAGBOSO, ROSALINE   34, 210, 226

NWAPA, FLORA   2, 9-10, 22-3, 34-5, 109, 115, 122-3, 142-4, 170-71, 180, 199, 210, 217, 222, 226, 231, 244

NWIGWE, NKUKU   109, 205, 228

NXUMALO, NATALIE VICTORIA   199, 213

NYATE, FRANCES   110, 230

NYAYWA, ROSE   109

NYOKABI, SALLY   10, 199, 217

NZERIBE, EJINE   80, 210, 219

NZERIBE, GRACE NNENNE   144, 210

NZUJI, CAROLINE BALEKA BAMBA   80, 92, 145, 214, 219, 221

O

OBI, DOROTHY S.   70, 210, 224

ODAGA, ASENATH BOLE   10, 15, 80, 87, 92-3, 145, 199, 208, 217, 219, 221, 232, 245

ODOWELU, VIKKI EZINMA   10, 15, 199, 210, 217, 219

OGADA, PENNIAH   35, 208, 226

OGOT, GRACE AKINYI   23, 35-6, 43, 93, 115, 123, 145-47, 171-72, 180, 185, 200, 208, 218, 219, 221, 222, 226

OGOT, PAMELA also Pamela Ogot Kola   11, 81, 124, 147, 200, 208, 217

OGUNDIPE-LESLIE, OMOLARA   70, 85, 87, 93-4, 124, 200, 211, 221, 224, 232, 248

OHENE, ELIZABETH   12, 180, 228

OHENE, OOPOKUA   12, 206, 217

OKONKWO, JULIET I.   88, 94, 200, 211, 221

OKOYE, IFEOMA   12, 23, 200, 211, 217, 222

O'LANSEN, MALIKA   70, 204, 224

OLIMBA, MAUDE   36, 208, 226

OLISA, MARARET   70, 215

OLIVESI, DJAMILA   23, 215, 222

OLUDHE-MACGOYE, MARJORIE   147, 208, 237-8

OMANGA, CLARE   12, 81, 200, 208, 217, 219

OMODING, ANNA   12, 200, 214, 217

ONDITI, MARA   12, 201, 215

OPONDO, DIANA   110, 230

OTIENO, EVELYN   110, 228

OVBIAGELE, HELEN   211, 222, 247

OWANO, NANCY   228, 239

OWINO, ROSEMARIE   23, 172, 201, 208, 222

OWUSU-NIMOH, MERCY   12, 147, 172, 180-1, 201, 206, 217, 244

P

PALA, O. 94, 213, 221

PEARCE, ESTHER TAYLOR 48, 147, 212, 218

PEREIRA-EMANUEL, FRANCESCA YETUNDE 70, 148, 201, 211, 224

PHIRI, IRENE 71, 214, 224

PHUMLA 12, 201, 213, 217

PHUNGULA, NOMUSA CYNTHIA 71, 201, 213, 224

PIERCE, JACQUELINE 213, 241

PONTI-LAKO, AGNES 36, 213, 226

POPPIE 172, 242

Q

QUEEN HATSHEPSUT 71, 205, 224

QUTB, AMINA 36, 205, 226

R

RAHARIJAONA, BERTHE 229,

RAKOTOSON, MICHELE 23, 43, 173, 209, 218, 222

RAMALA, MAGGIE 23, 43, 209, 218, 222

RATSIFANDRIHAMANANA, CLARISSE 23, 201, 209, 222

RATSIMISERA, JASMINA 148, 209

RAZAFINIAINA, CHARLOTTE 148

REGGIE, MAE ALICE 228, 239

RIBEIRO, MARIANNA MARQUES, pseudonym Ytchyana 71, 207, 225

ROBERTS, MAIMA 36, 226

ROBY, MARIA EMILIA 71, 210, 225

ROSEMARY 36, 208, 226

RUSH, BRENDA UTAMU 71, 215, 225

RWAKYAKA, PROSCOVIA   71, 201, 214, 225

S

SAAD, SITI BINTI   67, 148, 214, 225

SA'ADU, A. B.   72, 211, 225

SACKEY, JULIANA   12, 94, 201, 206, 217, 221

SANGA, AMINATOU   110, 229

SEBBAR, LEILA   24, 173, 204, 222

SEFORA, RITA   201, 213

SEGUN, MABEL IMOUKHUEDE JOLAOSA   3, 12, 37, 72, 85, 110, 124, 173, 181, 201, 211, 217, 221, 225, 226, 229

SELLO , DORIS   35, 201, 213, 226

SELOLWANE, ONALENNA   204

SETIDISHO, EDITH   37, 149, 213, 226

SEYDOU AMADU, CHRISTIANE   81, 95, 215, 219

SHAFIK, DORIA   202, 228

SHEIKH, LELIA   110, 229

SHUAIB, YINKA   72, 211

SIBANE, NONA   37, 202, 213, 226

SIGANGA, JENIFER   37, 208, 226

SIGWILI, NAKUGCINA   72, 111, 202, 213, 225

SIKAKANE, JOYCE N.   3, 124, 202, 213

SIKANETA, CLARA   111, 230

SIKUADE, YEMI   211, 222, 247

SILVA, MARIA DE JESUS NUNES DA   37, 204, 226

SIWUNDHLA, ALICE PRINCESS MSUMBA   3, 174, 213

SOFOLA, ZULU   12, 16, 44, 88, 95, 115, 124, 149, 174, 202, 211, 217, 218, 220, 221

SOUSA, NOEMIA CAROLINA ABRANCHES SOARES DE   72-3, 150, 181, 185, 202, 210, 225

SOW FALL, AMINATA   24, 111, 124, 150, 174, 185, 211, 222, 247

SPIO-GARBRAH, ELIZABETH   115, 206

SUMBANE, NATALA   37, 81, 151, 219, 226

SUTHERLAND, EFUA THEODORA MORGUE   13, 38, 44, 48, 73, 95, 115, 125, 151-53, 174-75, 181, 202, 217, 218, 221, 225, 226

SWAARTBOOI, VICTORIA   3, 153, 202, 213

T

TADJO, VERONIQUE   73, 175, 181, 207

TAOS-AMROUCHE, MARGUERITE   24, 38, 74, 81, 95, 116, 153, 203, 213, 219, 221, 222, 225

TEAGE, HILARY   74, 153, 209, 225

TELIKO, RAHMATOULLAHI   74, 181, 206, 225

TEMBE, ROSARIA   74, 210

THIAM, AWA OR AOUA   95, 175, 215, 221

THOMAS, GLADYS   36, 74, 203, 213, 225, 226

TLALI, MIRIAM   24, 38, 96, 111, 116, 203, 213, 221, 222, 226, 229

TLALI, SOPHIA   74, 209, 225

TOL'ANDE, ELISABETH FRANCOISE MWEYA   74, 154, 214, 225

TOOKARAM, MERYL   81-2, 215, 219

TORO, PRINCESS ELIZABETH OF   3, 214

TSOGO, DELPHINE ZANGA   25, 205, 222

TULAY, ELIZABETH LOVO JALLAH   38, 209, 226

TUTU MALAMAFAMA, MATILDA   154, 205

U

UDENSI, UWA   45, 211, 218

ULASI, ADAORA LILY   25, 82, 125, 154, 175, 203, 219, 222, 229

UMELO, ROSINA   13, 215, 217, 222, 247

UREY-NGARA, ABIGAIL   39, 111, 215, 227, 230

UWECHUE, AUSTUA   111, 229

UWEMEDIMO, ROSEMARY   211, 238

V

VEIGA, AMELIA   75, 204, 225

W

WACIUMA, CHARITY   3, 13, 16, 79, 154, 176, 181, 203, 208, 217, 219, 220

WANGECI, AGATHA   75, 208, 225

WANJIRU, L. MUMBI   39, 208, 227

WANJIRU, PAULINE   16, 100, 208, 220, 221

WANNE, TEGBO   13, 207, 217

WARE, REBECCA J. N.   75, 209, 225

WARUHIU, DORIS MAY   16, 100, 208, 220, 221

WERE, JANE   39, 208, 227

WERE, MIRIAM KHAMADI   3, 16, 39, 154, 176, 203, 208, 220, 227

WHEATLEY, PHILLIS   75, 155, 203, 211, 225

WILLIAMS, DAPHNE   75, 212, 225

WILLIAMS, KATE NGOWO   25, 155, 205

WILSON, BEVERLY   76, 156, 209, 225

X

XAVIER, EMELINDA PEREIRA   76, 204, 225

Y

YAOU, REGINA   17, 207, 220

YEBOAH-AFARI, AJOA V.   39, 100, 206, 221, 227, 228

YEMBE, FAUSTINA   205

Z

ZAGBEDE, JOSEPHINE 76, 206, 225

ZELLEKE, SERK-ADDIS 76, 205, 225

ZERARI, ZEHOR 76, 204

ZINONDO, TOKOZILE 76, 210, 225

ZIRIMU, ELVANIA NAMUKWAYA 39, 45, 48, 76, 82, 85, 116, 125, 156, 176, 203, 214, 218-19, 225, 226

THE AUTHOR

Brenda F. Berrian is currently Associate Professor of Afro-American and African Literatures at the University of Pittsburgh. She received her B.S. and M.A. from Hampton Institute, and her "doctorat de 3^e cycle" from the University of Paris III-Sorbonne. Academic honors awarded her include a Social Science Research Council/American Council of Learned Societies fellowship for African Studies and a Southern Fellowships Fund.

Brenda F. Berrian has written the monograph Africa: Roots and Branches (1978) and has contributed book reviews, bibliographies, and articles to various literary journals. Works in progress are "A Critical Perspective of African Women Writers," and "Bibliography of Caribbean Women Writers."